FURTHER AFIELD
Pages 72–85
Street Finder maps 1–8

G000088487

ALFAMA
Pages 30–39
Street Finder map 8

BAIXA
AND
AVENIDA

BAIRRO ALTO
AND ESTRELA

ALFAMA

**BAIRRO ALTO
AND ESTRELA**
Pages 48–59
Street Finder maps 4, 7

BAIXA AND AVENIDA
Pages 40–47
Street Finder map 7

EYEWITNESS TRAVEL GUIDES

LISBON

EYEWITNESS TRAVEL GUIDES

LISBON

Main contributor: SUSIE BOULTON

LONDON, NEW YORK,
MELBOURNE, MUNICH AND DELHI
www.dk.com

PROJECT EDITORS Claire Folkard, Ferdie McDonald
ART EDITORS Jim Evoy, Vanessa Hamilton
EDITORS Francesca Machiavelli, Rebecca Miles,
Alice Peebles, Alison Stace
DESIGNERS Anthea Forlee, Carolyn Hewitson,
Nicola Rodway, Dooty Williams

CONTRIBUTORS AND CONSULTANTS
Clive Gilbert, Peter Gilbert, Sarah McAlister, Norman Renouf,
Joe Staines, Martin Symington, Tomas Tranæus

PHOTOGRAPHERS
Linda Whitwam, Peter Wilson

ILLUSTRATORS
Isidoro González-Adalid Cabezas/Acanto Arquitectura y Urbanismo S.L.,
Paul Guest, Claire Littlejohn, John Woodcock, Martin Woodward

Reproduced by Colourscan (Singapore)
Printed and bound by L. Rex Printing Company Limited, China

First published in Great Britain in 1997
by Dorling Kindersley Limited
80 Strand, London WC2R ORL
**Reprinted with revisions 1999, 2000, 2001,
2002, 2003, 2004, 2006**

Copyright 1997, 2006 © Dorling Kindersley Limited, London
A Penguin Company

◁ View of the Castelo de São Jorge at night

CONTENTS

Manueline vaulting in the cloister
in the Mosteiro dos Jerónimos

INTRODUCING
LISBON

A statue of St Antony, dressed up
for his feast day celebrations

View to the Sé across the Baixa from the Elevador de Santa Justa

Porco à alentejana, a popular dish in Lisbon

Atmospheric houses in the old Moorish district of Alfama

The Monument to the Discoveries

Palácio da Pena, Sintra

HOW TO USE THIS GUIDE

THIS GUIDE helps you get the most from a visit to Lisbon, providing expert recommendations as well as detailed practical information. The opening chapter *Introducing Lisbon* maps the city and sets it in its historical and cultural context. Each of the five area chapters, plus *The Lisbon Coast*, describe important sights, using maps, pictures and illustrations. Hotel and restaurant recommendations plus features on subjects such as entertainment and food and drink can be found in *Travellers' Needs*. The *Survival Guide* contains practical information on everything from transport to personal safety.

LISBON

Lisbon has been divided into five main sightseeing areas. Each of these areas has its own chapter, which opens with a list of the major sights described. All sights are numbered and plotted on an *Area Map*. Information on the sights is easy to locate as the order in which they appear in the chapter follows the numerical order used on the map.

Sights at a Glance lists the chapter's sights by category: Churches, Museums and Galleries, Historic Buildings, Parks and Gardens.

1 Area Map
For easy reference, the sights covered in the chapter are numbered and located on a map. The sights are also marked on the Street Finder *maps on pages 164–77.*

A locator map shows clearly where the area is in relation to other parts of the city.

Each area is indicated by a colour-coded thumb tab (see inside front cover).

2 Street-by-Street Map
This gives a bird's-eye view of the heart of each of the sightseeing areas.

A suggested route for a walk is shown in red.

Stars indicate the sights that no visitor should miss.

3 Detailed Information
All the sights in Lisbon are described individually. Addresses and practical information are provided. The key to the symbols used in the information block is shown on the back flap.

1 Introduction to The Lisbon Coast

The Lisbon Coast has its own introduction, which provides an overview of the history and character of the coast and countryside around Lisbon and outline what it has to offer the visitor today. The area covered by this section is highlighted on the map of Portugal shown on page 89. It covers coastal resorts and local wildlife, as well as beautiful palaces and historic towns.

2 Pictorial Map

This shows the main road network and gives an illustrated overview of the region. All entries are numbered and there are also useful tips on getting around the region.

The Lisbon Coast chapter is indicated by a green thumb tab.

3 Detailed Information

All the important towns and other places to visit are described individually. They are listed in order, following the numbering given on the Pictorial Map. Within each entry, there is further detailed information on important buildings and other sights.

Story boxes explore specific subjects further.

For all the top sights, a Visitors' Checklist provides the practical information you need to plan your visit.

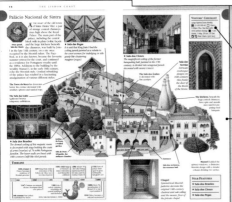

4 The Top Sights

These are given two or more full pages. Historic buildings are dissected to reveal their interiors; museums and galleries have colour-coded floorplans to help you locate the most interesting exhibits.

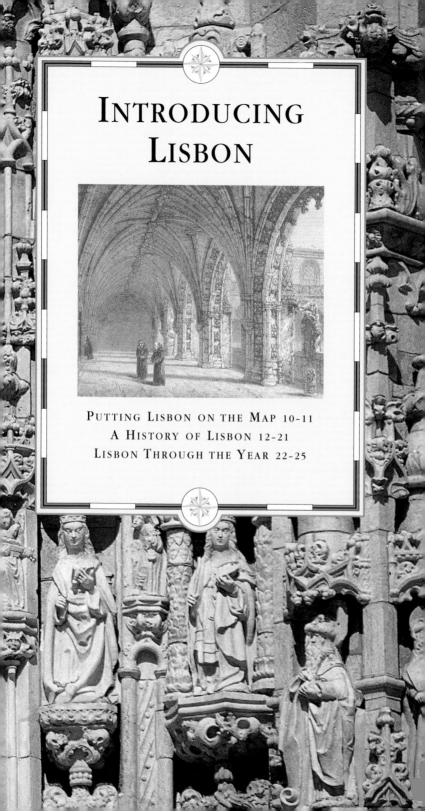

INTRODUCING
LISBON

Putting Lisbon on the Map

L ISBON, the capital of Portugal, is situated on the
Atlantic coast, in the southwest of the country.
It is approximately 300 km (180 miles) from the
Algarve in the south and around 400 km (250 miles)
from the Minho in the north. The political, economic
and cultural centre of Portugal, the city lies on the
steep hills on the north bank of the Tagus. The
greater Lisbon area occupies around 1,000 sq km
(300 sq miles) and has a population of 3.3 million.
The city has become increasingly popular as a holiday
destination and its proximity to the coast makes it an
ideal choice for both sightseeing and sunbathing.

Aerial view of Lisbon, showing the Tagus river

```
0 kilometres          100
0 miles          50
```

KEY

✈	Airport
⛴	Port
▬	Motorway
▬	Major road
═	Minor road
—	Main railway line
▪▪·	National boundary

ATLANTIC

OCEAN

Pontevedra
Vigo
Our
N120
Braga
Guim
Oporto (Porto)
IP5 (E80)
Vis
Figueira da Foz
Coimbra
POR
Santarém
LISBON (Lisboa)
Setúbal
Sines
Portimão N125

EUROPE

NORWAY
SWEDEN
ESTONIA
LATVIA
LITHUANIA
DENMARK
POLAND
UNITED
KINGDOM
GERMANY
CZECH
REPUBLIC
SLOVAKIA
REPUBLIC
OF
IRELAND
NETHERLANDS
BELGIUM
LUXEMBOURG
HUNGARY
AUSTRIA
SLOVENIA
SWITZERLAND
FRANCE
ITALY
PORTUGAL
SPAIN
Lisbon
Azores
TUNISIA
Madeira
MOROCCO
ALGERIA
LIBYA

Bragança
N122 (E82)
IP4 (E82)
Duero
aves
A6
Sil
N-52
IP5
N620 (E80)
Alagón
Tormes
N110
N403
MADRID
NII (E90)
NV (E90)
NIV (E5)
NIII (E901)
N401
Guarda

SPAIN

GAL
N630 (E803)
Plasencia
Tajo
stelo
anco
N521
Cáceres
N521
Portalegre
NV (E90)
N430
Mérida
Guadiana
N630 (E803)
N4 (E90)
Badajoz
NV (E90)
EX112
Ardila
N432
N433
N630 (E803)
A49 (E1)
Sevilla
Huelva
Genil
A92
A92
A92
Granada
N323 (E902)
A359
N331
N340 (E15)
Jerez de
la Frontera
Málaga
A4 (E5)

GREATER LISBON

N117
A9 (CREL)
IC 17 (CRIL)
Odivelas
Sacavém
A8
A1 (E1)
A12
Queluz
Amadora
IC 19
A5
N6
Belém
Cacilhas
Trafaria
Almada
Costa de
Caparica
Seixal
Barreiro
Moita
Coina
A2 (E1)
N10
IC 21
N11
Montijo
N119
Tejo

0 kilometres   10
0 miles   5

Lisbon and its Environs

*The sights in central Lisbon are described in detail on
pages 26–85 and a Street Finder is provided on pages
164–77. Sights in the Lisbon Coast region are covered
in a separate chapter on pages 88–109.*

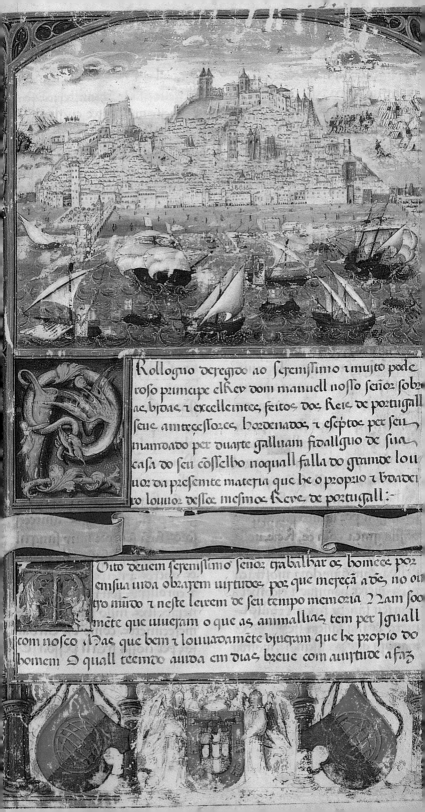

Rolloguo deregdo ao serenissimo i muito pode
roso principe elrey dom manuell nosso senor sobr
ae, bidas i excellentes, feitos dos reis de portugall
seus antecessores, hordenados, i escpto per seu
mandado per duarte galluam fidalguo de sua
casa do seu cosselho noquall falla do grande lou
uor da presente materia que he o proprio i bdadei
ro louuor destes mesmos reves de portugall:~

Oito deuem serenissimo senor trabalhar os homee por
emsua uida obrarem uirtudes por que mereça a ds no ou
tro mudo i neste leurem de seu tempo memoria Nam soo
mete que uiueram o que as animallias tem per iguall
com nosco Mas que bem i louuadamete biueram que he proprio do
homem O quall teendo ainda em dias breue com auirtude a faz

THE HISTORY OF LISBON

O VER THE CENTURIES, *Lisbon has both flourished and suffered. The city is most famous for its history of maritime successes, in particular the voyages of Vasco da Gama who first navigated a sea route to India. In recent years the city has flourished again, and is now a major European centre of commerce.*

According to myth, the Greek hero Odysseus (also known as Ulysses) founded Lisbon on his journey home from Troy. The Phoenicians are known to have established a trading post on the site in around 1200 BC. From 205 BC the town was in Roman hands, reaching the height of its importance when Julius Caesar became the governor in 60 BC.

St Vincent

With the collapse of the Roman Empire, barbarian tribes invaded from northern Europe. The Alans, who conquered the city in around AD 409, were superseded by the Suevi who in turn were driven out by the Visigoths. None of these tribes were primarily town-dwellers and Lisbon began to decline. In 711 North African Muslim invaders, the Moors, overran the peninsula and occupied the city for some 450 years. Lisbon was an important trading centre under the Moors and their legacy is evident today in the Castelo de São Jorge and the streets of the Alfama district.

The first king of Portugal, Afonso Henriques, finally ousted the Moors from Lisbon in 1147. Among those who helped was the English Crusader Gilbert of Hastings, who became Lisbon's first bishop. A new cathedral was built below the castle and, shortly afterwards, the remains of St Vincent, the patron saint of Portugal, were brought there. Lisbon received its charter early in the 13th century, but it was not until 1256, under Afonso III, that it became the capital.

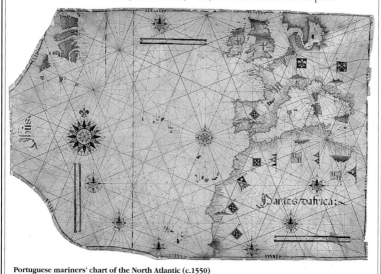

Portuguese mariners' chart of the North Atlantic (c.1550)

◁ Illuminated page from the *Chronica de Dom Afonso Henriques*, showing Lisbon in the 16th century

THE REIGN OF KING DINIS

Under King Dinis, the son of Afonso III, the court at Lisbon became a centre of culture and in 1290 the University of Lisbon was founded. Dinis extended the city away from the castle, developing the Baixa, and Lisbon flourished as trade with Europe grew.

In the 14th century, the city continued to expand westwards along the river, despite the ruin caused by the Black Death, which spread throughout Portugal from Lisbon. In 1373, after Lisbon was sacked by Enrique II of Castile, Fernando I built a new line of fortifications to protect his 40,000 citizens and to redefine the boundaries of the growing city. When Fernando died without an heir, the throne was claimed by his illegitimate half brother, João of Avis, who defeated Juan of Castile, in 1385 at the famous Battle of Ajubarrota.

Statue of Manuel I and St Jerome on the Mosteiro dos Jerónimos

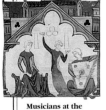

Musicians at the court of King Dinis

THE DISCOVERIES

Periodic outbreaks of plague continued to destabilize the economy and led to riots in Lisbon over grain shortages. Prosperity returned during the Age of Discovery (*see pp18–19*) when Vasco da Gama, setting out from Belém in 1497, successfully navigated a sea route to India. The resulting wealth from the spice trade made Lisbon the mercantile centre of Europe. In gratitude for this new-found prosperity, Manuel I ordered the building of the Torre de Belém (*see p70*) and the magnificent Mosteiro dos Jerónimos in Belém (*see pp66–7*); their ornate late-Gothic style, known as Manueline after the king,

reflects the Discoveries in the exotic and nautical nature of the detailed sculpture on the two monuments.

The 16th century saw major developments: a new square, the Terreiro do Paço (now the Praça do Comércio), was built on the waterfront, and a new district, the Bairro Alto, sprang up to house the many merchants drawn to Lisbon. The Inquisition, a Catholic movement which persecuted heretics and non-believers, began a reign of terror. Mass trials and executions of those that were condemned took place regularly in the Terreiro do Paço.

SPANISH CONTROL

The young King Sebastião I was killed at the battle of Alcácer-Quibir in a doomed attempt to invade Morocco in 1578. The lack of an heir led to conquest by Spain in 1580. Ignoring his advisers, Philip II of Spain refused to make Lisbon the capital of his extended kingdom and left the government of Portugal to a viceroy. The Spanish were ousted in 1640 and the Duke of Bragança crowned João IV.

With the discovery of Brazilian gold in 1697, Lisbon enjoyed a new wave of prosperity. From 1706, João V began an ambitious building programme in the city. The most valuable addition to Lisbon at this time was the Águas Livres aqueduct (*see p84*),

The battle of Alcácer-Quibir in Morocco, where 8,000 men were killed and 15,000 captured

which was carrying water across the Alcântara valley just a few years before the devastating earthquake struck the city in 1755 *(see pp20–21)*.

POMBAL'S VISION

Responsibility for rebuilding the ruined city fell to José I's chief minister, the Marquês de Pombal. Engineers drew up a plan that re-aligned Lisbon on a north–south axis and created a grid of streets with the Baixa at its heart. Pombal's vision was not continued by his successors; when the royal family fled to Brazil in 1807, ahead of Napoleon's invading army, Rio de Janeiro temporarily became the capital of the Portuguese empire, and Lisbon began to decline.

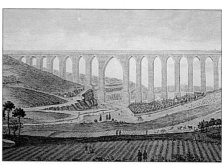

The Águas Livres aqueduct, completed in the 19th century

The Marquês de Pombal pointing to the new Lisbon

REGENERATION

In the second half of the 19th century a period of economic revival and industrialization commenced. Railways and new roads were built, trams were introduced, modern drains and sewers were constructed and work began on the embankment of the Tagus. In 1908 the king was assassinated and two years later the monarchy was overturned. Under António Salazar's lengthy dictatorship (1926–68), Lisbon's modernization continued at the expense of the rest of the country.

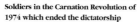

Soldiers in the Carnation Revolution of 1974 which ended the dictatorship

A suspension bridge across the Tagus was completed in 1966. Initially called the Ponte Salazar, it was later renamed Ponte 25 de Abril in commemoration of the peaceful Carnation Revolution in 1974 which finally ended the totalitarian regime instituted by Salazar.

MODERN LISBON

The years following the Revolution were a period of both euphoria and political chaos. Then, in 1986, Portugal joined the European Community and foreign companies began to set up in Lisbon. Under the leadership of the Social Democratic prime minister, Aníbal Cavaco Silva, Lisbon's economy recovered. Even the disastrous fire which swept through the Chiado district in 1988 failed to dampen the general optimism. To mastermind the rebuilding of this historic district, the city appointed Portugal's most prestigious architect, Álvaro Siza Vieira. Since then, Lisbon has enjoyed much prestige, and was voted European City of Culture in 1994. In 1998 the city hosted a World Exposition on the theme of the Oceans, in celebration of its maritime history. Today, Lisbon is a cosmopolitan city where the influence of its previous African and South American and colonies is still widely evident.

The Rulers of Portugal

Afonso Henriques declared himself Portugal's first king in 1139, but his descendants' ties of marriage to various Spanish kingdoms led to dynastic disputes. João I's defeat of the Castilians in 1385 established the House of Avis which presided over the golden age of Portuguese imperialism. Then in 1580, in the absence of a direct heir, Portugal was ruled by Spanish kings for 60 years before the Duke of Bragança became João IV. A Republican uprising ended the monarchy in 1910. However, in the first 16 years of the Republic there were 40 different governments, and in 1926 Portugal became a dictatorship under the eventual leadership of Salazar. Democracy was restored by the Carnation Revolution of 1974.

1481–95 João II

1438–81 Afonso V

1211–23 Afonso II

1185–1211 Sancho I

1248–79 Afonso III

1279–1325 Dinis

1100	1200	1300	1400	1500
HOUSE OF BURGUNDY			AVIS	
1100	1200	1300	1400	1500

1325–57 Afonso IV

1357–67 Pedro I

1223–48 Sancho II

1367–83 Fernando I

1139–85 Afonso Henriques (Afonso I)

1433–8 Duarte

152 João

1385–1433 João I

1495–1521 Manuel I

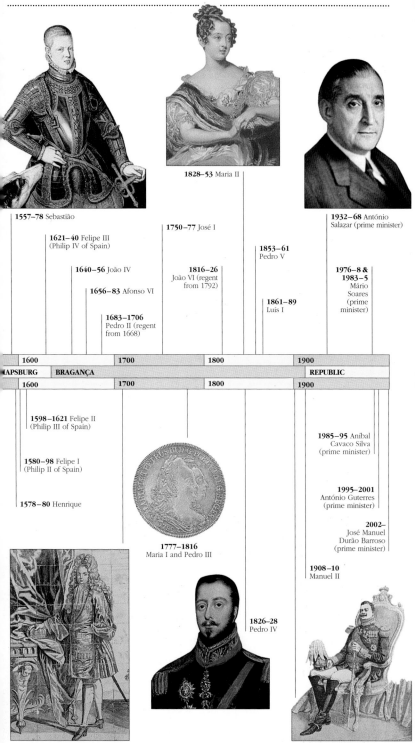

1828–53 Maria II

1557–78 Sebastião

1621–40 Felipe III
(Philip IV of Spain)

1640–56 João IV

1656–83 Afonso VI

1683–1706
Pedro II (regent
from 1668)

1750–77 José I

1816–26
João VI (regent
from 1792)

1932–68 António
Salazar (prime minister)

1853–61
Pedro V

1861–89
Luís I

1976–8 &
1983–5
Mário
Soares
(prime
minister)

1600		1700		1800		1900	

HAPSBURG   BRAGANÇA   REPUBLIC

1600		1700		1800		1900	

1598–1621 Felipe II
(Philip III of Spain)

1580–98 Felipe I
(Philip II of Spain)

1578–80 Henrique

1985–95 Aníbal
Cavaco Silva
(prime minister)

1995–2001
António Guterres
(prime minister)

2002–
José Manuel
Durão Barroso
(prime minister)

1908–10
Manuel II

1777–1816
Maria I and Pedro III

1826–28
Pedro IV

1706–50 João V

1889–1908 Carlos I

The Age of Discovery

PORTUGAL'S ASTONISHING PERIOD of conquest and exploration began in 1415 with the capture of the North African city of Ceuta. Maritime expeditions into the Atlantic and along the West African coast followed, motivated by conflict between Christianity and Islam and the desire for commercial gain. Great riches were earned from the gold and slaves taken from the Guinea coast, but the real breakthrough for Portuguese imperialism occurred in 1498 when Vasco da Gama *(see p68)* reached India. Portugal soon controlled the Indian Ocean and the spice trade, and established an eastern capital at Goa. With Pedro Álvares Cabral's "discovery" of Brazil, Portugal became a mercantile super-power rivalled only by her neighbour Spain.

Portuguese padrão

Armillary Sphere
This celestial globe with the ea[r] in its centre was used by nav[i] gators for measuring the positio of the stars. It became the personal emblem of Manuel I.

Magellan (c.1480–1521)
With Spanish funding, Portuguese sailor Fernão de Magalhães, known as Magellan, led the first circumnavigation of the globe (1519–22). He was killed in the Philippines before the voyage's end.

1500–1501 Gaspar Corte Real reaches Newfoundland.

1427 Diogo de Silves discovers the Azores.

1434 Gil Eanes rounds Cape Bojador (Western Sahara).

1460 Diogo Gomes discovers the Cape Verde archipelago.

1470s Discovery of island of São Tomé.

1482 Diogo Cão reaches the mouth of the Congo.

1500 Pedro Álvares Cabral reaches Brazil.

1485 On his third voyage Diogo Cão reaches Cape Cross (Namibia).

1488 Bartolo[meu] Dias rounds C[ape] of Good Ho[pe]

African Ivory Salt Cellar
This 16th-century ivory carving shows Portuguese warriors supporting a globe and a ship. A sailor peers out from the crow's nest at the top.

The Adoration of the Magi
Painted for Viseu Cathedral shortly after Cabral returned from Brazil in 1500, this panel is attributed to the artist Grão Vasco (c.1475–1540). King Baltazar is depicted as a Tupi Indian.

Japanese Screen (c.1600)
This screen shows traders unloading a nau, a great ship. Between 1575 and their expulsion in 1638, the Portuguese monopolized the carrying trade between China and Japan.

HENRY THE NAVIGATOR

Although he did not sail himself, Henry (1394–1460), the third son of João I, laid the foundations for Portugal's maritime expansion that were later built upon by João II and consolidated by Manuel I. As Master of the wealthy Order of Christ and Governor of the Algarve, Henry was able to finance expeditions along the African coast. By the time he died he had a monopoly on all trade south of Cape Bojador. Legend tells that he founded a school of navigation in the Algarve, at either Sagres or Lagos.

KEY

– – – Discoverers' routes

Cloves

Pepper

Nutmeg

Cinnamon

The Spice Trade
Exotic spices were a great source of wealth for Portugal. The much-disputed Moluccas, or Spice Islands, were purchased from Spain in 1528.

1543 Portuguese arrive in Japan.

1513 Trading posts set up in China at Macau and Canton.

1510 Capture of Goa.

1498 Vasco da Gama reaches Calicut in India.

1518 Fortress built in Colombo (Sri Lanka).

1512 Portuguese reach Ternate in the Moluccas (Spice Islands).

PORTUGUESE DISCOVERIES

The systematic attempt to find a sea route to India, which led to a monopoly of the spice trade, began in 1482 with the first voyage of Diogo Cão, who planted a *padrão* (stone cross) on the shores where he landed.

Crow's nest

Square sail on foremast

Cross of the Order of Christ

Lateen-rigged Caravel
These ships with three triangular sails were favoured by the first Portuguese explorers who sailed close to the African coast. For later journeys across the open ocean, square sails were found more effective.

The 1755 Lisbon Earthquake

Votive tile panel offered by survivors

THE FIRST TREMOR of the devastating earthquake was felt at 9:30am on 1 November. A few minutes later there was a second, far more violent shock, reducing over half the city to rubble. Although the epicentre was close to the Algarve, Lisbon, as the most populated area, bore the worst. Over 20 churches collapsed, crushing the crowds who had assembled for All Saints' Day. A third shock was followed by fires which quickly spread. An hour later, huge waves came rolling in from the Tagus and flooded the lower part of the city. Most of Portugal suffered damage and the shock was felt as far away as Italy. Perhaps 15,000 people lost their lives in Lisbon alone.

This anonymous painting of the arrival of a papal ambassador at court in 1693 shows how Terreiro do Paço looked before the earthquake.

Some buildings that might have survived an earthquake alone were destroyed by the fire that followed.

The old royal palace, the 16th-century Paço da Ribeira, was utterly ruined by the earthquake and ensuing flood.

The royal family was staying at the palace in Belém, a place far less affected than Lisbon, and survived the disaster unscathed. Here the king surveys the city's devastation.

Ships crammed full of people fleeing the fire were wrecked and anchors thrown up to water level.

This detail is from a votive painting dedicated to Nossa Senhora da Estrela, given by a grateful father in thanks for the sparing of his daughter's life in the earthquake. The girl was found miraculously alive after being buried under rubble for seven hours.

THE RECONSTRUCTION OF LISBON

Marquês de Pombal (1699–1782)

No sooner had the tremors abated than Sebastião José de Carvalho e Melo, chief minister to José I and later to become Marquês de Pombal, was outlining ideas for rebuilding the city. While philosophers moralized, Pombal reacted with practicality. "Bury the dead and feed the living" is said to have been his initial response. He then began a progressive town-planning scheme. His efficient handling of the crisis won him almost total political control.

REACTIONS TO THE DISASTER

The earthquake had a profound effect on European thought. Eyewitness accounts appeared in the papers, many written by foreigners living in Lisbon. A heated debate developed over whether the earthquake was a natural phenomenon or divine wrath. Pre-earthquake Lisbon had been a flourishing city, famed for its wealth – also for its Inquisition and idolatry. Interpreting the quake as punishment, preachers prophesied further catastrophes. Famous literary figures debated the significance of the event, among them the French writer Voltaire, who wrote a poem about the disaster, propounding his views that evil exists and man is weak and powerless, doomed to an unhappy fate on earth.

French author, Voltaire

The ancient castle walls succumbed to the reverberating shock waves.

Flames erupted as the candles lit for All Saints' Day ignited the city's churches. The fire raged for seven days.

Some of Lisbon's finest buildings were destroyed, along with gold, jewellery, priceless furniture, archives, books and paintings.

At 11am, tidal waves rolled into Terreiro do Paço. The Alcântara docks, to the west, bore the brunt of the impact.

Churches, homes and public buildings all suffered in the disaster. The Royal Opera House, here shown in ruins, was only completed in March the same year.

A CONTEMPORARY VIEW OF THE EARTHQUAKE

This anonymous German engraving of 1775 gives a vivid picture of the scale of the disaster. Many who fled the flames made for the Tagus, but were washed away in the huge waves which struck the Terreiro do Paço. The human and material losses were incalculable.

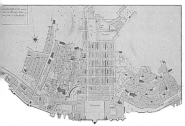

The reconstruction of the centre of Lisbon took place rapidly. By the end of November the Marquês de Pombal had devised a strikingly modern scheme for a grid of parallel streets running from the waterfront to Rossio. The new buildings are shown in yellow.

Modern-day Lisbon holds many reminders of the earthquake. Pombal's innovative grid system is clearly visible in this aerial view of the Baixa (see pp40–47). The scheme took many years to complete, and the triumphal arch that spans Rua Augusta was not finished until over a century later, in 1873.

LISBON THROUGH THE YEAR

WHILE THE SUMMER MONTHS are the most popular for visiting Lisbon and have many events on the calendar – the Festas dos Santos Populares, in June, are one of the highlights of the year – spring and autumn can also be rewarding if you want to tour the Lisbon Coast. In late winter, the colourful Carnaval celebrations attract many visitors to Lisbon. Other events during the year include music festivals, sporting fixtures and the many religious *festas*, which are great times of celebration for the Portuguese people.

SPRING

WITH THE ARRIVAL of springtime in Lisbon, the café and restaurant terraces begin to fill with people. Many events, such as concerts, start to take place in the open air again as the weather improves. At the weekends the coastal resorts of Cascais and Estoril become livelier when on warm, bright days local people take day trips there to enjoy the seaside.

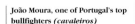

João Moura, one of Portugal's top bullfighters (cavaleiros)

MARCH

Festa da Primavera
(25 Mar). Music, theatre and dance performances, including many open-air events, are held at the Centro Cultural de Belém. The festival offers rock and pop as well as classical music.
Procissão dos Terceiros Franciscanos *(4th Sun before Easter)*. The colourful

procession through the streets of Mafra *(see p92)* starts at the convent. The ceremonial robes worn in the procession were given to the church by João V, in the 18th century.

APRIL

Lisbon's Half Marathon
(1 Apr). One of the city's most popular sporting events, the race crosses the Ponte 25 de Abril *(see p74)* and draws international runners .
Festa dos Merendeiros
(7 Apr). A traditional festival and procession held in Santo Isidoro, near Mafra *(see p92)*. There is a ceremony to bless the bread and the fields in the hope of a successful harvest later on in the year.
Estoril Open Tennis Championship
(early April). International players compete in Portugal's top tennis competition, held at the Jamor Tennis Courts.

Liberty Day *(25 Apr)*. The annual celebration of the Carnation Revolution that ended 48 years of dictatorship in 1974 *(see p15)* is also known as the Dia da Revoluçaõ. A public holiday throughout Portugal, commemorations include a military parade and political speeches at the Praça do Império. The unions organize festivities that take place all over the city.
Beginning of the bullfighting season *(Apr–Sep)*. The Campo Pequeno bullring in Lisbon is the usual venue for this traditional entertainment. However, the ring is being currently refurbished and is now scheduled to reopen in 2004. Bullfights may be seen at rings in Cascais *(see p102)* and Montijo.
Moda Lisboa *(April)*. This biannual fashion show attracts designers from all over the world, and is Portugal's principal fashion event.

MAY

Dia do Trabalhador *(1 May)*. Protest marches and political speeches throughout Lisbon are organized by the unions on Labour Day.
Gulbenkian Contemporary Music Encounters *(21 May–1 Jun)*. A forum for conferences, debates and performances by lesser-known composers and musicians.
Feira do Livro *(May–Jun)*. One of the main literary events in Lisbon, this book fair offers numerous bargains, such as second-hand books and signed copies. The event takes place at the Parque Eduardo VII, the city's largest park *(see p75)*.
Feira do Mar *(May–Jun)*. Held in Sesimbra *(see p106)*, this festival promotes the town's artists and local food.

Formal military parades are held in Lisbon in celebration of Liberty Day

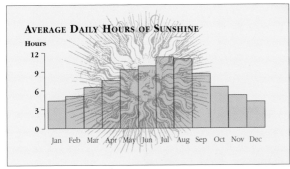

AVERAGE DAILY HOURS OF SUNSHINE

Hours

12
9
6
3
0

Jan Feb Mar Apr May Jun Jul Aug Sep Oct Nov Dec

Sunshine Chart
Although Lisbon enjoys a moderate amount of sunshine all year, the days are particularly hot and sunny in the summer months. Care should be taken to protect the skin against the sun, both when walking around Lisbon itself and when sunbathing along the coast on the beaches of Estoril or Cascais.

SUMMER

THE SUMMER MONTHS are a major holiday time in Lisbon, especially August when many Lisboetas retire to the coastal resorts, in particular Costa da Caparica and Cascais.

JUNE

Festas da Cidade *(throughout Jun)*. A celebration of the city of Lisbon itself, that includes all sorts of events from rock concerts to drive-in films. The festa is in addition to the three saints' festivals listed below.
Santo António *(12–13 Jun)*.
São João *(23–24 Jun)*.
São Pedro *(25 Jun–1 Jul)*.
Santo António is the major festival in Lisbon, honouring the city's patron saint, and the beginning of the Festas dos Santos Populares (Feasts of the People's Saints). Locals decorate the Alfama and bring out chairs for the hundreds who come for the celebrations.

Celebrating Santo António, one of Lisbon's most important festivals

The beach at Estoril, just one of the many popular bays along the Lisbon Coast

The festivities continue throughout June with the festas of São João and São Pedro.
Troia Internationl Film Festival *(throughout Jun)*. Based at Setúbal, south of Lisbon, this festival is aimed at countries with an annual production of less than 21 feature films.
Arraial Gay e Lésbico *(late Jun)*. Up to a week of events and celebrations held in one of Lisbon's parks or squares.
Feira Grande de São Pedro *(29 Jun)*. A market of crafts, antiques and local delicacies, in Sintra *(see pp96–9)*.
Festival de Música de Sintra *(mid-Jun–mid-Jul)*. A series of classical music concerts held in the parks and palaces of Sintra and Queluz *(see pp96–9)*.

JULY

Festival Internacional de Teatro (FIT) *(early–mid-July)*. This international festival is held in venues across Lisbon, and is one of Portugal's main theatrical events.
FIA-Lisbon International Handicraft Exhibition *(early Jul)*. This huge display of arts and crafts is held in the Parque de Nações.

Festival Estoril Jazz *(early Jul)*. A series of jazz concerts, lasting about a week, takes place in locations in and around Lisbon.
Feira de Artesanato *(Jul–Aug)*. This craft fair is held in Estoril *(see p102)*, and features folk music and dance performances.
Feira dos Alhos *(3rd Sun in Jul)*. Annual market of crafts, delicacies and wine- and cheese-tasting, near the Convent of Mafra *(see p92)*.
Capuchos Music Festival *(Jul–Aug)*. Centred on the Capuchos Monastery on the south side of the Tagus.
BaixAnima *(Jul–Sep)*. Street performances, music, dance and circus acts take place at weekends in the squares and streets of Baixa and Chiado.
Verão Em Sesimbra *(Jul–Sep)*. Popular entertainment festival held in the town of Sesimbra *(see p106)*.

AUGUST

Jazz em Agosto *(early Aug)*. Jazz music is performed in the gardens of the Calouste Gulbenkian Cultural Centre.
Noites de Bailado em Seteais *(weekends throughout Aug)*. Ballet performances are held in the Seteais palace gardens, near Sintra *(see pp96–7)*.
Romaria de São Mamede *(14–22 Aug)*. Farmers lead their animals around the chapel of Janas, north of Colares *(see p93)*, to be blessed. The tradition originates in the fact that the site of the church was once that of a Roman temple dedicated to Diana, goddess of hunting and animals.

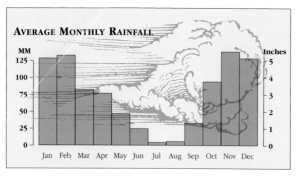

AVERAGE MONTHLY RAINFALL

Rainfall Chart
*Rainfall is fairly
heavy in the winter
months in Lisbon,
and then drops
steadily until the
height of summer,
when there is almost
no rain at all. The
autumn, although
still warm, can
produce some wet
days, the wettest
month on average
being November.*

AUTUMN

IN MANY WAYS, this is the best season for touring and sightseeing. The strong heat of the summer has passed but the weather is still pleasantly warm. The countryside around Sintra is particularly beautiful with the changing colours of the trees.

SEPTEMBER

Avante! *(1st weekend in Sep).*
This lively *festa* in Seixal, south of the Tagus, attracts large crowds. It includes rock and folk music, exhibitions and cultural events and an array of delicious food.
Nossa Senhora da Luz *(2nd weekend of Sep)*. A religious *festa* held in honour of Our Lady of the Light in Sampaio, near Sesimbra *(see p106)*.
Festa das Vindimas *(early Sep)*. At the foot of Palmela's medieval castle *(see p106)*, the first grape harvest is blessed, amid traditional entertainment, wine- and cheese-tasting and fireworks.

Nossa Senhora do Cabo Espichel *(last Sun of Sep)*.
Local fishermen honour the Virgin Mary with a procession up to the church at Cabo Espichel *(see p103)*.
Feira da Luz *(throughout Sep)*. This event focuses on arts and crafts, especially pottery. It takes place in the Carnide district of Lisbon.
Festa de Senhora da Consolação *(throughout Sep)*. This festival in the Assafora area of Sintra *(see p96–101)* celebrates Portugal's patron saint with a month of parties, music and food.
Encontros ACARTE *(throughout Sep)*. Organized by the Gulbenkian Foundation, this is a programme of activities designed to promote new talent in the arts. It runs all year round but a show is held in September. *Acarte* is an acronym standing for Animation, Creativity, Art and Education.

OCTOBER

Republic Day *(5 Oct)*. The revolution that brought the monarchy to an end in 1910 *(see p15)*, is commemorated annually in Lisbon with military parades.
Estoril Golf Open *(late Oct)*. A major golf tournament, in Estoril *(see p102)*.

An old lady laying flowers at a cemetery in Lisbon in honour of All Saints' Day

NOVEMBER

All Saints' Day *(1 Nov)*.
An important festival in the Portuguese religious calendar, many families light candles and lay flowers in local cemeteries throughout the area, in honour of their dead relatives.
Feira de Todos os Santos *(1 Nov)*. Also known as the Dried Fruits' Market, this is a lively fair held in Azureira, near Mafra *(see p92)*.
Dia do Magusto e de São Martinho *(11 Nov)*. The celebration of Roast Chestnut Day is based on the tradition of preparing for winter.
Circus *(late Nov–early Jan)*.
Before Christmas, circuses arrive in Lisbon. Check venues and dates with tourist offices.
Lisbon Marathon *(end Nov)*.
Festive celebrations in the city as the runners compete.

Blessing the grape harvest at the Festa das Vindimas in Palmela

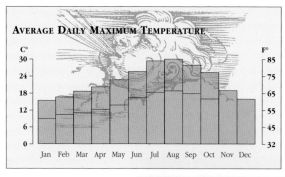

AVERAGE DAILY MAXIMUM TEMPERATURE

Temperature Chart
Lisbon is rarely very cold, and maintains a pleasantly mild climate, even during the winter months, making it a good city to visit in any season. However, the summer months bring days of consistent heat, and although the city is quiet in high summer, it can become humid and stifling.

WINTER

THOSE SEEKING MILD, sunny climes and an escape from the winter cold, will find this a good time of year to visit Lisbon. The nightlife is very lively and continues until the early hours, especially at weekends. Christmas is a time of great celebration and an important occasion for families to reunite and enjoy long meals together.

DECEMBER

Festa de Imaculada Conceição *(8 Dec)*. This festival of the Immaculate Conception is a national holiday throughout Portugal. There are special church services and Lisbon's population celebrate with their usual festive spirit.
Christmas *(24–25 Dec)*. Throughout the Lisbon area, churches and shops display nativity scenes and cribs. The main celebrations take place on Christmas Eve, when families get together and go to midnight mass. They then return home for a large traditional meal of *bacalhau* (salted dried cod) and *sonhos* (small fried cakes similar to doughnuts, usually flavoured with pumpkin or orange).
Nossa Senhora da Conceição *(26 Dec)*. A traditional religious procession held in honour of Our Lady of the Immaculate Conception, the saint protector of Alfarim, near Sesimbra *(see p106)*.

Colourful parades during the annual Carnaval celebrations in Lisbon

JANUARY

New Year *(31 Dec–1 Jan)*. In Lisbon, a spectacular firework display is held in Praça do Comércio to welcome the New Year.
Epiphany *(6 Jan)*. The traditional cake baked for the Epiphany is *bolo rei* (king's cake), a small fruit cake made with a lucky charm and a bean inside. Crown-shaped, it is topped with crystallized fruit, resembling gems. The person who gets the bean must then buy the next cake. *Bolo rei* is also made at Christmas time.

The celebratory cake, *bolo rei*

Opera season *(Jan–Nov)*. The opera season starts at the Teatro Nacional de São Carlos *(see p53)*.

FEBRUARY

Carnaval *(date varies)*. This is celebrated throughout Portugal with spectacular costumes and floats; there is an especially colourful parade in Sesimbra *(see p106)*.

Procissão do Senhor dos Passos da Graça *(second Sun in Lent)*. The figure of Christ *(Senhor dos Passos)* is taken out of the Igreja da Graça *(see p37)* and carried through the streets of Graça, in Lisbon. The procession dates back to the 16th century.

PUBLIC HOLIDAYS

New Year's Day (1 Jan)
Carnaval (Feb)
Good Friday (Mar or Apr)
Dia 25 de Abril, *commemorating 1974 revolution* (25 Apr)
Dia do Trabalhador, *Labour Day* (1 May)
Corpus Christi (6 Jun)
Camões Day (10 Jun)
Assumption Day (15 Aug)
Republic Day (5 Oct)
All Saints' Day (1 Nov)
Dia da Restauração, *commemorating Independence from Spain, 1640* (1 Dec)
Immaculate Conception (8 Dec)
Christmas Day (25 Dec)

LISBON AREA
BY AREA

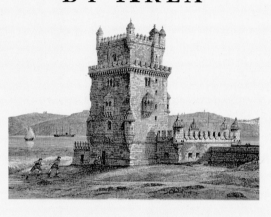

Lisbon at a Glance

PORTUGAL'S CAPITAL, a city of about 550,000 people, sits on the north bank of the Tagus estuary, 17 km (10 miles) from the Atlantic. Razed to the ground by the devastating earthquake of 1755 *(see pp20–21)*, the city centre, the Baixa, is essentially 18th century, with a carefully planned grid of elegant streets. On the hills on either side of the centre, the narrow streets of the Alfama and Bairro Alto make it a personal, approachable city. The construction of the 25 de Abril Bridge, in the 1960s, encouraged development on the Outra Banda (the other bank). The Vasco da Gama Bridge, completed in 1998, added interest to the Expo site, the Parque das Naçoes *(see p81)*. Since its days of glory when Lisbon was at the forefront of world trade, the city has been an important port. Today the docks have moved, but in Belém, along the river from the centre, the Mosteiro dos Jerónimos and the Torre de Belém bear witness to the city's maritime past.

The Museu Nacional de Arte Antig houses paintings and sculpture. There a notable Flemish-influenced Portugues works such as Jorge Afonso's Apparitic of Christ to the Virgin (see pp56–7).

The Mosteiro dos Jerónimos *is a magnificent 16th-century monastery. Commissioned by Manuel I, much of it is built in the peculiarly Portuguese style of architecture, known as Manueline. The extravagantly sculpted south portal of the church with its minute detailing was designed by João de Castilho in 1516. It is one of the finest examples of the style* (see pp66–7).

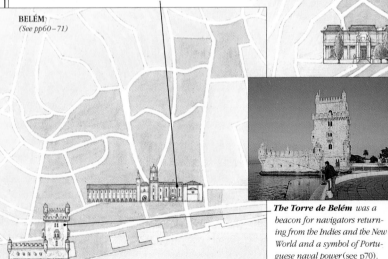

BELÉM
(See pp60–71)

The Torre de Belém *was a beacon for navigators returning from the Indies and the New World and a symbol of Portuguese naval power* (see p70).

◁ **View from the Tagus of Praça do Comércio with the statue of José I at the centre**

The Elevador de Santa Justa, built at the turn of the century, is a wrought-iron lift decorated with filigree that links the Baixa quarter with Largo do Carmo (see p46).

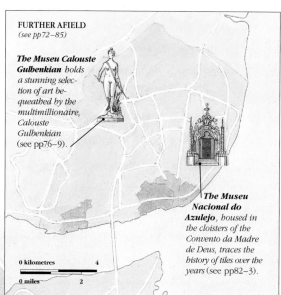

FURTHER AFIELD
(see pp72–85)

The Museu Calouste Gulbenkian holds a stunning selection of art bequeathed by the multimillionaire, Calouste Gulbenkian *(see pp76–9)*.

The Museu Nacional do Azulejo, housed in the cloisters of the Convento da Madre de Deus, traces the history of tiles over the years *(see pp82–3)*.

0 kilometres 4

0 miles 2

BAIXA AND AVENIDA
(See pp40–47)

BAIRRO ALTO AND ESTRELA
(See pp48–59)

ALFAMA
(See pp30–39)

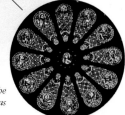

The Castelo de São Jorge, once a Moorish castle and then the abode of the Portuguese kings, was transformed in the 1930s into tranquil public gardens. The battlements afford spectacular views of the city *(see pp38–9)*.

The Sé, the city's greatly restored cathedral, is a sturdy Romanesque building noted for its beautiful rose window. Ornate silver and ecclesistical robes are among the many religious objects on display in the treasury *(see p36)*.

0 metres 500

0 yards 500

ALFAMA

I T IS DIFFICULT TO BELIEVE that this humble neighbourhood was once the most desirable quarter of Lisbon. For the Moors, the tightly packed alleyways around the fortified castle comprised the whole city. The seeds of decline were sown in the Middle Ages when wealthy residents moved west for fear of earthquakes, leaving the quarter to fishermen and paupers. The buildings survived the 1755 earthquake *(see pp20–21)* and, although there are no Moorish houses still standing, the quarter retains its kasbah-like layout. Compact houses line steep streets and stairways, their façades strung with washing.

Portugal's coat of arms in the treasury of the Sé

Long-overdue restoration is under way in the most dilapidated areas, but daily life still revolves around local grocery stores and small, cellar-like tavernas.

Above the Alfama, the imposing Castelo de São Jorge crowns Lisbon's eastern hill. This natural vantage point, a defensive stronghold and royal palace until the 16th century, is today a popular promenade, with spectacular views from its reconstructed ramparts.

West of the Alfama stand the proud twin towers of the Sé. To the north-east, the domed church of Santa Engrácia and the white façade of São Vicente de Fora dominate the skyline.

SIGHTS AT A GLANCE

Museums and Galleries
Museu de Artes Decorativas ②
Museu Militar ⑥

Historic Buildings
Casa dos Bicos ⑦
Castelo de São Jorge pp38–9 ⑩

Churches
Santo António à Sé ⑨

Santa Engrácia ⑤
São Vicente de Fora ③
Sé ⑧

Belvederes
Miradouro da Graça ⑪
Miradouro de Santa Luzia ①

Markets
Feira da Ladra ④

GETTING THERE
The 12 and 28 trams rattle up the narrow streets of the Alfama from the Baixa. Bus 37 does a circuit from the Castle to Rossio. Many buses run east along Avenida Dom Infante Henrique to Santa Apolónia station, and west to Belém.

KEY

▨	Street-by-Street: Alfama *pp32–3*
🚉	Railway station
P	Parking
ℹ	Tourist information
—	Castle walls

0 metres 　　250
0 yards 　　250

◁ **Ironwork balconies on a house in Rua dos Bacalhoeiros, beside the Casa dos Bicos**

Street-by-Street: Alfama

A FASCINATING QUARTER at any time of day, the Alfama comes to life in the late afternoon and early evening when the locals emerge at their doorways and the small tavernas start to fill. A new generation of younger residents has resulted in a small number of trendy shops and bars. Given the steep streets and steps of the quarter, the least strenuous approach is to start at the top and work your way down. A walk around the maze of winding alleyways will reveal picturesque corners and crumbling churches as well as panoramic views from the shady terraces, such as the Miradouro de Santa Luzia.

On Largo das Portas do Sol, café tables look out over the Alfama towards the Tagus estuary. Portas do Sol was one of the entrance gates to the old city.

Statue of St. Vincent

Largo das Portas do Sol has its own terrace viewpoint on a converted rooftop on the east side of the Santa Luzia church.

The church of Santa Luzia has 18th-century blue and white *azulejo* panels on its south wall.

L. DAS PORTAS DO SOL

BECO DE SANTA HELENA

R. DO

Castelo de São Jorge

RUA N. DE ARAÚJO

★ Museu de Artes Decorativas
Set up as a museum by the banker Ricardo do Espírito Santo Silva, the 17th-century Palácio Azurara houses fine 17th- and 18th-century Portuguese furniture and decorative arts **2**

KEY

- - - Suggested route

0 metres   25
0 yards   25

STAR SIGHTS

★ Miradouro de Santa Luzia

★ Museu de Artes Decorativas

★ Miradouro de Santa Luzia
The view from this bougainvillea-clad terrace spans the tiled roofs of the Alfama toward the Tagus. This is a pleasant place to rest after a walk around the area's steep streets **1**

Beco dos Cruzes, like most of the alleyways *(becos)* that snake their way through the Alfama, is a steep cobbled street. Locals often hang washing between the tightly packed houses.

LOCATOR MAP
See Lisbon Street Finder map 8

Rua de São Pedro is the scene of a lively early-morning fish market where the *varinas* sell the catch of the day. *Peixe espada* (scabbard fish) is one of the fish sold here.

Largo do Chafariz de Dentro is named after the 17th-century fountain *(chafariz)* that was originally placed within *(dentro)* rather than outside the 14th-century walls.

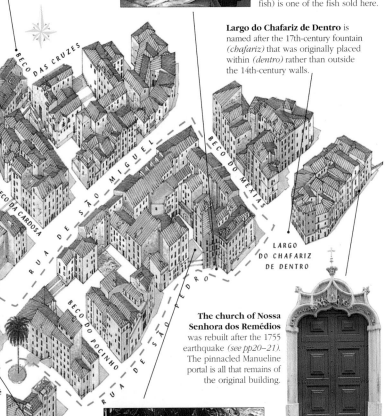

The church of Nossa Senhora dos Remédios was rebuilt after the 1755 earthquake *(see pp20–21)*. The pinnacled Manueline portal is all that remains of the original building.

São Miguel was rebuilt after it was damaged in the 1755 earthquake. It retains a few earlier features, including a fine ceiling of Brazilian jacaranda wood.

Popular restaurants hidden in the labyrinth of alleyways spill out onto open-air patios. The Lautasco *(see p128)*, in Beco do Azinhal, serves excellent Portuguese food.

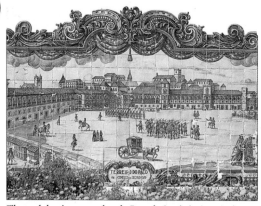

Tile panel showing pre-earthquake Praça do Comércio, Santa Luzia

Miradouro de Santa Luzia ❶

Rua do Limoeiro. **Map** 8 D4. 🚊 28.

THE TERRACE by the church of Santa Luzia provides a sweeping view over the Alfama and the River Tagus. Distinctive landmarks, from left to right, are the cupola of Santa Engrácia, the church of Santo Estêvão and the two startling white towers of São Miguel. While tourists admire the views, old men play cards under the bougainvillea-clad pergola. The south wall of Santa Luzia has two modern tiled panels, one of Praça do Comércio before it was flattened by the earthquake, the other showing the Christians attacking the Castelo de São Jorge (see pp38–9) in 1147.

Museu de Artes Decorativas ❷

Largo das Portas do Sol 2. **Map** 8 D3.
📞 21-888 19 91 or 881 46 00.
🚊 37. 🚋 12, 28. ◯ 10am–5pm
Tue–Sun. ◯ 1 Jan, Easter, 1 May,
25 Dec. 🏷 ♿ 🌐 www.fress.pt

ALSO KNOWN AS the Ricardo do Espírito Santo Silva Foundation, the museum was set up in 1953 to preserve the traditions and increase public awareness of the Portuguese decorative arts. The foundation was named after a banker who bought the 17th-century Palácio Azurara in 1947 to house his fine collection of furniture, textiles, silver and ceramics. Among the 17th- and 18th-century antiques displayed in this handsome four-storey mansion are many fine pieces in exotic woods, including an 18th-century rosewood back-gammon and chess table. Also of note are the collections of 18th-century silver and Chinese porcelain, and the Arraiolos carpets. The spacious rooms still retain some original ceilings and *azulejo* panels.

18th-century china cutlery case, Museu de Artes Decorativas

In the adjoining building are workshops where artisans preserve the techniques of cabinet-making, gilding, bookbinding and other traditional crafts. Temporary exhibitions, lectures and concerts are also held in the palace.

Stone figure of a woman praying by the tomb of Carlos I in São Vicente de Fora

São Vicente de Fora ❸

Largo de São Vicente. **Map** 8 E3.
📞 21-882 44 00. 🚋 12, 34.
🚊 28. ◯ 9am–6:30pm Tue–Sun.
🕇 📷 🌐 to cloisters.

ST VINCENT was proclaimed Lisbon's patron saint in 1173, when his relics were transferred from the Algarve, in southern Portugal, to a church on this site outside (*fora*) the city walls. Designed by the Italian architect Filippo Terzi, and completed in 1627, the off-white façade is sober and symmetrical, in Italian Renaissance style, with towers either side and statues of saints Augustine, Sebastian and Vincent over the entrance. Inside, one is drawn immediately to Machado de Castro's Baroque canopy over the altar, flanked by life-size wooden statues.

The adjoining former Augustinian monastery, reached via the nave, retains its 16th-century cistern and vestiges of the former cloister but is visited for its 18th-century *azulejos*. Among the panels in the entrance hall off the first cloister there are lively, though historically inaccurate, tile scenes of Afonso Henriques attacking Lisbon and Santarém. Around the cloisters, the tiled rural scenes are surrounded by floral designs and cherubs, illustrating the fables of La Fontaine. A passageway leads behind the church to the old refectory, transformed into the Bragança Pantheon in 1885. The stone sarcophagi of almost every king and queen are here, from João IV, who died in 1656, to Manuel II, last king of Portugal. Only Maria I and Pedro IV are not buried here. A stone mourner kneels at the tomb of Carlos I and his son Luís Felipe, assassinated in Praça do Comércio in 1908.

Feira da Ladra ➍

Campo de Santa Clara. **Map** 8 F2. ◯
7:30am–1pm Tue & Sat. 🚌 12. 🚋 28.

T HE STALLS of the so-called
"Thieves' Market" have
occupied this site on the edge
of the Alfama for over a century, laid out under the shade
of trees or canopies. As the
fame of this flea market has
grown, bargains are increasingly hard to find amongst the
mass of bric-a-brac, but a few
of the vendors have interesting
wrought-iron work, prints and
tiles, as well as second-hand
clothes. Evidence of Portugal's
colonial past is reflected in
the stalls selling African
statuary, masks and jewellery.
Fish, vegetables and herbs are
sold in the central wrought-
iron marketplace.

Bric-a-brac for sale in the Feira da Ladra

Santa Engrácia ➎

Campo de Santa Clara. **Map** 8 F2.
📞 21-814 96 17. 🚌 12. 🚋 28.
◯ 10am–5pm Tue–Sun. ⬤ public
hols. 🈂 🈳 ♿

O NE OF LISBON'S most striking
landmarks, the soaring
dome of Santa Engrácia punc-
tuates the skyline in the east
of the city. The original church
collapsed in a storm in 1681.
The first stone of the new
Baroque monument, laid in
1682, marked the beginning
of a 284-year saga which led
to the invention of a saying
that a Santa Engrácia job was
never done. The church was
not completed until 1966.
   The interior is paved with
coloured marble and crowned
by a giant cupola. As the
National Pantheon, it houses
cenotaphs of Portuguese
heroes, such as Vasco da
Gama (see p68) and Afonso

de Albuquerque, Viceroy of
India (1502–15) on the left,
and on the right Henry the
Navigator (see p19). More
contemporary tombs include
that of the fadista, Amália
Rodrigues (see p143). A lift up
to the dome offers a 360-
degree panorama of the city.

Museu Militar ➏

Largo do Museu de Artilharia. **Map**
8 D3. 📞 21-884 25 69. 🚌 9, 25,
28, 35, 39, 46. 🚋 28. ◯ 10am–
5pm Tue–Sun. ⬤ public hols. 🈂
🌐 www.geira.pt/mmilitar

L OCATED on the site of a 16th-
century cannon foundry
and arms depot, the military
museum contains an extensive
display of arms, uniforms and
historical documents. Visits
begin in the Vasco da
Gama Room with a col-
lection of old cannons
and modern murals
depicting the discovery
of the sea route to India.
The Salas da Grande
Guerra, on the first floor,
display exhibits related
to World War I. Other
rooms focus on the
evolution of weapons in
Portugal, from primitive
flints through spears to
rifles. The large court-
yard, flanked by cannons, tells
the story of Portugal in tiled
panels, from the Christian Re-
conquest to World War I. The
Portuguese artillery section in
the oldest part of the museum
displays the wagon used to
transport the triumphal arch
to Rua Augusta (see p47).

**The multicoloured marble interior
beneath Santa Engrácia's dome**

Casa dos Bicos ➐

Rua dos Bacalhoeiros. **Map** 8 D4.
📞 21-881 09 00. 🚌 9, 28, 46, 59.
🚋 18, 25. ◯ 9:30am–5:30pm Mon–
Fri (ground floor only). ⬤ public hols.

T HIS CONSPICUOUS house,
faced with diamond-shaped
stones (bicos), was built in
1523 for Brás de Albuquerque,
illegitimate son of Afonso,
Viceroy of India and conqueror
of Goa and Malacca. The
façade is an adaptation of a
style popular in Europe during
the 16th century. The two top
storeys, ruined in the earthquake of 1755, were restored
in the 1980s, recreating the
original from old views of
Lisbon in tile panels and
engravings. In the interim the
building was used for salting
fish (Rua dos Bacalhoeiros
means street of the cod fishermen). The modern interior of
the lower floors is used for
temporary exhibitions.

The curiously faceted Casa dos Bicos, and surrounding buildings

The façade of the Sé, the city's cathedral

Sé ❽

Largo da Sé. **Map** 8 D4. 🕾 21-886
67 52. 🚋 37. 🚌 12, 28. ⏰ 9am–
7pm Tue–Sat (cloister & treasury
10am–5pm), 9am–5pm Sun, Mon &
public hols. ✝ 📷 💰 to cloister
& treasury.

I N 1150, THREE YEARS after
Afonso Henriques recap-
tured Lisbon from the Moors,
he built a cathedral for the first
bishop of Lisbon, the English
crusader Gilbert of Hastings,
on the site of the old mosque.
Sé is short for Sedes Episco-
palis, the seat (or see) of a
bishop. Devastated by three
earth tremors in the 14th century, as well as the earthquake
of 1755, and
renovated over the
centuries, the
cathedral you see
today blends a
variety of archi-
tectural styles.
The façade, with
twin castellated
belltowers and a
splendid rose win-
dow, retains its
solid Romanesque
aspect. The gloomy
interior, for the most
part, is simple and
austere, and hardly
anything remains
of the embellish-
ment lavished
upon it by King
João V in the first
half of the 18th
century. Beyond
the renovated Romanesque
nave the ambulatory has nine
Gothic chapels. The Capela de
Santo Ildefonso contains the
14th-century sarcophagi of
Lopo Fernandes Pacheco,
companion in arms to King
Afonso IV, and his wife, Maria
Vilalobos. The bearded figure
of the nobleman, sword in

**Tomb of the 14th-century nobleman Lopo
Fernandes Pacheco in the ambulatory**

Detail of the Baroque nativity scene
by Joaquim Machado de Castro

hand, and his wife, clutching
a prayer book, are carved
onto the tombs with their
dogs sitting faithfully at their
feet. In the adjacent chancel
are the tombs of Afonso IV
and his wife Dona Beatriz.

The Gothic **cloister**, reached
via the third chapel in the ambulatory, has elegant double
arches with some finely carved
capitals. One of the chapels is
still fitted with its 13th-century
wrought-iron gate. Archaeological excavations in the
cloister have unearthed various
Roman and other remains.

To the left of the cathedral
entrance the
Franciscan chapel
contains the font
where the saint
was baptized in
1195 and is decor-
ated with a charm-
ing tiled scene of St
Antony preaching
to the fishes. The
adjacent chapel
contains a Baroque
nativity scene made of cork,
wood and terracotta by
Machado de Castro (1766).

The **treasury** is at the top
of the staircase on the right.
It houses silver, ecclesiastical
robes, statuary, illustrated
manuscripts and a few relics
associated with St Vincent
which were transferred to
Lisbon from Cape St Vincent
in southern Portugal in 1173.
Legend has it that two sacred
ravens kept a vigil over the
boat that transported the
relics. The ravens and the
boat became a symbol of the
city of Lisbon, still very much
in use today. It is also said
that the ravens' descendants
used to dwell in the cloisters
of the cathedral.

SANTO ANTÓNIO (C.1195–1231)

To the chagrin of the Lisboetas, their best-loved
saint is known as St Antony of Padua. Although
born and brought up in Lisbon, he spent
the last months of his life in Padua, Italy.
St Antony joined the Franciscan Order in
1220, impressed by some crusading friars he
had met at Coimbra where he was studying.
The Franciscan friar was a learned and pas-
sionate preacher, renowned for his devotion
to the poor and his ability to convert heretics.
Many statues and paintings of St Antony depict
him carrying the Infant Jesus on a book,
while others show him preaching to the
fishes, as St Francis preached to the birds.
In 1934 Pope Pius XI declared St Antony
a patron saint of Portugal. On 13 June, the
anniversary of his death, there are celebrations in the Alfama district and a costumed
procession along Avenida da Liberdade.

Santo António à Sé ❾

Largo Santo António à Sé, 24. **Map** 7 C4. 📞 21-886 91 45. 🚌 37. 🚋 12, 28. ⏰ 8am–7:30pm daily. ⛪ public hols. 🏛 **Museu Antoniano** 📞 21-886 04 47. ⏰ 10am–1pm, 2–6pm Tue–Sun. ♿

THE POPULAR LITTLE church of Santo António allegedly stands on the site of the house in which St Antony was born. The crypt, reached via the tiled sacristy on the left of the church, is all that remains of the original church destroyed by the earthquake of 1755. Work began on the new church in 1757 headed by Mateus Vicente, architect of the Basílica da Estrela *(see p55)* and was partially funded by donations collected by local children with the cry "a small coin for St Antony". Even today the floor of the tiny chapel in the crypt is strewn with escudos and the walls are scrawled with devotional messages from worshippers.

The church's façade blends the undulating curves of the Baroque style with Neo-Classical Ionic columns on either side of the main portal. Inside, on the way down to the crypt, a modern *azulejo* panel commemorates the visit of Pope John Paul II in 1982. In 1995 the church was given a facelift for the saint's eighth centenary. It is traditional for young couples to visit the

The Miradouro and Igreja da Graça seen from the Castelo de São Jorge

church on their wedding day and leave flowers for St Antony who is believed to bring good luck to new marriages.

Next door the small **Museu Antoniano** houses artefacts, relating to St Antony, as well as gold and silverware which used to decorate the church. The most charming exhibit is a 17th-century tiled panel of St Antony preaching to the fishes.

Castelo de São Jorge ❿

See pp38–9.

Miradouro da Graça ⓫

Map 8 D2. 🚌 37. 🚋 12, 28.

THE WORKING-CLASS quarter of Graça developed at the end of the 19th century. Today, it is visited chiefly for the views from its *miradouro* (belvedere). The panorama of rooftops and skyscrapers is less spectacular than the view from the castle, but it is a popular spot, particularly in the early evenings when couples sit at café tables under the pines. Behind the *miradouro* stands an Augustinian monastery, founded in 1271 and rebuilt after the earthquake. Once a flourishing complex, the huge building is nowadays used as barracks but the church, the **Igreja da Graça**, can still be visited. Inside, in the right transept, is the *Senhor dos Passos*, a representation of Christ carrying the cross on the way to Calvary. This figure, clad in brilliant purple clothes, is carried on a procession through Graça on the second Sunday in Lent. The *azulejos* on the altar front, dating from the 17th century, imitate the brocaded textiles usually draped over the altar.

Tiled panel recording Pope John Paul II's visit to Santo António à Sé

Castelo de São Jorge ⑩

Stone head of Martim Moniz

F OLLOWING THE RECAPTURE of Lisbon from the Moors in 1147, King Afonso Henriques transformed their hilltop citadel into the residence of the Portuguese kings. In 1511 Manuel I built a more lavish palace in what is now the Praça do Comércio and the castle was used variously as a theatre, prison and arms depot. After the 1755 earthquake the ramparts remained in ruins until 1938 when Salazar *(see p15)* began a complete renovation, rebuilding the "medieval" walls and adding gardens and wild-fowl. The castle may not be authentic but the gardens and the narrow streets of the Santa Cruz district within the walls make a pleasant stroll and the views are the finest in Lisbon.

Torre de Ulisses has a camera obscura that projects views of Lisbon onto the inside walls of the tower.

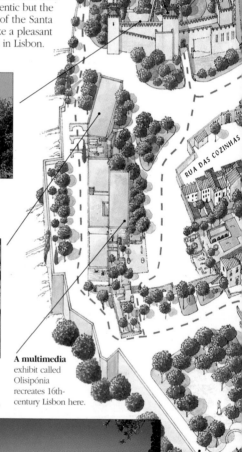

RUA DAS COZINHAS

★ Battlements
Visitors can climb the towers and walk along the reconstructed ramparts of the castle walls.

Casa do Leão Restaurant
Part of the former royal residence can be booked for evening meals and parties (see p128).

A multimedia exhibit called Olisipónia recreates 16th-century Lisbon here.

★ Observation Terrace
This large shaded square affords spectacular views over Lisbon and the Tagus. Local men play backgammon and cards under the trees.

KEY

– – – Suggested route

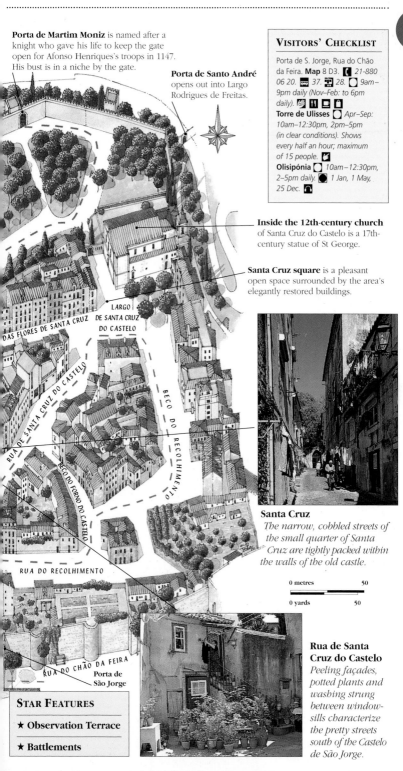

Porta de Martim Moniz is named after a knight who gave his life to keep the gate open for Afonso Henriques's troops in 1147. His bust is in a niche by the gate.

Porta de Santo André opens out into Largo Rodrigues de Freitas.

VISITORS' CHECKLIST

Porta de S. Jorge, Rua do Chão da Feira. **Map** 8 D3. 📞 *21-880 06 20.* 🚌 *37.* 🚋 *28.* 🕐 *9am– 9pm daily (Nov–Feb: to 6pm daily).* 🚫 🚻 🛒 🔒
Torre de Ulisses 🕐 *Apr–Sep: 10am–12:30pm, 2pm–5pm (in clear conditions). Shows every half an hour; maximum of 15 people.* 🚫
Olisipónia 🕐 *10am–12:30pm, 2–5pm daily.* ⬤ *1 Jan, 1 May, 25 Dec.* 🔒

Inside the 12th-century church of Santa Cruz do Castelo is a 17th-century statue of St George.

Santa Cruz square is a pleasant open space surrounded by the area's elegantly restored buildings.

LARGO DE SANTA CRUZ DO CASTELO

DAS FLORES DE SANTA CRUZ

RUA DE SANTA CRUZ DO CASTELO

BECO DO RECOLHIMENTO

BECO DO FORNO DO CASTELO

RUA DO RECOLHIMENTO

RUA DO CHÃO DA FEIRA

Porta de São Jorge

Santa Cruz
The narrow, cobbled streets of the small quarter of Santa Cruz are tightly packed within the walls of the old castle.

0 metres   50
0 yards   50

Rua de Santa Cruz do Castelo
Peeling façades, potted plants and washing strung between window-sills characterize the pretty streets south of the Castelo de São Jorge.

STAR FEATURES

★ **Observation Terrace**

★ **Battlements**

BAIXA AND AVENIDA

FROM THE RUINS of Lisbon, devastated by the earthquake of 1755 (*see pp20–21*), the Marquês de Pombal created an entirely new centre. Using a grid layout of streets, he linked Praça do Comércio with the busy central square of Rossio. The streets were flanked by uniform, Neo-Classical buildings and named according to the shopkeepers and craftsmen who traded there. The Arco Triumfal was built 80 years later.

Detail on statue of José I in Praça do Comércio

The Baixa (lower town) is still the commercial hub of the capital, housing banks, offices and shops. At its centre, Rossio is a popular meeting point with cafés, theatres and restaurants. The geometric layout of the area has been retained, but most of the buildings constructed since the mid-18th century have not adhered to Pombaline formality. The streets are crowded by day, particularly the lively Rua Augusta, but after dark the quarter is almost deserted.

SIGHTS AT A GLANCE

Museums and Galleries
Museu da Sociedade de Geografia **4**

Churches
Nossa Senhora da Conceição Velha **9**

Parks and Gardens
Jardim Botânico **1**

Lifts
Elevador de Santa Justa **7**

Historic Streets and Squares
Avenida da Liberdade **2**
Praça do Comércio **10**
Praça da Figueira **6**
Praça dos Restauradores **3**
Rossio **5**
Rua Augusta **8**

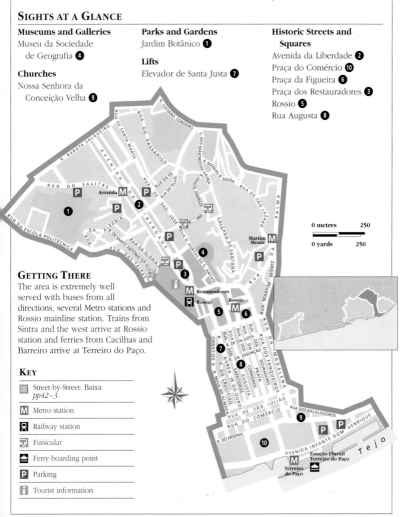

GETTING THERE
The area is extremely well served with buses from all directions, several Metro stations and Rossio mainline station. Trains from Sintra and the west arrive at Rossio station and ferries from Cacilhas and Barreiro arrive at Terreiro do Paço.

KEY

▨	Street-by-Street: Baixa *pp42–3*
Ⓜ	Metro station
🚆	Railway station
🚡	Funicular
⛴	Ferry boarding point
P	Parking
ℹ	Tourist information

◁ **The triumphal arch in Praça do Comércio leading into Rua Augusta and the Baixa**

Street-by-Street: Restauradores

Tʜɪs ɪs ᴛʜᴇ ʙᴜsɪᴇsᴛ ᴘᴀʀᴛ of the city, especially the central squares of Rossio and Praça da Figueira. Totally rebuilt after the earthquake of 1755 *(see pp20–21)*, the area was one of Europe's first examples of town planning. Today, the large Neo-Classical buildings on the wide streets and squares house business offices. The atmosphere and surroundings are best absorbed from one of the busy pavement cafés. Rua das Portas de Santo Antão, a pedestrianized street where restaurants display tanks of live lobsters, is more relaxing for a stroll.

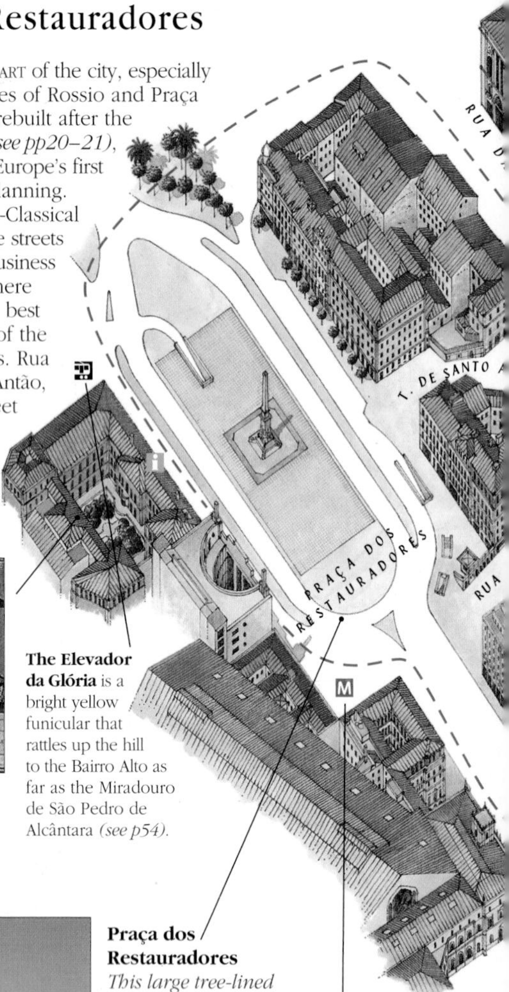

Tiled panel on façade of the Tabacaria Monaco

Palácio Foz, once a magnificent 18th-century palace built by the Italian architect Francesco Fabri, now houses a tourist office.

The Elevador da Glória is a bright yellow funicular that rattles up the hill to the Bairro Alto as far as the Miradouro de São Pedro de Alcântara *(see p54).*

Praça dos Restauradores
This large tree-lined square, named after the men who gave their lives during the War of Restoration, is a busy through road with café terraces on the pat-terned pavements ❸

Restauradores

KEY

— — — Suggested route

STAR SIGHT

★ **Rossio**

Rossio station, designed by Jos[é] Luís Monteiro, is an eye-catching late 19th-century Neo-Manueline building with tw[o] Moorish-style horseshoe arch[es]

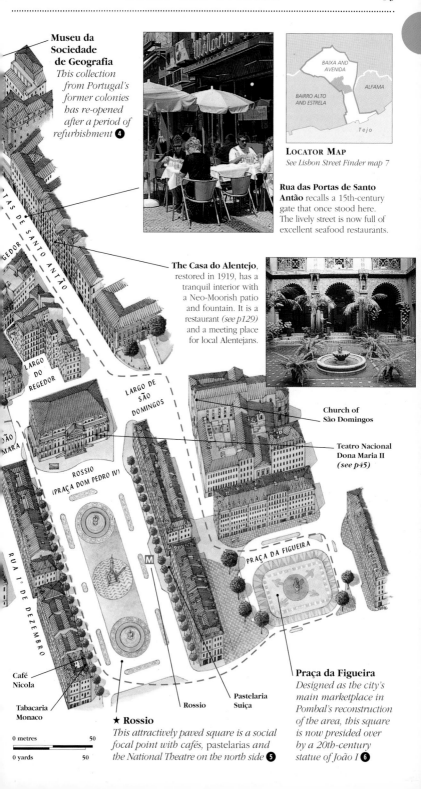

Museu da Sociedade de Geografia
This collection from Portugal's former colonies has re-opened after a period of refurbishment ④

LOCATOR MAP
See Lisbon Street Finder map 7

Rua das Portas de Santo Antão recalls a 15th-century gate that once stood here. The lively street is now full of excellent seafood restaurants.

The Casa do Alentejo, restored in 1919, has a tranquil interior with a Neo-Moorish patio and fountain. It is a restaurant *(see p129)* and a meeting place for local Alentejans.

Church of São Domingos

Teatro Nacional Dona Maria II *(see p45)*

LARGO DO REGEDOR

LARGO DE SÃO DOMINGOS

ROSSIO (PRAÇA DOM PEDRO IV)

RUA 1.º DE DEZEMBRO

PRAÇA DA FIGUEIRA

Café Nicola

Tabacaria Monaco

Rossio

Pastelaria Suiça

★ **Rossio**
This attractively paved square is a social focal point with cafés, pastelarias and the National Theatre on the north side ⑤

Praça da Figueira
Designed as the city's main marketplace in Pombal's reconstruction of the area, this square is now presided over by a 20th-century statue of João I ⑥

0 metres 50
0 yards 50

**Bridge and pond shaded by trees
in the Jardim Botânico**

Jardim Botânico ❶

Rua da Escola Politécnica 58. **Map** 4 F1.
⚃ *21-392 18 93.* 🚌 *15, 58, 100.* Ⓜ
Rato. **Gardens** ◯ *9am–6pm (Apr–
Sep: to 8pm) Mon–Fri, 10am–6pm
(Apr–Sep: to 8pm) Sat & Sun.* ● *1 Jan,
25 Dec.* 🈲 ⚿ 🆆 *www.jb.ul.pt*
Museu de História Natural ⚃ *21-
392 18 00.* ◯ *for exhibitions only.*
🈲 **Museu de Ciência** ⚃ *21-392
18 08.* ◯ *10am–1pm, 2–5pm
Mon–Fri, 3–6pm Sat.* ● *public hols.*
🈲 🆆 *www.museu-de-ciencia.ul.pt*

T HE COMPLEX, owned by
the university of Lisbon,
comprises two museums and
four hectares (10 acres) of
gardens. The botanical gardens
have a distinct air of neglect.
However, it is worth paying the
entrance fee to wander among
the exotic trees and dense
paths of the gardens as they
descend from the main entrance
towards Rua da Alegria. A
magnificent avenue of lofty
palms connects the two levels.

The **Museu de História
Natural** (Natural History
Museum) opens only for temporary exhibitions and these
are well advertised throughout
the city. The **Museu de
Ciência** (Science Museum),
whose exhibits demonstrate
basic scientific principles, is
popular with school children.

Avenida da Liberdade ❷

Map 7 A2. 🚌 *2, 9, 36 & many other
routes.* Ⓜ *Restauradores, Avenida.*

F OLLOWING THE earthquake
of 1755 *(see pp20–21)*, the
Marquês de Pombal created
the Passeio Público (public
promenade) in the area now
occupied by the lower part of
Avenida da Liberdade and
Praça dos Restauradores.

Despite its name,
enjoyment of the
park was restricted to
Lisbon's high society
and walls and gates
ensured the exclu-
sion of the lower
classes. In 1821,
when the Liberals
came to power, the
barriers were pulled
down and the
Avenida and square
became open to all.

The boulevard
you see today was
built in 1879–82 in
the style of the
Champs-Elysées
in Paris. The wide
tree-lined avenue
became a focus for
pageants, festivities
and demonstrations.
A war memorial
stands as a tribute to
those who died in
World War I. The
avenue still retains
a certain elegance
with fountains and
café tables shaded by trees,
however, it no longer makes
for a peaceful stroll. The once
majestic thoroughfare, 90 m
(295 ft) wide and decorated
with abstract pavement patterns, is now divided by seven
lanes of traffic linking Praça
dos Restauradores and Praça
Marquês de Pombal to the
north. Some of the original
mansions have been preserved,
including the Neo-Classical
Tivoli cinema at No. 188, with
an original 1920s kiosk outside,
and Casa Lambertini with its
colourful mosaic decoration at
No. 166. However, many of
the Art Nouveau façades have
unfortunately given way to
newer ones occupied by
offices, hotels or shopping
complexes.

**Detail from the memorial to the dead of
World War I in Avenida da Liberdade**

**19th-century monument in honour of the
Restoration in Praça dos Restauradores**

Praça dos Restauradores ❸

Map 7 A2. 🚌 *2, 9, 36, 46 & many
other routes.* Ⓜ *Restauradores.*

T HE SQUARE, distinguished by
its soaring obelisk, erected
in 1886, commemorates
Portugal's liberation from
the Spanish yoke in 1640. The
bronze figures on the pedestal
depict Victory, holding a palm
and a crown, and Freedom.
The names and dates that are
inscribed on the sides of the
obelisk are those of the battles
of the War of Restoration.

On the west side the Palácio
Foz now houses a small tourist
and other offices. It was built
by Francesco Savario
Fabri in 1755–77
for the Marquês
de Castelo-Melhor
and renamed after
the Marquês de Foz,
who lived here in the
19th century. The smart
Avenida Palace Hotel *(see
p115)*, on the southwest
side of the square, was
designed by José Lúis
Monteiro (1849–1942),
who also built Rossio
railway station *(see p42)*.

Museu da Sociedade de Geografia ❹

Rua das Portas de Santo Antão 100.
Map 7 A2. 🅒 21-342 54 01.
🚌 1, 2, 9, 11, 21, 80, 90.
Ⓜ *Restauradores.* 🕐 *10am–6pm
Mon–Fri.* 📷 *compulsory.* 🖼 &

Located in the Geographical Society building, the museum houses an idiosyn-cratic ethnographical collection brought back from Portugal's former colonies. On display are circumcision masks from Guinea Bissau, musical instru-ments and snake spears. From Angola there are neckrests to sustain coiffures and the ori-ginal *padrão* – the stone pillar erected by the Portuguese in 1482 to mark their sovereignty over the colony. Most of the exhibits are arranged along the splendid Sala Portugal.

Rossio ❺

Map 6 B3. 🚌 2, 36, 44, 45 & many other routes. Ⓜ *Rossio.*

Formally called Praça de Dom Pedro IV, this large square has been Lisbon's nerve centre for six centuries. During its history it has been the stage of bullfights, festivals, military parades and the burning of heretics during the Inquisition (*see p14*). Today there is little more than an occasional political rally, and the sober

Teatro Nacional Dona Maria II in Rossio illuminated by night

Pombaline buildings, disfigured on the upper level by neon signs, are occupied at street level by souvenir shops and cafés. Centre stage is a statue of Dom Pedro IV, the first emperor of independent Brazil. At the foot of the statue, the four female figures are allegories of Justice, Wisdom, Strength and Moderation.

In the mid-19 century the square was paved with wave-patterned mosaics which gave it the nickname of "Rolling Motion Square". The hand-cut grey and white stone cubes were the first such designs to decorate the city's pavements. Today, only a small central section of the design survives.

On the north side of Rossio is the Teatro Nacional Dona Maria II, named after Dom

Pedro's daughter. The Neo-Classical structure was built in the 1840s by the Italian archi-tect Fortunato Lodi. The inte-rior was destroyed by fire in 1964 and reconstructed in the 1970s. On top of the pediment is Gil Vicente (1465–1536), the founder of Portuguese theatre.

Café Nicola on the west side of the square was a favourite meeting place among writers, including the poet Manuel du Bocage (1765–1805), who was notorious for his satires. Café Suiça, on the opposite side, is popular with tourists for its sunlit terrace.

Praça da Figueira ❻

Map 6 B3. 🚌 14, 43, 59, 60 & many other routes. 🚋 12, 15. Ⓜ *Rossio.*

Before the 1755 earthquake (*see pp20–21*) the square next to Rossio was the site of the Hospital de Todos-os-Santos (All Saints). In Pombal's new design for the Baixa, the square took on the role of the city's central marketplace. In 1885 a covered market was introduced, but this was pulled down in the 1950s. Today, the four-storey buildings are given over to hotels, shops and cafés and the square is no longer a marketplace. Perhaps its most eye-catching feature is the multitude of pigeons that perch on the pedestal supporting Leopoldo de Almeida's bronze equestrian statue of João I, erected in 1971.

Bronze statue of King João I in Praça da Figueira

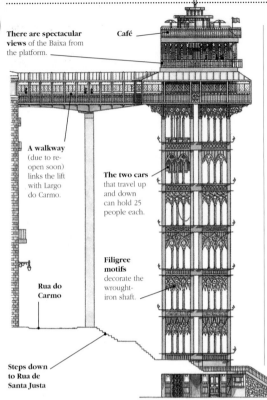

There are spectacular views of the Baixa from the platform.

Café

A walkway (due to re-open soon) links the lift with Largo do Carmo.

The two cars that travel up and down can hold 25 people each.

Rua do Carmo

Filigree motifs decorate the wrought-iron shaft.

Steps down to Rua de Santa Justa

Elevador de Santa Justa ❼

Rua de Santa Justa & Largo do Carmo.
Map 7 B3. 21-342 79 44.
8:30am–9:30pm Mon–Sat,
9am–9:30pm Sun.

A LSO KNOWN as the Elevador do Carmo, this Neo-Gothic lift, was built at the turn of the century by the French architect Raoul Mesnier du Ponsard, an apprentice of Alexandre Gustave Eiffel. Made of iron, and embellished with filigree, it is one of the more eccentric features of the Baixa. The ticket office is located behind the tower on the steps up to Rua do Carmo.

Passengers can travel up and down inside the tower in one of two smart wood-panelled cabins with brass fittings, but the walkway linking them to the Largo do Carmo in the Bairro Alto, 32 m (105 ft) above is currently closed for works.

The very top of the tower, reached via a tight spiral stairway, is given over to café tables. This high vantage point commands splendid views of Rossio, the grid pattern of the Baixa, the castle on the opposite hill, the river and the nearby ruins of the Carmo church. The fire that gutted the Chiado district in 1988 (see p52) was extinguished very close to the lift.

Café on the top platform of the Elevador de Santa Justa

Rua Augusta ❽

Map 7 B4. Rossio. 2, 14, 36, 40 & many other routes.

A LIVELY PEDESTRIANIZED street decorated with mosaic pavements and lined with boutiques and open-air cafés, Rua Augusta is the main tourist thoroughfare and the smartest in the Baixa. Street performers provide entertainment, while vendors sell lottery tickets, street art, books and souvenirs. The triumphal Arco da Rua Augusta frames the equestrian statue of José I in Praça do Comércio. Designed by the architect Santos de Carvalho to commemorate the city's recovery from the earthquake (see pp20–21), the arch was completed only in 1873.

The other main thorough-fares of the Baixa are Rua da Prata (silversmiths' street) and Rua do Ouro or Rua Aurea (goldsmiths' street). Cutting across these main streets full of shops and banks are smaller streets that give glimpses up to the Bairro Alto to the west and the Castelo de São Jorge (see pp38–9) to the east. Many of the streets retain shops that gave them their name: there are jewellers in Rua da Prata and Rua do Ouro, shoemakers in Rua dos Sapateiros and banks in Rua do Comércio.

The most incongruous sight in the heart of the Baixa is a small section of the Roman baths, located within the Banco Comercial Português in Rua dos Correeiros. The ruins and mosaics can be seen from the street window at the rear side of the bank; alternatively you can book ahead to visit the "museum" on 21-321 10 00.

Shoppers and strollers in the pedestrianized Rua Augusta

Nossa Senhora da Conceição Velha ❾

Rua da Alfândega. **Map** 7 C4. 📞 21-887 02 02. 🚌 9, 46, 90. 🚊 18. 🕐 8am–6pm Mon–Sat; Sun (morning mass only). ⬤ Aug. 🚻 📷 ♿

THE ELABORATE Manueline doorway of the church is the only feature that survived from the original 16th-century Nossa Senhora da Misericórdia, which stood here until the 1755 earthquake. The portal is decorated with a profusion of Manueline detail including angels, beasts, flowers, armillary spheres and the cross of the Order of Christ. In the tympanum, the Virgin Mary spreads her protective mantle over various contemporary figures. These include Pope Leo X, Manuel I and his sister, Queen Leonor, widow of João II. It was Leonor who founded the original Misericórdia (alms-house) on the site of a former synagogue.

Detail from portal of Conceição Velha

Enjoyment of the portal is hampered by the constant stream of traffic along Rua da Alfândega and the cars parked right in front of the church. The interior has an unusual stucco ceiling; in the second chapel on the right is a statue of Our Lady of Restelo. This came from the Belém chapel where navigators prayed before embarking on their historic voyages east.

destroyed in the earthquake of 1755. In the rebuilding of the city, the square became the *pièce de résistance* of Pombal's Baixa design. The new palace occupied spacious arcaded buildings that extended around three sides of the square. After the revolution of 1910 *(see p15)* these were converted into government administrative offices and painted Republican pink. However, they have since been repainted royal yellow.

The south side, graced by two square towers, looks across the wide expanse of the Tagus. This has always been the finest gateway to Lisbon, where royalty and ambassadors would alight and take the marble steps up from the river. You can still experience the dramatic approach by taking a ferry across from Cacilhas on the southern bank. However, today the spectacle is spoilt by the busy Avenida Infante Dom Henrique, which runs along the waterfront.

In the centre of Praça do Comércio is the equestrian statue of King José I erected in 1775 by Machado de Castro, the leading Portuguese sculptor of the 18th century. The bronze horse, depicted trampling on serpents, earned the square its third name of "Black Horse Square", used by English travellers and merchants. Over the years, however, the horse has acquired a green patina.

Shaded arcades along the north side of Praça do Comércio

The impressive triumphal arch on the north side of the square leads into Rua Augusta and is the gateway to the Baixa. Opened in January 2001, in the northwest of the square, the Lisboa Welcome Centre has a tourist information service, gallery, restaurants and shops. In the opposite corner, stands Lisbon's oldest café, the Martinho da Arcada, formerly a haunt of the city's literati.

On 1 February 1908, King Carlos and his son, Luís Felipe, were assassinated as they were passing through the square. In 1974 the square saw the first uprising of the Armed Forces Movement which overthrew the Caetano regime in a bloodless revolution *(see p15)*. For many years the area was requisitioned as a car park, but today this is a vast open space used for cultural events and festivals.

Praça do Comércio ❿

Map 7 C5. 🚌 2, 9, 11, 14, 40, 46 & many other routes. 🚊 15, 18, 25.

MORE COMMONLY known by the locals as *Terreiro do Paço* (Palace Square), this huge open space was the site of the royal palace for 400 years. Manuel I transferred the royal residence from Castelo de São Jorge to this more convenient location by the river in 1511. The first palace, along with its library and 70,000 books, was

Statue of King José I in Praça do Comércio

BAIRRO ALTO AND ESTRELA

**Tile panel in Largo
Rafael Bordalo
Pinheiro, Bairro Alto**

L AID OUT IN A GRID pattern in the late 16th century, the hilltop Bairro Alto is one of the most picturesque districts of the city. First settled by rich citizens who moved out of the disreputable Alfama, by the 19th century it had become a run-down area frequented by prostitutes. Today, its small workshops and family-run *tascas* (cheap restaurants) exist alongside a thriving nightlife.

Very different in character to the heart of the Bairro Alto is the elegant commercial district known as the Chiado, where affluent Lisboetas do their shopping. To the northwest, the Estrela quarter is centred on the huge domed basilica and popular gardens. The mid-18th century district of Lapa, to the southwest, is home to foreign embassies and large, smart residences.

SIGHTS AT A GLANCE

Museums and Galleries
Museu do Chiado **5**
*Museu Nacional de Arte
  Antiga pp56–9* **11**
Museu da Marioneta **6**

Churches
Basílica da Estrela **13**
Igreja do Carmo **2**
São Roque **1**

Historic Buildings
and Districts
Chiado **3**
Palácio de São Bento **10**
Solar do Vinho
  do Porto **7**
Teatro
  Nacional
  de São
  Carlos
  (Opera) **4**

Gardens and Belvederes
Jardim da Estrela **12**
Miradouro de São Pedro
  de Alcântara **8**
Praça do Príncipe Real **9**

GETTING THERE
This area is reached via the Elevador da Glória from Praça dos Restauradores, the Elevador de Santa Justa from the Baixa, or by a steep, but pleasant walk. There is also a metro station on Largo do Chiado. Tram 28 passes Bairro Alto on its way between Graça and Estrela.

KEY

	Street-by-Street: Bairro Alto and Chiado *pp50–51*
M	Metro station
R	Railway station
	Funicular
	Ferry boarding point
P	Parking
=	Railway line

◁ **Art Nouveau decoration in the Chiado's Café Brasileira, once popular with writers and intellectuals**

Street-by-Street: Bairro Alto and Chiado

T HE BAIRRO ALTO (high quarter) is a
fascinating area of cobbled streets
adjacent to the Carmo and Chiado areas.
Since the 1980s, this has been Lisbon's
best-known nightlife zone, with countless
small bars and restaurants alongside the older
casas de fado. Much restoration work has taken
place over the last four years, and many new
buildings now stand side by side to old, peeling
houses and tiny grocery shops. In contrast,
the Chiado is an area of elegant shops and
old-style cafés that extends down from Praça Luís
de Camões towards Rua do Carmo and the
Baixa. Major renovation work has taken
place since a fire in 1988 *(see p52)*
destroyed many of the buildings.

**Baroque cherub,
Igreja do Carmo**

**Praça Luís
de Camões**

Once a haunt of writers and
intellectuals, Chiado is now
an elegant shopping district.
The 1920s Brasileira café, on
Largo do Chiado, is adorned
with gilded mirrors.

**Largo do
Chiado** is flanked
by the churches
of Loreto and Nossa
Senhora da Encarnação.

**The statue of Eça de
Queirós** (1845–1900), by
Teixeira Lopes, was erected
in 1903. The great novelist
takes inspiration from a
scantily veiled muse.

Baixa/Chiado

Rua Garrett
is the main shopping
street of the Chiado.

Chiado

0 metres   50

0 yards   50

KEY

– – – Suggested route

Tavares, at No. 3
Rua da Misericórd
first opened as a
café in 1784. Toda
it is an elegant re
taurant *(see p129)*
decorated at the t
of the century wi
mirrors and elabo
rate stucco desig

Elevador da Glória

The Museu de Arte Sacra has an interesting exhibition of religious artefacts and explains the history of the treasures in the church of São Roque next door.

BAIXA AND AVENIDA

BAIRRO ALTO AND ESTRELA

Tejo

LOCATOR MAP
See Lisbon Street Finder map 7

Cervejaria Trindade is a popular beer hall and restaurant decorated with *azulejo* panels.

Teatro da Trindade

★ São Roque
Opulent mosaics and semiprecious stones adorn the Baroque Capela de São João inside the 16th-century church of São Roque ❶

The tile decoration on the façade of this house, erected in 1864 on Largo Rafael Bordalo Pinheiro, features allegorical figures of Science, Agriculture Industry and Commerce.

★ Igreja do Carmo
The graceful skeletal arches of this Carmelite church, once the largest in Lisbon, stand as a reminder of the earthquake of 1755. The chancel, and main body of the church house an archaeological museum ❷

Elevador de Santa Justa is due to re-open shortly, after some restoration work.

The shops in Rua do Carmo have been restored and renewed after the devastating fire in 1988 *(see p52)*.

STAR SIGHTS

★ São Roque

★ Igreja do Carmo

Ruins of the 14th-century Igreja do Carmo seen from the Baixa

São Roque ❶

Largo Trindade Coelho. **Map** 7 A3.
[21-323 53 80.] 58, 100 &
Glória lift.] 8am–5pm Mon–Fri;
9:30am–5pm Sat & Sun. ✝
Museu de Arte Sacra [21-323
53 81.] 10am–5pm Tue–Sun.
] public hols. ✎ ◙

Sᴀ̃ᴏ ʀᴏǫᴜᴇ's plain façade
belies a remarkably rich
interior. The church
was founded at the
end of the 16th
century by the Jesuit
Order, then at the
peak of its power. In
1742 the Chapel of
St John the Baptist
(last on the left) was
commissioned by the
prodigal João V from
the Italian architects
Luigi Vanvitelli and
Nicola Salvi. Con-
structed in Rome
and embellished with lapis
lazuli, agate, alabaster, ameth-
yst, precious marbles, gold,
silver and mosaics, the chapel
was given the Pope's blessing
in the church of Sant'Antonio
dei Portoghesi in Rome, dis-
mantled and sent to Lisbon in
three ships.

Tile detail in the Chapel of St Roch

Among the many tiles in the
church, the oldest and most
interesting are those in the
third chapel on the right, dating
from the mid-16th century
and dedicated to São Roque
(St Roch), protector against
the plague. Other features of
the church are the scenes of
the Apocalypse painted on the
ceiling and the sacristy, with its
coffered ceiling, as well as
painted panels of the life of St
Francis Xavier, the 16th-century
missionary. Treasures from the
Chapel of St John, including
the silver and lapis lazuli altar
front, are in the adjoining
Museu de Arte Sacra.

Igreja do Carmo ❷

Largo do Carmo. **Map** 7 B3. [21-
347 86 29.] 58.] 28.] Baixa-
Chiado.] May–Sep: 10am–6pm
Tue–Sun; Oct–Apr: 10am–5pm
Tue–Sun.] 1 Jan, Easter,
1 May, 25 Dec. ✎

Tʜᴇ ɢᴏᴛʜɪᴄ ʀᴜɪɴs
of this Carmelite
church, built on a
slope overlooking the
Baixa, are evocative
reminders of the dev-
astation left by the
earthquake of 1755. As
the congregation were
attending mass the
shockwaves caused
the church to collapse,
depositing tons of masonry
on to the people below.

Founded in the late 14th
century by Nuno Álvares
Pereira, the commander who
became a member of the
Carmelite Order, the church
was at one time the biggest
in Lisbon.

Nowadays the main body
of the church and the chancel,
whose roof withstood the
earthquake, house an
archaeological museum
with a small, heterogeneous
collection of sarcophagi,
statuary, ceramics and mosaics.

Among the more ancient
finds from Europe are a
remnant from a Visigothic
pillar and a Roman tomb
carved with reliefs depicting
the Muses. There are also
finds from Mexico and South
America, including ancient
mummies.

Outside the ruins, in the
Largo do Carmo, stands the
Chafariz do Carmo, an 18th-
century fountain designed by
Ângelo Belasco, elaborately
decorated with four dolphins.

Chiado ❸

Map 7 A4.] 58.] 28.] Chiado.

Hʏᴘᴏᴛʜᴇsᴇs abound for the
origin of the word Chiado,
in use since 1567. One of the
most interesting recalls the
creak *(chiar)* of the wheels of
the carts as they negotiated the
area's steep slopes. A second
theory refers to the nickname
given to the 16th-century poet
António Ribeiro, "O Chiado".
An area traditionally known

THE CHIADO FIRE

On 25 August 1988 a disastrous fire began in a store in
Rua do Carmo, the street that
links the Baixa with the Bairro
Alto. Fire engines were unable
to enter this pedestrianized
street and the fire spread into
Rua Garrett. Along with shops
and offices, many important
18th-century buildings were
destroyed, the worst damage
being in Rua do Carmo. The
renovation project, which is
now complete, has preserved
many original façades, and
was headed by Portuguese
architect, Álvaro Siza Vieira.

Firemen attending the raging fire in Rua do Carmo

Stalls and circle of the 18th-century Teatro Nacional de São Carlos

for its intellectual associations, various statues of literary figures can be found here. Fernando Pessoa, Portugal's most famous 20th-century poet, is seated at a table outside the Café Brasileira. Established in the 1920s, this was a favourite rendezvous of intellectuals.

The name Chiado is often used to mean just Rua Garrett, the main shopping street of the area, named after the author and poet João Almeida Garrett (1799–1854). This elegant street, which descends from Largo do Chiado towards the Baixa, is known for its clothes shops, cafés and bookshops. Devastated by fire in 1988, the former elegance of this quarter has been recently restored.

On Largo do Chiado stand two Baroque churches: the Italian church, Igreja do Loreto, on the north side and opposite, Nossa Senhora da Encarnação, whose exterior walls are partly decorated with *azulejos*.

Teatro Nacional de São Carlos ❹

Rua Serpa Pinto 9. **Map** 7 A4.
📞 21-325 30 00. 🚌 58, 100.
🚊 28. Ⓜ Baixa-Chiado. ⃝ for
performances. ⓦ www.saocarlos.pt

REPLACING a former opera house which was ruined by the earthquake of 1755, the Teatro de São Carlos was built in 1792–5 by José da Costa e Silva. Designed on the lines of La Scala in Milan, the building has a beautifully proportioned façade and an enchanting Rococo interior. Views of the exterior, however, are spoiled by the car park, invariably crammed, which occupies the square in front. The opera season lasts from September to June, but concerts and ballets are also staged here at other times of the year.

Museu do Chiado ❺

Rua Serpa Pinto 4–6. **Map** 7 A5.
📞 21-343 21 48. 🚌 58, 85, 100.
🚊 20, 28. Ⓜ Baixa-Chiado. ⃝
2–6pm Tue, 10am–6pm Wed–Sun.
⬤ 1 Jan, Easter, 1 May, 25 Dec.
ⓦ www.museudochiado-ipmuseus.pt

THE NATIONAL MUSEUM of Contemporary Art, whose collection of 1850–1950 paintings could no longer be described as contemporary, changed its name in 1994 and moved to a stylishly restored warehouse. The paintings and sculpture are arranged over three floors in 12 rooms. Each room has a different theme illustrating the development

from Romanticism to Modernism. The majority are works by Portuguese, often showing the marked influence from other European countries. This is particularly noticeable in the 19th-century landscape painters who had contact with artists from the French Barbizon School. The few international works of art on display include a collection of drawings by Rodin (1840–1917) and some French sculpture from the late 19th century. There are also temporary exhibitions which are held for "very new artists, preferably inspired by the permanent collection".

Grotesque puppet in Museu da Marioneta

Museu da Marioneta ❻

Convento das Bernardas, Rua da
Esperança 146. **Map** 4 D3. 📞 21-
394 28 10. 🚌 6, 13, 27, 49, 60.
🚊 15, 25. Ⓜ Cais do Sodré. 🚉
Santos. ⃝ 10am–1pm, 2–6pm
Tue–Sun. ⬤ 1 Jan, 1 May, 25 Dec.
ⓦ (free 10am–2pm Sun).

THIS SMALL PUPPET museum, housed in an elegantly refurbished convent building, includes characters dating from 17th- and 18th-century theatre and opera, among them jesters, knights, devils and satirical figures. Many of the puppets possess gruesome, contorted features that are unlikely to appeal to small children. The museum explains the history of the art form and runs videos of puppet shows. Call ahead to see if a live performance is being held on the small stage. There is also a space for pedagogical activities.

Art Nouveau façade of the popular Café Brasileira in the Chiado

The wide selection of port at the Solar do Vinho do Porto

Solar do Vinho do Porto **❼**

Rua de São Pedro de Alcântara 45.
Map 4 F2. 🄲 *21-347 57 07.*
🚌 *58.* 🚋 *28, Elevador da Glória.*
⭕ *11am–midnight Mon–Sat.*
⬤ *public hols.*

THE PORTUGUESE WORD *solar* means mansion or manor house and the Solar do Vinho do Porto occupies the ground floor of an 18th-century mansion. The building was once owned by the German architect, Johann Friedrich Ludwig (Ludovice), who built the monastery at Mafra *(see p92)*. The port wine institute of Oporto runs a pleasant if dated bar here for the promotion of port. Nearly 200 types of port are listed in the lengthy drinks menu, with every producer represented and including some rarities. Unfortunately, many of the listed wines are often unavailable. All but the vintage ports are sold by the glass, with prices ranging from one euro for the simplest ruby to 70 euros for a glass of 40-year-old tawny.

Miradouro de São Pedro de Alcântara **❽**

Rua de São Pedro de Alcântara. **Map** 7 A2. 🚌 *58.* 🚋 *28, Elevador da Glória.*

THE BELVEDERE *(miradouro)* commands a sweeping view of eastern Lisbon, seen across the Baixa. A tiled map, conveniently placed against the balustrade, helps you locate the landmarks in the city below. The panorama extends from the battlements of the Castelo de São Jorge *(see pp38–9)*, clearly seen surrounded by trees on the hill to the southeast, to the 18th-century church of Penha da França in the northwest. The large monastery complex of the Igreja da Graça *(see p37)* is also visible on the hill, and in the distance São Vicente de Fora *(see p35)* is recognizable by the symmetrical towers that flank its white façade.

Benches and ample shade from the trees make this terrace a pleasant stop after the steep walk up Calçada da Glória from the Baixa. Alternatively, the yellow funicular, Elevador da Glória, will drop you off nearby.

The memorial in the garden, erected in 1904, depicts Eduardo Coelho (1835–89), founder of the newspaper *Diário de Notícias*, and below him a ragged paper boy running with copies of the famous daily. This area was once the centre of the newspaper industry, however the modern printing presses have now moved to more spacious premises west of the city.

The view is most attractive at sunset and by night when the castle is floodlit and the terrace becomes a popular meeting point for young Lisboetas.

Praça do Príncipe Real **❾**

Map 4 F1. 🚌 *58, 100.*

Playing cards in Praça do Príncipe Real

LAID OUT IN 1860 as a prime residential quarter, the square still retains an air of affluence. Smartly painted mansions surround a particularly pleasant park with an open-air café, statuary and some splendid robinia, magnolia and Judas trees. The branches of a huge cedar tree have been trained on a trellis, creating a wide shady spot for the locals who play cards beneath it. On the large square, at No. 26, the eye-catching pink and white Neo-Moorish building with domes and pinnacles is part of Lisbon university.

View across the city to Castelo de São Jorge from Miradouro de São Pedro de Alcântara

Attractive wrought-iron music pavilion in Jardim da Estrela

Palácio de São Bento ⑩

Largo das Cortes, Rua de São Bento.
Map 4 E2. 🔇 21-391 90 00.
🚌 6, 49, 100. 🚋 28. ◯ by appt only. 🔇 call 21-391 94 46 or 21-391 96 25. 🔲 www.parlamento.pt

ALSO KNOWN as the Assembleia da República, this massive white Neo-Classical building started life in the late 1500s as the Benedictine monastery of São Bento. After the dissolution of the religious orders in 1834, the building became the seat of the Portuguese Parliament, known as the Palácio das Cortes. The interior is suitably grandiose with marble pillars and Neo-Classical statues.

Museu Nacional de Arte Antiga ⑪

See pp56–9.

Jardim da Estrela ⑫

Praça da Estrela. **Map** 4 D2. 🚌 9, 20, 38. 🚋 25, 28. ◯ 7am–midnight daily.

LAID OUT IN the middle of the 19th century, opposite the Basílica da Estrela, the popular gardens are a focal part of the Estrela quarter. Local families congregate here at weekends to feed the ducks and carp in the lake, sit at the waterside café or wander among the flower beds, plants and trees. The formal gardens are planted with herbaceous borders and shrubs surrounding plane trees and elms. The central feature of the park is a green wrought-iron bandstand, decorated with elegant filigree, where musicians strike up in the summer months. This was built in 1884 and originally stood on the Passeio Público, before the creation of Avenida da Liberdade *(see p44)*.

The English Cemetery to the north of the gardens is best known as the burial place of Henry Fielding (1707–54), the English novelist and playwright who died in Lisbon at the age of 47. The *Journal of a Voyage to Lisbon,* published posthumously in 1775, recounts his last voyage to Portugal made in a fruitless attempt to recover his failing health.

Basílica da Estrela ⑬

Praça da Estrela. **Map** 4 D2.
🔇 21-396 09 15. 🚌 9, 20, 38. 🚋 25, 28. ◯ 8am–1pm, 3–8pm daily. 🔲 📷

The tomb of the pious Maria I in the Basílica da Estrela

IN THE SECOND half of the 18th century Maria I *(see p105),* daughter of José I, vowed she would build a church if she bore a son and heir to the throne. Her wish was granted and construction of the basilica began in 1779. Her son José, however, died of smallpox two years before the completion of the church in 1790. The huge domed basilica, set on a hill in the west of the city, is one of Lisbon's great landmarks. A simpler version of the basilica at Mafra *(see p92),* this church was built by architects from the Mafra School in late Baroque and Neo-Classical style. The façade is flanked by twin belltowers and decorated with an array of statues of saints and allegorical figures.

The spacious, somewhat awe-inspiring interior, where light streams down from the pierced dome, is clad in grey, pink and yellow marble. The elaborate Empire-style tomb of Queen Maria I, who died in Brazil, lies in the right transept. Locked in a room nearby is Machado de Castro's extraordinary Nativity scene, composed of over 500 cork and terracotta figures. (To see it, ask the sacristan.)

Neo-Classical façade and stairway of Palácio de São Bento

Museu Nacional de Arte Antiga ⓫

PORTUGAL'S NATIONAL ART COLLECTION is housed in a 17th-century palace that was built for the counts of Alvor. In 1770 it was acquired by the Marquês de Pombal and remained in the possession of his family for over a century. Inaugurated in 1884, the museum is known to locals as the Museu das Janelas Verdes, referring to the former green windows of the palace. In 1940 a modern annexe (including the main façade) was added. This was built on the site of the St Albert Carmelite monastery, which was partially demolished between 1910 and 1920. The only surviving feature was the chapel, now integrated into the museum.

15th-century wood carving of St George

★ St Jerome
This masterly portrayal of old age by Albrecht Dürer expresses one of the central dilemmas of Renaissance humanism: the ephemeral nature of man (1521).

GALLERY GUIDE

The ground floor contains 14th–19th-century European paintings, as well as some decorative arts and furniture. Oriental and African art, Chinese and Portuguese ceramics and silver, gold and jewellery are on display on the first floor. The top floor is dedicated to Portuguese art and sculpture.

The Temptations of St Antony by Hieronymus Bosch

Stairs down to
📺 🍴 ♿

St Augustine by Piero della Francesca

The Virgin and Child and Saints
Hans Holbein the Elder's balanced composition of a Sacra Conversazione (1519) is set among majestic Renaissance architecture with saints in detailed contemporary costumes sewing or reading.

Ecce Homo
Painted in the 16th century by an artist of the Portuguese school, the unusual depiction of the accused Jesus, with the shroud lowered over his eyes, retains an air of dignified calm, despite the crown of thorns, the rope and the specks of blood.

KEY TO FLOORPLAN

- ☐ European art
- ☐ Portuguese painting and sculpture
- ☐ Portuguese and Chinese ceramics
- ☐ Oriental and African art
- ☐ Silver, gold and jewellery
- ☐ Decorative arts
- ☐ Chapel of St Albert
- ☐ Textiles and furniture
- ☐ Non-exhibition space

STAR EXHIBITS

- **★ St Jerome by Dürer**
- **★ Namban Screens**
- **★ Adoration of St Vincent by Gonçalves**

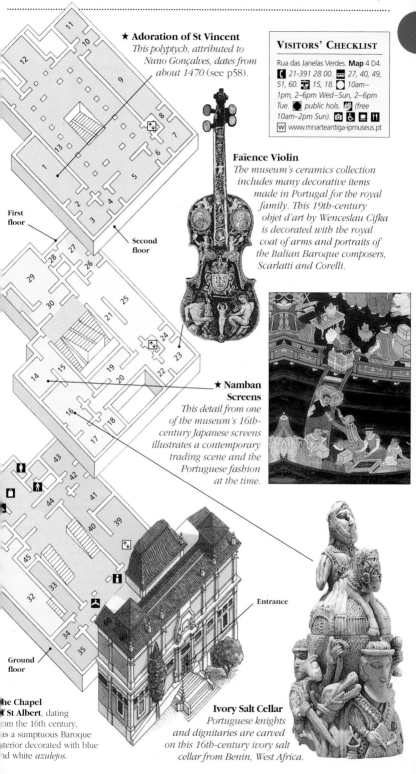

★ Adoration of St Vincent
This polyptych, attributed to Nuno Gonçalves, dates from about 1470 (see p58).

VISITORS' CHECKLIST

Rua das Janelas Verdes. **Map** 4 D4.
21-391 28 00. 27, 40, 49, 51, 60. 15, 18. 10am–1pm, 2–6pm Wed–Sun, 2–6pm Tue. public hols. (free 10am–2pm Sun).
www.mnarteantiga-ipmuseus.pt

Faïence Violin
The museum's ceramics collection includes many decorative items made in Portugal for the royal family. This 19th-century objet d'art by Wenceslau Cifka is decorated with the royal coat of arms and portraits of the Italian Baroque composers, Scarlatti and Corelli.

First floor

Second floor

★ Namban Screens
This detail from one of the museum's 16th-century Japanese screens illustrates a contemporary trading scene and the Portuguese fashion at the time.

Entrance

Ground floor

Ivory Salt Cellar
Portuguese knights and dignitaries are carved on this 16th-century ivory salt cellar from Benin, West Africa.

he Chapel f St Albert, dating om the 16th century, s a sumptuous Baroque terior decorated with blue nd white *azulejos*.

Exploring the Collections of the Museu Nacional de Arte Antiga

THE MUSEUM has the largest collection of paintings in Portugal and is particularly strong on early religious works by Portuguese artists. The majority of exhibits came from convents and monasteries following the suppression of religious orders in 1834. There are also extensive displays of sculpture, silverware, porcelain and applied arts giving an overview of Portuguese art from the Middle Ages to the 19th century, complemented by many fine European and Oriental pieces. The theme of the discoveries is ever-present, illustrating Portugal's links with Brazil, Africa, India, China and Japan.

EUROPEAN ART

PAINTINGS by European artists, dating from the 14th to the 19th century, are arranged chronologically on the ground floor. Unlike the Portuguese art, most of the works were donated from private collections, contributing to the great diversity of works on display. The first rooms, dedicated to the 14th and 15th centuries, trace the transition from medieval Gothic taste to the aesthetic of the Renaissance.

The painters best represented in the European Art section are 16th-century German and Flemish artists. Notable works are *St Jerome* by Albrecht Dürer (1471–1528), *Salomé* by Lucas Cranach the Elder (1472–1553), *Virgin and Child* by Hans Memling (c.1430–94) and *The Temptations of St Antony* by the great Flemish master of fantasy, Hieronymus Bosch (1450–1516). Of the small number of Italian works, the finest are *St Augustine* by

the Renaissance painter, Piero della Francesca (c.1420–92) and a graceful early altar panel representing the Resurrection by Raphael (1483–1520).

Some Portuguese painters, including Josefa de Óbidos (1631–84) and Gregório Lopes (1490–1550), are also displayed in the galleries of European art.

PORTUGUESE PAINTING AND SCULPTURE

MANY OF THE EARLIEST works of art are by the Portuguese primitive painters who were influenced by the realistic detail of Flemish artists. There had always been strong trading links between Portugal and Flanders and in the 15th and 16th centuries several painters of Flemish origin, for example Frey Carlos of Évora, set up workshops in Portugal.

Pride of place, however, goes to the São Vicente de Fora polyptych, the most important painting of 15th-century Portuguese art and one that has

Cistercian monks from Alcobaça in central Portugal   **Friar**

Fisherman

become a symbol of national pride in the Age of Discovery. Painted in about 1467–70, and generally believed to be by Nuno Gonçalves, the altarpiece portrays the *Adoration of St Vincent*, patron saint of Portugal, surrounded by dignitaries, knights and monks as well as fishermen and beggars. The accurate portrayal of contemporary figures makes the painting an invaluable historical and social document.

Later works include a 16th-century portrait of the young Dom Sebastião (1557–78) by Cristóvão de Morais and paintings by Neo-Classical artist Domingos António de Sequeira.

The museum's sculpture collection has many Gothic polychrome stone and wood statues of Christ, the Virgin and saints. There are also statues from the 17th century and an 18th-century nativity scene by Machado de Castro in the Chapel of St Albert.

PORTUGUESE AND CHINESE CERAMICS

THE EXTENSIVE collection of ceramics enables visitors to trace the evolution of Chinese porcelain and Portuguese faïence and to see the influence of oriental designs on

Central panel of *The Temptations of St Antony* by Hieronymus Bosch

Nuno Gonçalves, self-portrait of the artist

Queen Eleonor of Aragon, the Queen mother

Henry the Navigator *(see p49)*

Archbishop of Lisbon, Jorge da Costa

Moorish knight

Jewish scholar

Beggar

Queen Isabel

Infante João (King João II)

King Afonso V

Infante Fernão, the king's brother

St Vincent

Knight

Duke of Bragança

Priest holding a fragment of St Vincent's skull

Portuguese pieces, and vice versa. From the 16th century Portuguese ceramics show a marked influence of Ming, and conversely the Chinese pieces bear Portuguese motifs such as coats of arms. By the mid-18th century individual potters had begun to develop an increasingly personalized, European style, with popular, rustic designs. The collection also includes ceramics from Italy, Spain and the Netherlands.

Chinese porcelain vase, 16th century

ORIENTAL AND AFRICAN ART

THE COLLECTION of ivories and furniture, with their European motifs, further illustrates the reciprocal influences of Portugal and her colonies. The 16th-century predilection for the exotic gave rise to a huge demand for items such as carved ivory hunting horns from Africa. The fascinating 16th-century Japanese Namban screens show the Portuguese trading in Japan. *Namban-jin* (barbarians from the south) is the name the Japanese gave to the Portuguese.

SILVER, GOLD AND JEWELLERY

AMONG THE MUSEUM'S fine collection of ecclesiastical treasures are King Sancho I's gold cross (1214) and the Belém monstrance (1506). Also on display is the 16th-century Madre de Deus reliquary which allegedly holds a thorn from the crown of Christ. Highlight of the foreign collection is a sumptuous set of rare 18th-century silver tableware. Commissioned by José I from the Paris workshop of Thomas Germain, the 1,200 pieces include intricately decorated tureens, sauce boats and salt cellars. The rich collection of jewels came from the convents, originally donated by members of the nobility and wealthy bourgeoisie on entering the religious orders.

APPLIED ARTS

FURNITURE, tapestries and textiles, liturgical vestments and bishops' mitres are among the wide range of objects on display. The furniture collection

includes many Medieval and Renaissance pieces, as well as Baroque and Neo-classical items from the reigns of King João V, King José and Queen Maria I. Of the foreign furniture, French pieces from the 18th century are prominent.

The textiles include 17th-century bedspreads, tapestries, many of Flemish origin, such as the *Baptism of Christ* (16th century), embroidered rugs and Arraiolos carpets.

Gold Madre de Deus reliquary inlaid with precious stones (c.1502)

Belém

AT THE MOUTH of the River Tagus, where the caravels set sail on their voyages of discovery, Belém is inextricably linked with Portugal's golden age of discovery. When Manuel I came to power in 1495 he reaped the profits of those heady days of expansion, building grandiose monuments and churches that mirrored the spirit of the time. Two of the finest examples of the exuberant and exotic Manueline style of architecture are the Mosteiro dos Jerónimos and the Torre de Belém. Today Belém is a

Generosity, statue at entrance to Palácio da Ajuda

spacious, relatively green suburb with many museums, parks and gardens, as well as an attractive riverside setting with cafés and a promenade. On sunny days there is a distinct seaside feel to the river embankment.

Before the Tagus receded, the monks in the monastery used to look out onto the river and watch the boats set forth. In contrast today several lanes of traffic along the busy Avenida da Índia cut central Belém off from the picturesque waterfront, and silver and yellow trains rattle regularly past.

SIGHTS AT A GLANCE

Museums and Galleries
Museu de Arte Popular ⑩
Museu de Marinha ⑦
Museu Nacional
   de Arqueologia ⑤
Museu Nacional
   dos Coches ②
Planetário Calouste
   Gulbenkian ⑥

Parks and Gardens
Jardim Agrícola Tropical ③
Jardim Botânico da Ajuda ⑭

Churches and Monasteries
Ermida de São Jerónimo ⑫
Igreja da Memória ⑬
*Mosteiro dos Jerónimos
   pp66–7* ④

Historic Buildings
Palácio de Belém ①
Palácio Nacional da Ajuda ⑮
Torre de Belém p70 ⑪

Monuments
Monument to the
   Discoveries ⑨

Cultural Centres
Centro Cultural
   de Belém ⑧

KEY

	Street-by-Street: Belém pp62–3
🚉	Railway station
⛴	Ferry boarding point
🅿	Parking
=	Railway line

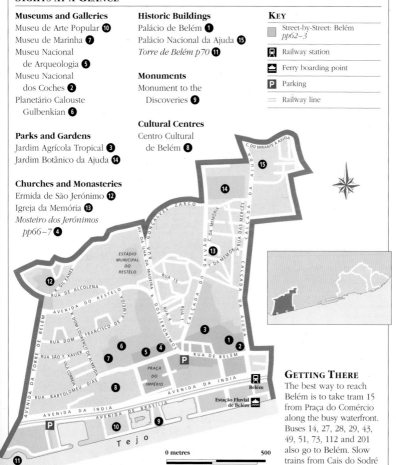

GETTING THERE
The best way to reach Belém is to take tram 15 from Praça do Comércio along the busy waterfront. Buses 14, 27, 28, 29, 43, 49, 51, 73, 112 and 201 also go to Belém. Slow trains from Cais do Sodré to Oeiras stop at Belém.

◁ **Nave of Santa Maria de Belém, the church of the Jerónimos monastery**

Street-by-Street: Belém

Stone caravel, Jerónimos monastery

Portugal's former maritime glory, expressed in the imposing, exuberant buildings such as the Jerónimos monastery, is evident all around Belém. In Salazar's *(see p15)* attempted revival of awareness of Portugal's Golden Age, the area along the waterfront, which had silted up since the days of the caravels, was restructured to celebrate the former greatness of the nation. Praça do Império was laid out for the Exhibition of the Portuguese World in 1940 and Praça Afonso de Albuquerque was dedicated to Portugal's first viceroy of India. The royal Palácio de Belém, restored with gardens and a riding school by João V in the 18th century, briefly housed the royal family after the 1755 earthquake.

★ Mosteiro dos Jerónimos
Vaulted arcades and richly carved columns adorned with foliage, exotic animals and navigational instruments decorate the Manueline cloister of the Jerónimos monastery ❹

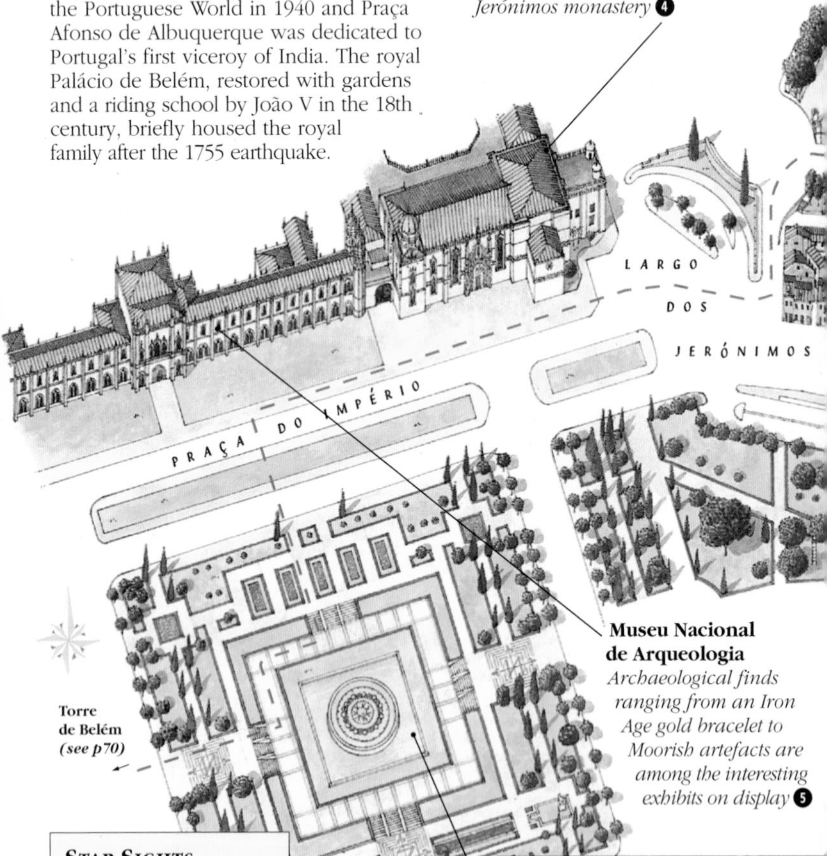

LARGO

DOS

JERÓNIMOS

PRAÇA DO IMPÉRIO

Museu Nacional de Arqueologia
Archaeological finds ranging from an Iron Age gold bracelet to Moorish artefacts are among the interesting exhibits on display ❺

Torre de Belém
(see p70)

STAR SIGHTS

★ **Mosteiro dos Jerónimos**

★ **Museu Nacional dos Coches**

KEY

— — — Suggested route

Praça do Império, an impressive square that opens out in front of the monastery, is lit up on special occasions with a colourful light display in the central fountain.

Rua Vieira Portuense runs along a small park. Its colourful 16th- and 17th-century houses contrast with the typically imposing buildings in Belém.

Jardim Agrícola Tropical
Exotic plants and trees gathered from Portugal's former colonies fill these peaceful gardens that were once part of the Palácio de Belém ❸

LOCATOR MAP
See Lisbon Street Finder maps 1 & 2

Antiga Confeitaria de Belém, a 19th-century café, sells *pastéis de Belém*, rich custard in a flaky pastry cup.

AVESSA DOS FERREIROS

T MARTA PINTO

RUA DE BELÉM

RUA VIEIRA PORTUENSE

Central Lisbon

Palácio de Belém
Also known as the Palácio Cor de Rosa (pink palace) because of its faded pink façade, the former royal palace is the residence of the Portuguese president. It also houses the Museu da Presidencia ❶

0 metres 50
0 yards 50

★ Museu Nacional dos Coches
This 18th-century coach used by the ambassador to Pope Clement XI is part of the collection in the old riding school of the Palácio de Belém ❷

Praça Afonso de Albuquerque is named after the first Portuguese viceroy of India. A Neo-Manueline column in the centre bears his statue, with scenes from his life carved on the base.

Palácio de Belém ❶

Praça Afonso de Albuquerque.
Map 1 C4. 📞 21-361 46 00.
🚌 14, 27, 28, 43, 49, 51. 🚊 15.
🚉 Belém. ⭕ 10am–5:30pm Sat.
🎫 compulsory (21-341 46 60). 📷

BUILT BY the Conde de
Aveiras in 1559, before the
Tagus had receded, this palace
once had gardens bordering
the river. In the 18th century
it was bought by João V, who
radically altered it, rendering
the interior suitably lavish for
his many amorous liaisons.

When the great earthquake
struck in 1755 *(see pp20–21)*,
the king, José I, and his family
were staying here and thus
survived the devastation of
central Lisbon. Fearing another
earth tremor, the royal family
temporarily set up camp in
tents in the palace grounds
and the interior was used as
a hospital. Today the elegant
pink building, is the residence
of the President of Portugal.

A new museum with state-
of-the-art technology, the
Museu da Presidencia, has
now opened on the premises
of the palace.

Pink façade of the Palácio de Belém, home of the President of Portugal

Museu Nacional dos Coches ❷

Praça Afonso de Albuquerque. **Map** 2
D4. 📞 21-361 08 50. 🚌 14, 27,
28, 43, 49, 51. 🚊 15. 🚉 Belém.
⭕ 10am–5:30pm Tue–Sun. ⬤ 1 Jan,
Easter, 1 May, 25 Dec. 🎫 (free Sun).
📷 ♿ ground floor only. 🌐 www.
museudoscoches-ipmuseus.pt

THE MUSEUM'S collection of
coaches is arguably the
finest in Europe. Occupying
the east wing of the Palácio de
Belém, this was formerly the
riding school built by
the Italian
architect Giacomo Azzolini
in 1726. Seated in the upper
gallery, the royal family used to
watch their beautiful Lusitanian
horses performing in the arena.
In 1905 the riding school was
turned into a museum by King
Carlos's wife, Dona Amélia,
whose riding cloak is on show.

Made in Portugal, Italy,
France, Austria and Spain, the
coaches span three centuries
and range from the plain to
the preposterous. The main
gallery, in Louis XVI style
with splendid painted ceiling,
is the setting for two straight,
regimented rows of coaches
created for Portuguese royalty.

The collection starts with
the comparatively plain
17th-century red leather
and wood coach of Philip
II of Spain. The coaches
become more sumptuous,
the interiors are lined
with red velvet and gold,
the exteriors are carved and
decorated with allegories and
royal coats of arms. The rows
end with three huge Baroque
coaches made in Rome for
the Portuguese ambassador
to the Vatican, Dom Rodrigo
Almeida e Menezes, the
Marquês de Abrantes.
The epitome of pomp
and extravagance, these
5-tonne carriages are
embellished with a plush
interior and life-size
gilded statues.

The neighbouring gallery
has further examples of
royal carriages, including
two-wheeled cabriolets,
landaus and pony-drawn
chaises used by young
members of the royal
family. There is also a 19th-
century Lisbon cab, painted
black and green, the colours of

Rear view of a coach built in 1716 for the Marquês de
Abrantes, the Portuguese ambassador to Pope Clement XI

taxis right up to the 1990s. The 18th-century Eyeglass Chaise, whose black leather hood is pierced by sinister eye-like windows, was made during the era of Pombal *(see p15)* when lavish decoration was discouraged. The upper gallery has a collection of harnesses, court costumes and portraits of members of the royal family.

Jardim Agrícola Tropical ❸

Rua da Junqueira 86. **Map** 1 C4. 21-362 02 10. 27, 28, 43, 49, 51, 112. 15. 10am–5pm Tue–Fri, 11am–6pm Sat & Sun. public hols. Tue–Fri only. **Museu Tropical** 21-361 63 40. by appt only.

A LSO KNOWN AS the Jardim do Ultramar, this peaceful park with ponds, waterfowl and peacocks, attracts surprisingly few visitors. Designed at the beginning of the 20th century as the research centre of the Institute for Tropical Sciences, it is more of an arboretum than a flower garden. The emphasis is on rare and endangered tropical and subtropical trees and plants. Among the most striking are dragon trees, native to the Canary Islands and Madeira, monkey puzzle trees from South America and a handsome avenue of lofty Washington palms. The oriental garden with its streams, bridges and hibiscus is heralded by a large Chinese-style gateway which represented Macau in the Exhibition of the Portuguese World in 1940 *(see p62)*.

The research buildings and **Museu Tropical** are housed in the Palácio dos Condes da Calheta, whose interior walls are covered with *azulejos* spanning three centuries. The museum has 50,000 dried plant specimens and 2,414 samples of wood.

Mosteiro dos Jerónimos ❹

See pp66–7.

Washington palms in the Jardim Agrícola Tropical

Museu Nacional de Arqueologia ❺

Praça do Império. **Map** 1 B4. 21-362 00 00. 27, 28, 29, 43, 49, 51, 112. 15, 16, 17. 2–6pm Tue, 10am–6pm Wed–Sun. 1 Jan, Easter, 1 May, 25 Dec. www.mnarqueologia-ipmuseus.pt

T HE LONG west wing of the Mosteiro dos Jerónimos *(see pp66–7)*, formerly the monks' dormitory, has been a museum since 1893. Reconstructed in the middle of the 19th century, the building is a poor imitation of the Manueline original. The museum houses Portugal's main archaeological research centre and the exhibits, from sites all over the country, include a gold Iron Age bracelet, Visigothic jewellery found in the Alentejo in southern Portugal, Roman ornaments and early 8th-century Moorish artefacts. The main Greco-Roman and Egyptian section is strong on funerary art, featuring figurines, tombstones, masks, terracotta amulets and funeral cones inscribed with hieroglyphics alluding to the solar system. The dimly lit Room of Treasures has a fine collection of coins, necklaces, bracelets and other jewellery dating

Visigothic gold buckle, Museu de Arqueologia

from 1800–500 BC. This room has been refurbished to allow more of the magnificent jewellery, unseen by the public for decades, to be shown.

Planetário Calouste Gulbenkian ❻

Praça do Império. **Map** 1 B4. 21-362 00 02. 27, 28, 43, 49, 51, 112. 15. for refurbishment. www.planetario.online.pt

F INANCED BY the Gulbenkian Foundation *(see p79)* and built in 1965, this modern building sits incongruously beside the Jerónimos monastery. Inside, the Planetarium reveals the mysteries of the cosmos. There are shows in Portuguese, English and French explaining the movement of the stars and our solar system, as well as presentations on more specialist themes, such as the constellations or the Star of Bethlehem (Belém).

The dome of the Planetário Calouste Gulbenkian

Mosteiro dos Jerónimos ❹

A MONUMENT TO THE WEALTH of the Age of Discovery (see pp18–19), this monastery is the culmination of Manueline architecture in this period. Commissioned by Manuel I in around 1501, after Vasco de Gama's return from his historic voyage, it was financed largely by "pepper money," a tax levied on spices, precious stones and gold.

Armillary sphere in the cloister

Various masterbuilders worked on the building, the most notable of whom was Diogo Boitac, replaced by João de Castilho in 1517. The monastery was cared for by the Order of St Jerome (Hieronymites) until 1834, when all religious orders were disbanded.

Tomb of Vasco da Gama
The 19th-century tomb of the explorer (see p68) is carved with ropes, armillary spheres and other seafaring symbols.

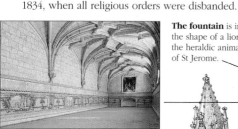

The fountain is in the shape of a lion, the heraldic animal of St Jerome.

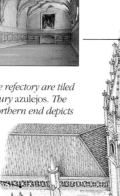

Refectory
The walls of the refectory are tiled with 18th-century azulejos. The panel at the northern end depicts the Feeding of the Five Thousand.

The modern wing, built in 1850 in Neo-Manueline style, houses the Museu Nacional de Arqueologia (see p65).

The west portal was designed by the French sculptor Nicolau Chanterène.

Entrance to church and cloister

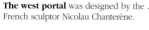

Gallery

View of the Monastery
This 17th-century scene by Felipe Lobo shows women at a fountain in front of the Mosteiro dos Jerónimos.

STAR FEATURES

★ **South Portal**

★ **Cloister**

★ **Cloister**
João de Castilho's pure Manueline creation was completed in 1544. Delicate tracery and richly carved images decorate the arches and balustrades.

Nave
The spectacular vaulting in the church of Santa Maria is held aloft by slender octagonal pillars. These rise like palm trees to the roof creating a feeling of space and harmony.

VISITORS' CHECKLIST

Praça do Império. **Map** 1 B4. [C]
21-362 00 34. [=] 27, 28, 43, 49,
51, 112. [=] 15. [R] Belém. [O]
10am–6pm Tue–Sun (Oct–Apr: to
5pm). [●] pub hols. [†] [♿] (free
10am–2pm Sun). [◎] [&] cloisters.

The chapterhouse holds the tomb of Alexandre Herculano (1810–77), historian and first mayor of Belém.

The chancel was commissioned in 1572 by Dona Catarina, wife of João III.

The tombs of Manuel I, his wife Dona Maria, João III and Catarina are supported by elephants.

★ **South Portal**
The strict geometrical architecture of the portal is almost obscured by the exuberant decoration. João de Castilho unites religious themes, such as this image of St Jerome, with the secular, exalting the kings of Portugal.

Tomb of King Sebastião
The tomb of the "longed for" Dom Sebastião stands empty. The young king never returned from battle in 1578.

Façade of the Museu de Marinha

Museu de Marinha 🔟

Praça do Império. **Map** 1 B4.
🕿 21-362 00 19. 🚌 14, 27, 28,
29, 43, 49, 51, 73, 112. 🚋 15.
🕙 10am–6pm Tue–Sun (Oct–Mar:
to 5pm). ⬤ public hols. 🎫 (21-362
00 10). 🎫 (free 10am–1pm Sun).
📷 ♿ 🌐 www.museumarinha.pt

THE MARITIME MUSEUM was
inaugurated in 1962 in the
west wing of the Jerónimos
monastery (see p66–7). It was
here, in the chapel built by
Henry the Navigator (see p19),
that mariners took mass before
embarking on their voyages.

A hall devoted to the
Discoveries illustrates
the progress in ship-
building from the
mid-15th century,
capitalizing on the
experience of long-
distance explorers.
Small replicas show
the transition from
the bark to the
lateen-rigged caravel,
through the faster
square-rigged caravel,
to the Portuguese
nau. Also here are
navigational instru-
ments, astrolabes and
replicas of 16th-cen-
tury maps showing
the world as it was
known then. The
stone pillars, carved
with the Cross of the
Knights of Christ, are
replicas of the types
of *padrão* set up as
monuments to Portu-
guese sovereignty on
the lands discovered.
A series of rooms displaying
models of modern Portuguese
ships leads on to the Royal
Quarters, where you can see
the exquisitely furnished
wood-panelled cabin of King
Carlos and Queen Amélia
from the royal yacht *Amélia*,
built in Scotland in 1900.
   The modern, incongruous
pavilion opposite houses original royal barges, the most
extravagant of which is the
royal brig built in 1780 for
Maria I. The collection ends
with a display of seaplanes,
including the *Santa Clara*
which made the first crossing
of the South Atlantic in 1922.

Centro Cultural de Belém 🔟

Praça do Império. **Map** 1 B5.
🕿 21-361 24 00. 🚌 14, 27, 28,
29, 43, 49, 51, 73, 112, 201. 🚋 15.
🚉 Belém. **Exhibition Centre and
Design Museum** 🕙 11am–8pm.
🎫 ♿ 🌐 www.ccb.pt

THE CONSTRUCTION of a stark
modern building between
the Jerónimos monastery and
the Tagus was controversial.
Built as the headquarters of
the Portuguese presidency of
the European Community,
it opened as a cultural and
conference centre in 1993.
It stresses music, performing
arts and photography, with a
large **Exhibition Centre and
Design Museum** that displays
choice pieces dating from 1937.
   Both the café and restaurant
spill out onto the ramparts of
the building whose peaceful
gardens of olive trees and
geometric lawns look out
over the quay and the river.

**The modern complex of the
Centro Cultural de Belém**

Monument to the Discoveries 🔟

Padrão dos Descobrimentos, Avenida
de Brasília. **Map** 1 C5. 🕿 21-303
19 50. 🚌 14, 28, 29, 43, 49, 51,
73, 112, 201. 🚋 15. 🚉 Belém.
🕙 9am–5pm (Jul–Aug: 7pm)
Tue–Sun. ⬤ public hols. 🎫 for lift.
📷 🌐 www.egeac.pt

STANDING PROMINENTLY on the
Belém waterfront, this massive angular monument, the
Padrão dos Descobrimentos,
was built in 1960 to mark the
500th anniversary of the death
of Henry the Navigator (see
p19). The 52-m (170-ft) high
monument, commissioned by
the Salazar regime, commemorates the mariners, royal
patrons and all those who took

VASCO DA GAMA (c.1460–1524)

In 1498 Vasco da Gama sailed
around the Cape of Good Hope
and opened the sea route to India
(see pp18–9). Although the Hindu
ruler of Calicut, who received him
wearing diamond and ruby rings,
was not impressed by his humble
offerings of cloth and wash basins,
da Gama returned to Portugal
with a cargo of spices. In 1502 he
sailed again to India, establishing
Portuguese trade routes in the
Indian Ocean. João III nominated
him Viceroy of India in 1524, but
he died of a fever soon after.

**16th-century painting of
Vasco da Gama in Goa**

The huge pavement compass in front of the Monument to the Discoveries

Museu de Arte Popular ⑩

Avenida de Brasília. **Map** 1 B5.
📞 21- 301 12 82. 🚌 9, 27, 28, 43, 49, 51, 112. 🚃 15. 🚉 Belém.
🕐 10am–12:30pm, 2–5pm Tue–Sun. ⬤ 1 Jan, Easter, 1 May, 25 Dec. ♿ Ⓦ www.ipmuseus.pt

THE DRAB BUILDING on the waterfront, between the Monument to the Discoveries and the Torre de Belém (see p70), houses the museum of Portuguese folk art and traditional handicrafts, opened in 1948. While the rooms housing the permanent collections are closed indefinitely for renovations, a temporary exhibition space is open. The exhibits, arranged by province, include pottery, costumes, agricultural tools, musical instruments, jewellery and brightly coloured saddles. The display gives a vivid indication of the diversity between the regions of Portugal. Each area has its speciality, such as the colourful ox yokes and ceramic cocks from the Minho and basketware from Trás-os-Montes, and cowbells and terracotta casseroles from the Alentejo. If you are planning to travel around Portugal the museum offers an excellent preview to the handicrafts of the various provinces.

Traditional costume from Trás-os-Montes

part in the development of the Portuguese Age of Discovery. The monument is designed in the shape of a caravel, with Portugal's coat of arms on the sides and the sword of the Royal House of Avis rising above the entrance. Henry the Navigator stands at the prow with a caravel in hand. In two sloping lines either side of the monument are stone statues of Portuguese heroes linked with the Age of Discovery. On the western face these include Dom Manuel I holding an armillary sphere, the poet Camões with a copy of *Os Lusíadas* and the painter Nuno Gonçalves with a paint pallet.

On the monument's north side, the huge mariner's compass cut into the paving stone was a present from the Republic of South Africa

in 1960. The central map, dotted with galleons and mermaids, shows the routes of the discoverers in the 15th and 16th centuries. Inside the monument a lift whisks you up to the sixth floor where steps then lead to the top for a splendid panorama of the river and Belém. The basement level is used for temporary exhibitions, but not necessarily related to the Discoveries.

The rather ostentatious Padrão is not to everyone's taste but the setting is undeniably splendid and the caravel design is imaginative. The monument looks particularly dramatic when viewed from the west in the light of the late afternoon sun.

EASTERN FACE OF THE MONUMENT TO THE DISCOVERIES

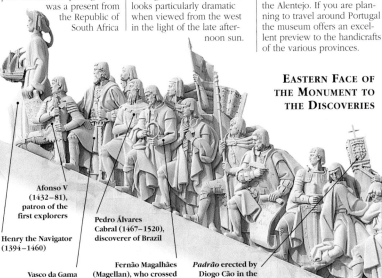

Afonso V (1432–81), patron of the first explorers

Henry the Navigator (1394–1460)

Pedro Álvares Cabral (1467–1520), discoverer of Brazil

Vasco da Gama (1460–1524)

Fernão Magalhães (Magellan), who crossed the Pacific in 1520–21

Padrão erected by Diogo Cão in the Congo in 1482

Torre de Belém ⑪

C OMMISSIONED BY Manuel I, the tower was
built as a fortress in the middle of the
Tagus in 1515–21. The starting point for the
navigators who set out to discover the trade
routes, this Manueline gem became a symbol
of Portugal's great era of expansion. The
real beauty of the tower lies in the decoration
of the exterior. Adorned with rope carved in
stone, it has openwork balconies, Moorish-
style watchtowers and distinctive battlements in the
shape of shields. The Gothic interior below the terrace,
which served as a storeroom for arms and a prison, is
very austere but the private quarters in the tower are
worth visiting for the loggia and the panorama.

**Arms of
Manuel I**

VISITORS' CHECKLIST

Avenida da India. **Map** 1 A5.
21-362 00 34. 14, 27, 28, 29,
43, 49, 51, 73, 112, 201. 15.
Belém. 10am–6pm Tue–
Sun (Oct–Apr: to 5). pub hols.
(free Sun am). partial.

Renaissance Loggia
*The elegant arcaded loggia,
inspired by Italian architecture,
gives a light touch
to the defensive
battlements of
the tower.*

Armillary spheres
and nautical rope
are symbols
of Portugal's
seafaring
prowess.

**Royal
coat of
arms of
Manuel I**

Chapel

Battlements are
decorated with
the cross of the
Order of Christ.

**Governor's
room**

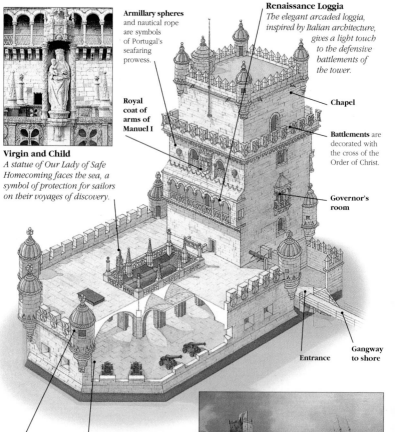

Virgin and Child
*A statue of Our Lady of Safe
Homecoming faces the sea, a
symbol of protection for sailors
on their voyages of discovery.*

**Gangway
to shore**

Entrance

**Sentry
posts**

The vaulted dungeon
was used as a prison
until the 19th century.

The Torre de Belém in 1811
*This painting of a British ship navigating the Tagus,
by JT Serres, shows the tower further from the shore
than it is today. Land on the north bank was reclaimed
in the 19th century, making the river narrower.*

The simple Manueline chapel, Ermida de São Jerónimo

Ermida de São Jerónimo ⑫

Rua Pero de Covilhã. **Map** 1 A3. 〖 21-301 86 48. 🚌 14, 28, 29, 43, 49, 51, 73, 201. ⏰ Wed (by appt only).

ALSO KNOWN AS the Capela de São Jerónimo, this elegant little chapel was constructed in 1514 when Diogo Boitac was working on the Jerónimos monastery (see pp66–7). Although a far simpler building, it is also Manueline in style and may have been built to a design by Boitac. The only decorative elements on the monolithic chapel are the four pinnacles, corner gargoyles and Manueline portal. Perched on a quiet hill above Belém, the chapel has fine views down to the River Tagus and a path from the terrace winds down the hill towards the Torre de Belém.

Igreja da Memória ⑬

Calçada do Galvão, Ajuda. **Map** 1 C3. 〖 21-363 52 95. 🚌 14, 27, 28, 32. 🚊 18. ⏰ 4–6pm Mon–Sat. ✝ 🚻

BUILT IN 1760, the church was founded by King José I in gratitude for his escape from an assassination plot on this site in 1758. The king was returning from a secret liaison with a lady of the noble Távora family when his carriage was attacked and a bullet hit him in the arm. Pombal (see p15), whose power had now become absolute, used this as an excuse to get rid of his enemies in the Távora family,

accusing them of conspiracy. In 1759 they were savagely tortured and executed. Their deaths are commemorated by a pillar in Beco do Chão Salgado, off Rua de Belém.

The Neo-Classical domed church has a marble-clad interior and a small chapel, on the right, containing the tomb of Pombal. He died at the age of 83, a year after he had been banished from Lisbon.

Jardim Botânico da Ajuda ⑭

Calçada da Ajuda. **Map** 1 C2. 〖 21-362 25 03. 🚌 14, 27, 28, 29, 32, 73, 201. 🚊 18. ⏰ 9am–6pm Thu–Tue (Apr–Sep: to 8pm). ● public hols. 🉑 (free 10am–2pm Sun). 🚻

LAID OUT on two levels by Pombal (see p15) in 1768, these Italian-style gardens provide a pleasant respite from the noisy suburbs of Belém. The entrance (wrought-iron gates in a pink wall) is easy to miss. The park comprises 5,000 plant species from Africa, Asia and America. Notable features are the 400-year-old dragon tree, native of Madeira, and the flamboyant 18th-century fountain decorated with serpents, winged fish, sea horses and mythical creatures. A majestic terrace looks out over the lower level of the gardens.

Palácio Nacional da Ajuda ⑮

Calçada da Ajuda. **Map** 2 D2. 〖 21-363 70 95. 🚌 14, 27, 28, 32, 42, 60. 🚊 18. ⏰ 10am–5pm Thu–Tue. ● Feb, public hols. 🉑 (free Sun). 🚻 🅿 🆆 www.ipmuseus.pt

THE ROYAL PALACE, destroyed by fire in 1795, was replaced in the early 19th century by this Neo-Classical building. It was left incomplete when the royal family was forced into exile in Brazil in 1807.

The palace only became a permanent residence of the royal family when Luís I became king in 1861 and married an Italian Princess, Maria Pia di Savoia. No expense was spared in furnishing the apartments. The ostentatious rooms are decorated with silk wallpaper, Sèvres porcelain and crystal chandeliers. A prime example of regal excess is the extraordinary Saxe Room, a wedding present to Maria Pia from the King of Saxony, in which every piece of furniture is decorated with Meissen porcelain. On the first floor the huge

19th-century throne from the Palácio Nacional da Ajuda

Banqueting Hall, with crystal chandeliers, silk-covered chairs and an allegory of the birth of João VI on the frescoed ceiling, is truly impressive. At the other end of the palace, Luís I's Neo-Gothic painting studio is a more intimate display of intricately carved furniture.

Manicured formal gardens of the Jardim Botânico da Ajuda

FURTHER AFIELD

THE MAJORITY of the outlying sights, which include some of Lisbon's finest museums, are easily accessible by bus or metro from the city centre. A ten-minute walk north from the gardens of the Parque Eduardo VII brings you to Portugal's great cultural complex, the Calouste Gulbenkian Foundation, set in a pleasant park. Few tourists go further north than the Gulbenkian, but the Museu da Cidade on Campo Grande is worth a detour for its fascinating overview of Lisbon's history.

Azulejo **panel from Palácio Fronteira**

The charming Palácio Fronteira, decorated with splendid tiles, is one of the many villas built for the aristocracy that now overlook the city suburbs. Those interested in tiles will also enjoy the Museu Nacional do Azulejo in the cloisters of the Madre de Deus convent. Visitors with a spare half day can cross the Tagus to the Cristo Rei monument. Northeast of Lisbon is the vast oceanarium, Oceanário de Lisboa, in the Parque das Nações, which includes other family-oriented attractions, hotels and shops.

SIGHTS AT A GLANCE

Museums and Galleries
Centro de Arte Moderna **7**
Museu da Água **9**
Museu Calouste Gulbenkian pp76–9 **6**
Museu da Cidade **13**
Museu Nacional do Azulejo pp82–3 **10**

Modern Architecture
Amoreiras Shopping Centre **3**
Cristo Rei **1**
Parque das Nações **11**
Ponte 25 de Abril **2**

Historic Architecture
Aqueduto das Águas Livres **15**
Campo Pequeno **8**
Palácio Fronteira **16**
Praça Marquês de Pombal **4**

Parks and Gardens
Parque Eduardo VII **5**
Parque do Monteiro-Mor **17**

Zoos
Jardim Zoológico **14**
Oceanário de Lisboa **12**

KEY

▢	Main sightseeing areas
✈	Airport
⚓	Ferry boarding point
▬	Motorway
▬	Major road
▬	Minor road

0 kilometres   4

0 miles   2

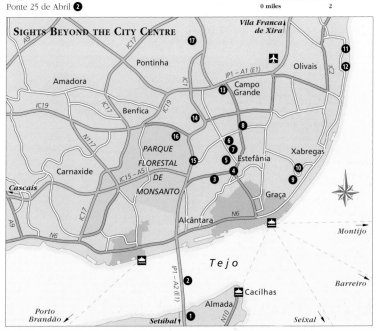

SIGHTS BEYOND THE CITY CENTRE

⊲ **Nymph fountain among tropical vegetation inside the Estufa Fria, Parque Eduardo VII**

Cristo Rei ❶

Santuário Nacional do Cristo Rei, Alto do Pragal, Almada. ☎ 21-275 10 00. 🚢 from Praça do Comércio & Cais do Sodré to Cacilhas then 🚌 1. 🕐 9:30am–6pm daily (Nov–Feb: to 7pm). 📷

MODELLED ON the more famous Cristo Redentor in Rio de Janeiro, this giant-sized statue stands with arms outstretched on the south bank of the Tagus. The 28 m (92 ft) tall figure of Christ, mounted on a huge pedestal, was built by Francisco Franco in 1949–59 at the instigation of Prime Minister Salazar.

You can see the monument from various viewpoints in the city, but it is fun to take a ferry to the Outra Banda (the other bank), then a bus or taxi to the monument. A lift, plus some steps, takes you up 82 m (269 ft) to the top of the pedestal, affording fine views of the city and river.

Ponte 25 de Abril ❷

Map 3 A5. 🚌 52, 53.

ORIGINALLY CALLED the Ponte Salazar after the dictator who had it built in 1966, Lisbon's suspension bridge was renamed (like many other

The towering monument of Cristo Rei overlooking the Tagus

monuments) to commemorate the revolution of 25 April 1974 which restored democracy to Portugal (see p15).

Inspired by San Francisco's Golden Gate Bridge in the United States, this steel con-struction stretches for 1 km (half a mile). The lower tier was modified in 1999 to accommodate the Fertagus, a much-needed railway across the Tagus.

The bridge's notorious traffic congestion has been partly resolved by the opening of the 11-km (7-mile) Vasco da Gama bridge. Spanning the river from Montijo to Sacavém, north of the Parque das Nações, this bridge was completed in 1998.

Amoreiras Shopping Centre ❸

Avenida Engenheiro Duarte Pacheco. **Map** 5 A5. ☎ 21-381 02 00. 🚌 11, 18, 23, 48, 51, 53, 58, 74, 83. 🕐 10am–11pm daily. ⬤ 25 Dec. ♿ Ⓦ www.amoreiras.com

IN THE 18TH CENTURY, the Marquês de Pombal (see p15) planted mulberry trees (amoreiras) on the western edge of the city to create food for silk worms. Hence the name of the futuristic shopping centre that was built here in 1985. This vast complex, with pink and blue towers, houses 370 shops, ten cinemas, and numerous restaurants. Once an incongruous feature, it now draws the crowds, particularly the young, and has been joined by other new buildings and shopping centres in the area.

Ponte 25 de Abril linking central Lisbon with the Outra Banda, the south bank of the Tagus

Tropical plants in the Estufa Quente glasshouse, Parque Eduardo VII

Praça Marquês de Pombal ❹

Map 5 C5. **M** *Marquês de Pombal.* 🚌 *2, 6, 9, 11, 12, 20, 22, 23, 27, 32, 36, 38 & many other routes.*

AT THE TOP of the Avenida da Liberdade *(see p44)*, traffic thunders round the "Rotunda" (roundabout), as the praça is also known. At the centre is the lofty monument to Pombal. The despotic statesman, who virtually ruled Portugal from 1750–77, stands on the top of the column, his hand on a lion (symbol of power) and his eyes directed down to the Baixa, whose creation he masterminded *(see p15)*.

Detail representing agricultural toil on the base of the monument in Praça Marquês de Pombal

Allegorical images depicting Pombal's political, educational and agricultural reforms decorate the base of the monument. Standing figures represent Coimbra University where he introduced a new Faculty of Science. Although greatly feared, this dynamic politician propelled the country into the Age of Enlightenment. Broken blocks of stone at the foot of the monument and tidal waves flooding the city are an allegory of the destruction caused by the 1755 earthquake.

An underpass, which is not always open, leads to the centre of the square where the sculptures on the pedestal and the inscriptions relating to Pombal's achievements can be seen. Nearby, the well-tended Parque Eduardo VII extends northwards behind the square. The paving stones around the Rotunda are decorated with a mosaic of Lisbon's coat of arms. Similar patterns in small black and white cobbles decorate many of the city's streets and squares.

Parque Eduardo VII ❺

Praça Marquês de Pombal. **Map** 5 B4. **C** *21-388 22 78.* **M** *Marquês de Pombal.* 🚌 *2, 12, 22, 38.* **Estufa Fria** **C** *21-388 22 78.* ☐ *Apr–Sep: 9am–6pm daily; Oct–Mar: 9am–5pm daily (last admission 30 mins before closing).* ● *public hols.* 🅰️

THE LARGEST PARK in central Lisbon was named in honour of King Edward VII of England who came to Lisbon in 1902 to reaffirm the Anglo-Portuguese alliance. The wide grassy slope, that extends for 25 hectares (62 acres), was laid out as Parque da Liberdade, a continuation of Avenida da Liberdade *(see p44)*, in the late 19th century. Neatly clipped box hedging, flanked by mosaic patterned walkways, stretches uphill from the Praça Marquês de Pombal to a belvedere at the top. Here are a flower-filled garden dedicated to the memory of Amália Rodrigues and a pleasant café. From here there are fine views of the city. On clear days it is possible to see as far as the Serra da Arrábida *(see p107)*.

Located at the northwest corner, the most inspiring feature of this rather monotonous park is the jungle-like **Estufa Fria**, or greenhouse, where exotic plants, streams and waterfalls provide an oasis from the city streets. There are in fact two greenhouses: in the Estufa Fria (cold greenhouse), palms push through the slatted bamboo roof and paths wind through a forest of ferns, fuchsias, flowering shrubs and banana trees; the warmer Estufa Quente, or hot-house, is a glassed-over garden with lush plants, water-lily ponds and cacti, as well as tropical birds in cages.

Near the estufas a pond with carp and a galleon-shaped play area are popular with children. On the east side the **Pavilhão Carlos Lopes**, named after the 1984 Olympic marathon winner, is now used for concerts and conferences. The façade is decorated with tiled scenes by *azulejo* artist, Jorge Colaço, mainly of Portuguese battles.

Museu Calouste Gulbenkian ❻

Thanks to a wealthy Armenian oil magnate, Calouste Gulbenkian (*see p79*), with wide-ranging tastes and an eye for a masterpiece, the museum has one of the finest collections of art in Europe. Inaugurated in 1969, the purpose-built museum was created as part of the charitable institution bequeathed to Portugal by the multimillionaire. The design of the building, set in a spacious park allowing natural light to fill some of the rooms, was devised to create the best layout for the founder's varied collection.

Mustard Barrel
This 18th-century silver mustard barrel was made in France by Antoine Sébastien Durand.

Lalique Corsage Ornament
The sinuous curves of the gold and enamel snakes are typical of René Lalique's Art Nouveau jewellery.

★ Diana
This fine marble statue (1780) by the French sculptor Jean-Antoine Houdon, was once owned by Catherine the Great of Russia and was considered too obscene to exhibit. The graceful Diana, goddess of the hunt, stands with a bow and arrow in hand.

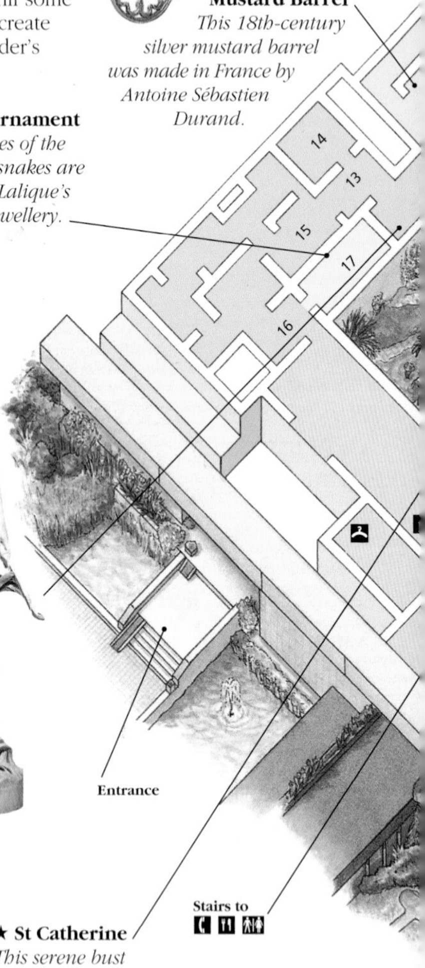

Entrance

Stairs to

★ St Catherine
This serene bust of St Catherine was painted by the Flemish artist Rogier Van der Weyden (1400–64). The thin strip of landscape on the left of the wooden panel brings light and depth to the still portrait.

STAR EXHIBITS

★ **Portrait of an Old Man by Rembrandt**

★ **Diana by Houdon**

★ **St Catherine by Van der Weyden**

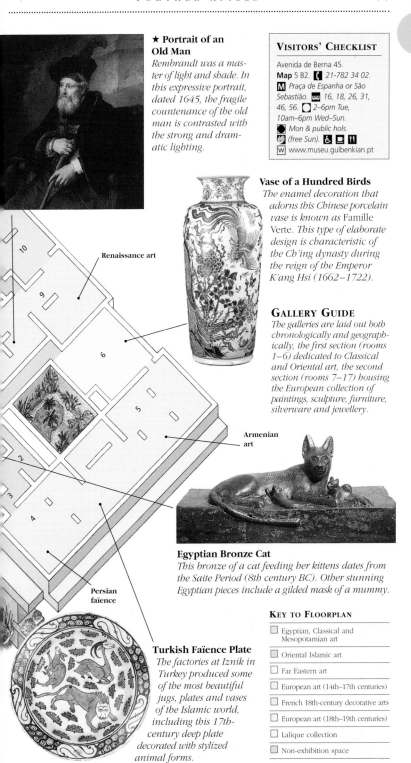

★ **Portrait of an Old Man**
Rembrandt was a master of light and shade. In this expressive portrait, dated 1645, the fragile countenance of the old man is contrasted with the strong and dramatic lighting.

Vase of a Hundred Birds
The enamel decoration that adorns this Chinese porcelain vase is known as Famille Verte. This type of elaborate design is characteristic of the Ch'ing dynasty during the reign of the Emperor K'ang Hsi (1662–1722).

GALLERY GUIDE
The galleries are laid out both chronologically and geographically, the first section (rooms 1–6) dedicated to Classical and Oriental art, the second section (rooms 7–17) housing the European collection of paintings, sculpture, furniture, silverware and jewellery.

Renaissance art

Armenian art

Persian faïence

Egyptian Bronze Cat
This bronze of a cat feeding her kittens dates from the Saite Period (8th century BC). Other stunning Egyptian pieces include a gilded mask of a mummy.

Turkish Faïence Plate
The factories at Iznik in Turkey produced some of the most beautiful jugs, plates and vases of the Islamic world, including this 17th-century deep plate decorated with stylized animal forms.

KEY TO FLOORPLAN

- Egyptian, Classical and Mesopotamian art
- Oriental Islamic art
- Far Eastern art
- European art (14th–17th centuries)
- French 18th-century decorative arts
- European art (18th–19th centuries)
- Lalique collection
- Non-exhibition space

Exploring the Gulbenkian Collection

HOUSING CALOUSTE GULBENKIAN'S unique collection of art, the museum ranks with the Museu de Arte Antiga *(see pp56–9)* as the finest in Lisbon. The exhibits, which span over 4,000 years from ancient Egyptian statuettes, through translucent Islamic glassware, to Art Nouveau brooches, are displayed in spacious and well-lit galleries, many overlooking the gardens or courtyards. The museum is quite small, however each individual work of art, from the magnificent pieces that make up the rich display of Oriental and Islamic art, to the selection of European paintings and furniture, is worthy of attention.

Late 16th-century Persian faïence tile from the School of Isfahan

EGYPTIAN, CLASSICAL AND MESOPOTAMIAN ART

PRICELESS TREASURES chart the evolution of Egyptian art from the Old Kingdom (c.2700 BC) to the Roman Period (1st century BC). The exhibits range from an alabaster bowl of the 3rd Dynasty to a surprisingly modern-looking blue terracotta torso of a statuette of *Venus Anadyomene* from the Roman period.

Outstanding pieces in the Classical art section are a magnificent red-figure Greek vase and 11 Roman medallions, found in Egypt. These are believed to have been struck to commemorate the athletic games held in Macedonia in AD 242 in honour of Alexander the Great. In the Mesopotamian art section the large Assyrian

5th-century BC Greek vase

alabaster bas-relief represents the winged genius of Spring, carrying a container of sacred water (9th century BC).

ORIENTAL ISLAMIC ART

BEING ARMENIAN, Calouste Gulbenkian had a keen interest in art from the Near and Middle East. The Oriental Islamic gallery has a fine collection of Persian and Turkish carpets, textiles, costumes and ceramics. In the section overlooking the courtyard, the Syrian mosque lamps and bottles commissioned by princes and sultans, are beautifully decorated with coloured enamel on glass. The Armenian section has some exquisite illustrated manuscripts from the 16th to 18th centuries, produced by Armenian refugees in Istanbul, Persia and the Crimea.

French ivory triptych of
Scenes from the Life of the Virgin **(14th century)**

FAR EASTERN ART

CALOUSTE GULBENKIAN acquired a large collection of Chinese porcelain between 1910 and 1930. One of the rarest pieces is the small blue-glazed bowl from the Yüan Dynasty (1279–1368), on the right as you go into the gallery. The majority of exhibits, however, are the later, more exuberantly decorated *famille verte* porcelain and the K'ang Hsi biscuitware of the 17th and 18th centuries. Further exhibits from the Far East are translucent Chinese jades and other semi-precious stones, Japanese prints, brocaded silk hangings and bound books, and lacquerwork.

EUROPEAN ART (14TH–17TH CENTURIES)

ILLUMINATED MANUSCRIPTS, rare printed books and medieval ivories introduce the section on Western art. The delicately sculpted 14th-century ivory diptychs and triptychs, made in France, show scenes from the lives of Christ and the Virgin.

The collection of early European paintings starts with panels of *St Joseph* and *St Catherine* by Rogier van der Weyden, leading painter of the mid-15th century in Flanders. Italian Renaissance painting is represented by Cima da Conegliano's *Sacra Conversazione* from the late 15th century and Domenico Ghirlandaio's *Portrait of a Young Woman* (1485).

The collection progresses to Flemish and Dutch works of the 17th century, including two works by Rembrandt: *Portrait of an Old Man* (1645), a masterpiece of psychological penetration, and *Alexander the Great* (1660), said to have been modelled on Rembrandt's son, Titus, and previously thought to have portrayed the Greek goddess Pallas Athena. Rubens is represented by three paintings, the most remarkable of which is the *Portrait of Hélène Fourment* (1630), the artist's second wife.

The gallery beyond the Dutch and Flemish paintings has tapestries and textiles from Italy and Flanders, Italian ceramics, rare 15th-century medallions and sculpture.

FRENCH 18TH-CENTURY DECORATIVE ARTS

SOME REMARKABLY elaborate Louis XV and Louis XVI pieces, many commissioned by royalty, feature in the collection of French 18th-century furniture. The exhibits, many of them embellished with laquer panels, ebony and bronze, are grouped together according to historical style with Beauvais and "chinoiserie" Aubusson tapestries decorating the walls.

The French silverware from the same period, much of which once adorned the dining tables of Russian palaces, includes lavishly decorated soup tureens, salt-cellars and platters.

Louis XV chest of drawers inlaid with ebony and bronze

EUROPEAN ART (18TH–19TH CENTURIES)

THE ART of the 18th century is dominated by French painters, including Watteau (1684–1721), Fragonard (1732–1806) and Boucher (1703–70). The most celebrated piece of sculpture is a statue of *Diana* by Jean-Antoine Houdon. Commissioned in 1780 by the Duke of Saxe-Gotha for his

View of the Molo with the Ducal Palace (1790) by Francesco Guardi

gardens, it became one of the principal exhibits in the Hermitage in Russia during the 19th and early 20th centuries.

One whole room is devoted to views of Venice by the 18th-century Venetian painter Francesco Guardi, and a small collection of British art includes works by leading 18th-century portraitists, such as Gainsborough's *Portrait of Mrs Lowndes-Stone* (c.1775) and Romney's *Portrait of Mrs Constable* (1787). There are also two stormy seascapes by JMW Turner (1775–1851). French 19th-century landscape painting is well represented here, reflecting Gulbenkian's preference for naturalism, with works by the Barbizon school, the Realists and the Impressionists. The best-known paintings in the section, however, are probably Manet's *Boy with Cherries*, painted in about 1858 at the beginning of the artist's career, and *Boy Blowing*

Bubbles, painted about 1867. Renoir's *Portrait of Madame Claude Monet* was painted in about 1872 when the artist was staying with Monet at his country home in Argenteuil, in the outskirts of Paris.

LALIQUE COLLECTION

THE TOUR of the museum ends with an entire room filled with the flamboyant creations of French Art Nouveau jeweller, René Lalique (1860–1945). Gulbenkian was a close friend of Lalique's and he acquired many of the pieces of jewellery, glassware and ivory on display here directly from the artist. Inlaid with semi-precious stones and covered with enamel or gold leaf, the brooches, necklaces, vases and combs are decorated with the dragonfly, peacock or sensual female nude motifs characteristic of Art Nouveau.

CALOUSTE GULBENKIAN

Born in Scutari (Turkey) in 1869, Gulbenkian started his art collection at the age of 14 when he bought some ancient coins in a bazaar. In 1928 he was granted a 5 per cent stake in four major oil companies, including BP and Shell, in thanks for his part in the transfer of the assets of the Turkish Petroleum Company to those four companies. He thereby earned himself the nickname of "Mr Five Percent". With the wealth he accumulated, Gulbenkian was able to indulge his passion for fine works of art. During World War II, he went to live in neutral Portugal and, on his death in 1955, bequeathed his estate to the Portuguese in the form of a charitable trust. The Foundation supports many cultural activities and has its own orchestra, libraries, ballet company and concert halls.

A light-filled gallery at the Centro de Arte Moderna

Centro de Arte Moderna **❼**

Rua Dr Nicolau de Bettencourt.
Map 5 B3. 🎫 *21-782 30 00.*
Ⓜ *São Sebastião.* 🚌 *16, 18, 26, 31, 42, 46, 56, 115.* 🚇 *24.* ⏰ *2–6pm Tue, 10am–6pm Wed–Sun.* ● *1 Jan, Easter, 1 May, 25 Dec.* 📷 *(free Sun).*
♿ Ⓦ *www.gulbenkian.pt*

THE MODERN ART MUSEUM lies across the gardens from the Calouste Gulbenkian museum and is part of the same cultural foundation *(see p59)*.

The permanent collection features paintings and sculpture by Portuguese artists from the turn of the 20th century to the present day. The most famous painting is the striking portrait of poet Fernando Pessoa in the Café Irmãos Unidos (1964) by José de Almada Negreiros (1893– 1970), a main exponent of Portuguese Modernism. Also of interest are paintings by Eduardo Viana (1881–1967), Amadeo de Sousa Cardoso (1887–1910), as well as contemporary artists such as Paula Rego, Rui Sanches, Graça Morais and Teresa Magalhães.

The museum is light and spacious, with pleasant gardens and a busy cafeteria.

Campo Pequeno **❽**

Map 5 C1. Ⓜ *Campo Pequeno.* 🚌 *22, 45.* **Bullring** 🎫 *21-793 24 42.* ● *for renovation.* 📷 ♿

THIS SQUARE is dominated by the red-brick Neo-Moorish bullring built in the late 19th century. Temporarily closed, the building is undergoing major works to build an underground car park and leisure centre. Much of the bullring's distinctive architecture, such as keyhole-shaped windows and double cupolas will be retained. Call the tourist office or the number listed above for information on this and other bull fight venues.

Renovated 19th-century steam pump in the Museu da Água

Museu da Água **❾**

Rua do Alviela 12. 🎫 *21-810 02 15.*
🚌 *35, 104, 105, 107.* ⏰ *1 Mar– 30 Nov: 10am–6pm Mon–Sat.* ● *public hols.* 📷 📷

DEDICATED TO the history of Lisbon's water supply, this small but informative museum was imaginatively created around the city's first steam pumping station. It commemorates Manuel da Maia, the 18th-century engineer who masterminded the Águas Livres aqueduct *(see p84)*. The excellent layout of the museum earned it the Council of Europe Museum Prize in 1990.

Pride of place goes to four lovingly preserved steam engines, one of which still functions (by electricity) and can be switched on for visitors. The development of technology relating to the city's water supply is documented with photographs. Particularly interesting are the sections on the Águas Livres aqueduct and the Alfama's 17th-century Chafariz d'El Rei, one of Lisbon's first fountains. Locals used to queue at one of six founts, depending on their social status.

Museu Nacional do Azulejo **❿**

Neo-Moorish façade of the bullring in Campo Pequeno

See pp82–3.

The impressive Oriente Station, located next to Parque das Nações

Parque das Nações ⑪

Avenida Dom João II. 🕿 21-891 98 98. Ⓜ *Oriente.* 🚌 *5, 10, 19, 21, 25, 28, 44, 50, 68, 114.* 🚃 *Gare do Oriente.* ⏰ *10am–8pm daily.* ♿
🏛 🖼 **Pavilhão do Conhecimento – Ciencia Viva** 🕿 *21-891 71 00.* ⏰ *10am–6pm Tue–Fri, 11am–7pm Sat & Sun.* ⬤ *1 Jan, 24, 25 & 31 Dec.* 📷

ORIGINALLY THE SITE of Expo '98, Parque das Nações has become a new focus for Lisbon. With its contemporary architecture, family-oriented attractions and modern living spaces, the park has renewed the eastern waterfront, an industrial wasteland as recently as 1990. Even from a distance, the soaring geometry of the platform canopies over Santiago Calatrava's Oriente Station set the architectural tone for the development. The impressive **Portugal Pavilion**, designed by the Portuguese architect Álvaro Siza Vieira, has an enormous reinforced-concrete roof suspended almost miraculously, like a sailcloth, above its forecourt.

The **Pavilhão do Conhecimento – Ciencia Viva** (Knowledge and Science Pavilion) is a modern museum of science and technology that houses several interactive exhibitions. Views can be had from the cable car that lifts visitors from one end of the park to the other or the **Torre Vasco da Gama**, Lisbon's tallest building. The promenade along the river, which offers delightful views of the Tagus at its widest and the impressive Vasco da Gama bridge, is not to be missed.

The 10-mile (17-km) long **Vasco da Gama** bridge is the longest in Europe and was completed in 1998. Also in the area are the Sony Plaza and Pavilhão Atlantico, which host concerts and sporting events.

Oceanário de Lisboa ⑫

Esplanada D. Carlos 1, Parque das Nações. 🕿 *21-891 70 02.* Ⓜ *Oriente.* 🚌 *5, 10, 19, 21, 28, 44, 50, 68, 82.* 🚃 *Gare do Oriente.* ⏰ *Apr–Oct: 10am–8pm daily; Nov–Mar: 10am–7pm daily.* 📷 ♿

CENTREPIECE OF Expo 98 and now the main attraction at Parque das Nações, the somewhat aircraft carrier-like oceanarium was designed by American architect Peter Chermayeff, and is perched on the end of a pier, surrounded by water. It is the second-largest aquarium in the world, and holds an impressive array of species – birds and some mammals as well as fish and other underwater dwellers.

Four separate sea- and landscapes represent the habitats of the Atlantic, Pacific, Indian and Antarctic oceans, with suitable fauna and flora. The main attraction for most visitors, though, is the vast central tank with a dazzling variety of fish, large and small, swimming round and round. Hammerhead sharks co-exist peaceably with bream, barracudas with rays.

18th-century Indian toy, Museu da Cidade

The softly-lit waters can be viewed through any number of glass panes, on two levels.

Museu da Cidade ⑬

Campo Grande 245. 🕿 *21-751 32 00.* Ⓜ *Campo Grande.* 🚌 *1, 3, 7, 33, 36, 47, 50, 68, 85, 101, 108.* ⏰ *10am–1pm, 2–6pm Tue–Sun.* ⬤ *public hols.* 📷 *(free 10am–2pm Sun).* ♿

PALÁCIO PIMENTA was allegedly commissioned by João V *(see p17)* for his mistress Madre Paula, a nun from the nearby convent at Odivelas. When the mansion was built, in the middle of the 18th century, it occupied a peaceful site outside the capital. Nowadays it has to contend with the traffic of Campo Grande. The house itself, however, retains its period charm and the city museum is one of the most interesting in Lisbon.

The displays follow the development of the city, from prehistoric times, through the Romans, Visigoths and Moors, traced by means of tiles, drawings, paintings, models and historical documents. Some of the most fascinating exhibits are those depicting the city before the earthquake of 1755, including a highly detailed model made in the 1950s and an impressive 17th-century oil painting by Dirk Stoop (1610–86) of *Terreiro do Paço*, as Praça do Comércio was known then *(see p47)*. One room is devoted to the Águas Livres aqueduct *(see p84)* with detailed architectural plans for its construction as well as prints and watercolours of the completed aqueduct.

The earthquake theme is resumed with pictures of the city amid the devastation and various plans for its reconstruction. The museum brings you into the 20th century with a large colour poster celebrating the Revolution of 1910 and the proclamation of the new republic *(see p15)*.

Museu Nacional do Azulejo ⑩

Pelican on the Manueline portal

ᴰONA LEONOR, widow of King João II, founded the Convento da Madre de Deus in 1509. Originally built in Manueline style, the church was restored under João III using simple Renaissance designs. The striking Baroque decoration was added by João V. The convent cloisters provide a stunning setting for the National Tile Museum. Decorative panels, individual tiles and photographs trace the evolution of tile-making from its introduction by the Moors, through Spanish influence and the development of Portugal's own style up to the present day.

Panorama of Lisbon
A striking 18th-century panel, along one wall of the cloister, depicts Lisbon before the 1755 earthquake (see pp20–21). This detail shows the royal palace on Terreiro do Paço.

Level 2

Hunting Scene
Artisans rather than artists began to decorate tiles in the 17th century. This detail shows a naive representation of a hunt.

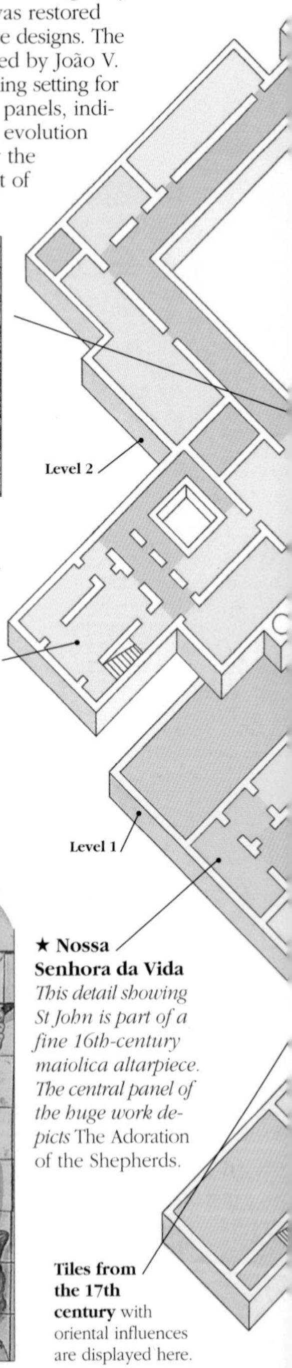

Level 1

KEY TO FLOORPLAN

- ☐ Moorish tiles
- ☐ 16th-century tiles
- ☐ 17th-century tiles
- ☐ 18th-century tiles
- ☐ 19th-century tiles
- ☐ 20th-century tiles
- ☐ Temporary exhibition space
- ☐ Non-exhibition space

STAR FEATURES

★ **Madre de Deus**

★ **Manueline Cloister**

★ **Nossa Senhora da Vida**

★ **Nossa Senhora da Vida**
This detail showing St John is part of a fine 16th-century maiolica altarpiece. The central panel of the huge work depicts The Adoration of the Shepherds.

Tiles from the 17th century with oriental influences are displayed here.

Café Tiles
The walls of the restaurant are lined with 20th-century tiles showing hanging game, including wild boar and pheasant.

Level 3

Moorish Tiles
Decorated with a stylized animal motif, this 15th-century tile is typical of Moorish azulejo patterns.

Entrance

The Renaissance cloister
is the work of Diogo de Torralva (1500–66).

VISITORS' CHECKLIST

Rua da Madre de Deus 4. 21-810 03 40. 18, 42, 104, 105. 2–6pm Tue, 10am–6pm Wed–Sun (last adm: 30 mins before closing). pub hols. (free 10am–2pm Sun). W www.mnazulejo-ipmuseus.pt

★ Madre de Deus
Completed in the mid-16th century, it was not until two centuries later, under João V, that the church of Madre de Deus acquired its ornate decoration. The sumptuous Rococo altarpiece was added after the earthquake of 1755.

GALLERY GUIDE
The rooms around the central cloister are arranged chronologically with the oldest tiles on the ground floor. Access to the Madre de Deus is via level 2 of the museum. The front entrance of the church is used only during religious services.

The carved Manueline portal was recreated from a 16th-century painting.

★ Manueline Cloister
An important surviving feature of the original convent is the graceful Manueline cloister. Fine geometrical patterned tiles were added to the cloister walls in the 17th century.

Jardim Zoológico ^⓭

Estrada de Benfica 158–60. ⓒ 21-
723 29 10. Ⓜ Jardim Zoológico.
▦ 16, 31, 55, 58 and other routes.
◯ 10am–6pm (Apr–Sep: 8pm)
daily. 🅿 📷

Dolphins performing in the aquarium of the Jardim Zoológico

THE GARDENS of the Jardim
Zoológico are as much
a feature as the actual zoo.
Opened in 1905, the zoo has
recently been revamped and
the majority of its aviaries
and cages now provide more
comfortable conditions for the
specimens. The most bizarre
feature is the dogs' cemetery,
complete with tombstones and
flowers. Current attractions of
the zoo include a cable car
touring the park, a reptile
house, dolphin shows and an
amusement park. The area is
divided into four zones and
the admission charge is based
on how many you visit.

Aqueduto das Águas Livres ^⓮

Best seen from Calçada da Quintinha.
▦ 6, 9, 20, 22, 27, 38, 49, 58, 74. ◯
for guided tours by appt (Apr–Oct only),
phone Museu da Água. ⓒ 21-813
55 22. **Mãe d'Água das Amoreiras**
Praça das Amoreiras. ⓒ 21-325 16
46. ◯ 10am–6pm Mon–Sat.

CONSIDERED THE most
beautiful sight in Lisbon
at the turn of the century, the
Aqueduto das Águas Livres
looms over the Alcântara valley
to the northwest of the city.
The construction of an aqueduct gave João V (see p17)
the opportunity to indulge his
passion for grandiose building

schemes, as the only area of
Lisbon with fresh drinking
water was the Alfama. A tax
on meat, wine, olive oil and
other comestibles funded the
project, and although not
complete until the 19th century,
it was already supplying the
city with water by 1748. The
main pipeline measures 19 km
(12 miles), but the total length,
including all the secondary
channels, is 58 km (36 miles).
The most visible part of this
imposing structure, classified as
a National Monument in 2002,
are the 35 arches that cross the
Alcântara valley, the tallest of
which rise to a spectacular 65
m (213 ft) above the ground.
The public walkway along
the aqueduct has been closed
since 1853. This is partly due
to Diogo Alves, the infamous
robber who threw his victims
over the edge. Today, it is
possible to take a lively guided
tour over the Alcântara arches.

There are also tours of the Mãe
d'Água reservoir and trips to
the Mãe d'Água springs, the
source of the water supply.
These tours can be irregular,
so it is best to contact the
Museu da Água (see p80) for
details of the trips on offer.
At the end of the aqueduct,
the **Mãe d'Água das
Amoreiras** is a castle-like
building which once served
as a reservoir for the water
supplied from the aqueduct.
The original design of 1745
was by the Hungarian architect, Carlos Mardel, who
worked under Pombal (see
pp20–21) in the rebuilding of
the Baixa. Completed in 1834,
it became a popular meeting
place and acquired a reputation as the rendezvous for
kings and their mistresses.
Today the space is used for
art exhibitions, fashion shows
and other events. There are
great views from the roof.

Imposing arches of the Aqueduto das Águas Livres spanning the Alcântara valley

Palácio Fronteira **15**

Largo São Domingos de Benfica 1.
(*21-778 20 23.* **M** *Jardim
Zoológico.* **▦** *70, 72.* **R** *Benfica.*
◯ *Mon–Sat:* **⏱** *Jun–Sep: 10:30,
11, & 11:30am & noon; Oct–May:
11am & noon.* **●** *public hols.* **▨**

Tiled terrace leading to the chapel of the Palácio Fronteira

THIS DELIGHTFUL country
manor house was built as
a hunting pavilion for João de
Mascarenhas, the first Marquês
de Fronteira, in 1640. Although
skyscrapers are visible in the
distance, it still occupies a
quiet spot, by the Parque
Florestal de Monsanto. Both
house and garden have *azulejo*
decoration whose subjects
include battle scenes and
trumpet-blowing monkeys.

Although the palace is still
occupied by the 12th Marquis,
some of the living rooms and
the library, as well
as the formal gar-
dens, are included
in the tour. The
Battles Room has
lively tiled panels
depicting scenes
of the War of
Restoration
(1640–1668), with
a detail of João de
Fronteira fighting
a Spanish general.
It was his loyalty
to Pedro II during
this war that earned him the
title of Marquis. Interesting
comparisons can be made between these naive 17th-century
Portuguese tiles and the Delft
ones from the same period in
the dining room, depicting
naturalistic scenes. The dining
room is also decorated with
frescoed panels and portraits
of Portuguese nobility by artists
such as Domingos António de
Sequeira (1768–1837).

The late 16th-century chapel
is the oldest part of the house.
The façade is adorned with
stones, shells, broken glass and
bits of china. These fragments
of crockery are believed to
have been used at the feast
inaugurating the palace and
then smashed to ensure no one
else could sup off the same set.
Visits to the **garden** start at the
chapel terrace, where tiled
niches are decorated with
figures personifying the arts
and mythological creatures.

Bust of João I in gardens
of Palácio Fronteira

In the formal Italian garden the
immaculate box hedges are
cut into shapes to represent
the seasons of the year. To
one end, tiled
scenes of dashing
knights on horse-
back, representing
ancestors of the
Fronteira family,
are reflected in the
waters of a large
tank. On either
side of the water,
a grand staircase
leads to a terrace
above. Here,
decorative niches
contain the busts
of Portuguese kings and colourful majolica reliefs adorn
the arcades. More blue and
white tiled scenes, realistic and
allegorical, decorate the wall
at the far end of the garden.

Entrance to the theatre museum
in Parque do Monteiro-Mor

Parque do Monteiro-Mor **16**

Largo Júlio Castilho. **(** *21-759 03
18.* **▦** *1, 3, 4, 7, 36, 101, 108.* **M**
Campo Grande. **Park ◯** *10am–6pm
Tue–Sun.* **●** *1 Jan, Easter, 1 May, 25
Dec.* **Museu Nacional do Traje
(** *21-759 03 18.* **◯** *10am–6pm
Tue–Sun.* **▨** *(free 10am–2pm Sun).*
**Museu Nacional do Teatro
(** *21-756 74 10.* **◯** *2–6pm Tue,
10am–6pm Wed–Sun.* **▨** *combined
ticket for park & museums.* **◉ ♿**

MONTEIRO-MOR PARK was
sold to the state in 1975
and the 18th-century palace
buildings were converted to
museums. The gardens are
attractive and rather more
romantic than the manicured
box-hedge gardens so typical
of Lisbon. Much of the land
is wooded, though the area
around the museums has
gardens with flowering shrubs,
duck ponds and tropical trees.

The rather old-fashioned
Museu Nacional do Traje
(costume museum) has a
vast collection of textiles,
accessories and costumes
worn by musicians, politicians,
poets, aristocrats and soldiers.

The **Museu Nacional do
Teatro** has two buildings, one
devoted to temporary exhibitions, the other containing a
small permanent collection.
Photographs, posters and
cartoons feature famous 20th-
century Portuguese actors and
one section is devoted to
Amália Rodrigues, the famous
fado singer *(see pp142–3).*

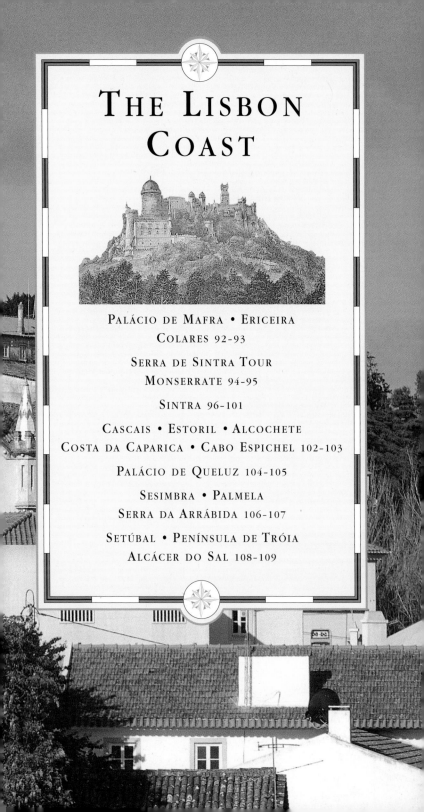

THE LISBON COAST

THE LISBON COAST

ITHIN AN HOUR'S DRIVE *northwest of Lisbon you can reach the rocky Atlantic coast, the wooded slopes of Sintra or countryside dotted with villas and royal palaces. South of Lisbon you can enjoy the sandy beaches and fishing towns along the coast or explore the lagoons of the Tagus and Sado river estuaries.*

Traders and invaders, from the Phoenicians to the Spanish, have left their mark in this region, in particular the Moors whose forts and castles, rebuilt many times over the centuries, can be found all along this coast. After Lisbon became the capital in 1256, Portuguese kings and nobles built summer palaces and villas in the countryside west of the city, particularly on the cool, green heights of the Serra de Sintra.

Across the Tagus, the less fashionable southern shore (Outra Banda) could be reached only by ferry, until the suspension bridge was built in 1966. Now, the long sandy beaches of the Costa da Caparica, the coast around the fishing town of Sesimbra and even the remote Tróia peninsula have become popular resorts during the summer months. Fortunately, large stretches of coast and unspoilt countryside are being protected as conservation areas and nature reserves.

Despite the region's rapid urbanization, small fishing and farming communities still survive. Lively fish markets offer a huge variety of fresh fish and seafood; Palmela and the Sado region are noted for their wine; sheep still roam the unspoilt Serra da Arrábida, providing milk for Azeitão cheese; and rice is the main crop in the Sado estuary. Traditional industries also survive, such as salt panning near Alcochete and marble quarries at Pero Pinheiro.

Though the sea is cold and often rough, especially on west-facing coasts, the beaches are among the cleanest in Europe. As well as surfing, fishing and scuba diving, the region provides splendid golf courses, horse riding facilities and a motor-racing track. Arts and entertainment range from music and cinema festivals to bullfights and country fairs where regional crafts, such as hand-painted pottery, lace and baskets, are on display.

Tiled façades of houses in Alcochete, an attractive town on the Tagus estuary

◁ **Brightly painted fishing boats moored in the harbour at Sesimbra**

Exploring the Lisbon Coast

NORTH OF THE TAGUS, the beautiful hilltown of Sintra is dotted with historic palaces and surrounded by wooded hills, at times enveloped in an eerie sea mist. On the coast, cosmopolitan Cascais and the traditional fishing town of Ericeira are both excellent bases from which to explore the rocky coastline and surrounding countryside. South of the Tagus, the Serra da Arrábida and the rugged coast around Cabo Espichel can be visited from the small port of Sesimbra. Inland, the nature reserves of the Tagus and Sado estuaries offer a quiet retreat.

SIGHTS AT A GLANCE

0 kilometres   10

0 miles   5

Torres Vedras

VILA FRANCA DO ROSÁRIO

ERICEIRA **2**

1 *PALÁCIO DE MAFRA*

N116

A8

N247   N9   N8

LOURES

MONSERRATE **5**

COLARES **3**   **6** *SINTRA*

CABO DA ROCA

SERRA DE SINTRA

4

IC19

A9   IC17

N117

PALÁCIO DE **9**
QUELUZ

A5

LISB

8 *ESTORIL*

CASCAIS **7**

COSTA DA CAPARICA **11**

Lagoa de Albufeira

CABO ESPICHEL
12

KEY

〰	Motorway
▬	Major road
⋯	Minor road
▬	Scenic route
〰	River
– –	Ferry route
⁂	Viewpoint

Cabo da Roca on the western edge of Serra de Sintra

**Convento da Arrábida in the hills
of the Serra da Arrábida**

GETTING AROUND

Motorways give quick access from
Lisbon to Sintra, Estoril, Palmela and
Setúbal. Main roads are generally
well signposted and surfaced, though
traffic congestion can be a problem,
particularly at weekends and holidays.
Watch out for potholes on smaller
roads. Fast, frequent trains run west
from Lisbon's Cais do Sodré station to
Estoril and Cascais, and from Rossio
station to Queluz and Sintra. For trains
south to Setúbal, Alcácer do Sal and
beyond, take a ferry to Barreiro on
the southern bank of the Tagus. There
are good bus services to all parts of
the region, most of which leave from
Lisbon's Praça de Espanha.

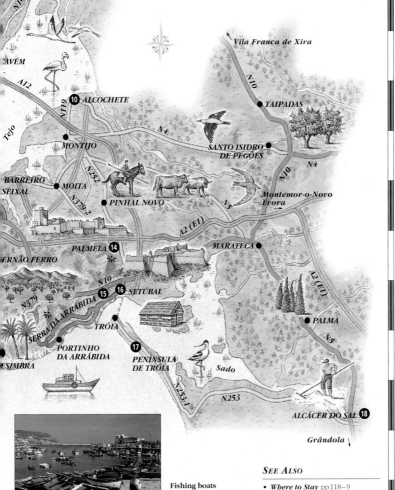

**Fishing boats
in the harbour
at Sesimbra**

The stunning library in the Palácio de Mafra, paved with chequered marble

Palácio de Mafra ①

Terreiro de Dom João V, Mafra.
C 261- 81 75 50. **■** from Lisbon.
M Campo Grande, then **■** 1
Mafrens. **○** 10am–4:30pm Wed–
Mon. **●** 1 Jan, Easter, 1 May, 25
Dec. **↑** **■** (free 10am–1pm Sun).
■ compulsory. **W** www.ippar.pt

THIS MASSIVE BAROQUE palace
and monastery dwarfs the
small town of Mafra. It was
built during the reign of João V,
and began with a vow by the
young king to build a new
monastery and basilica, sup-
posedly in return for an heir
(but more likely, to atone
for his well-known sexual
excesses). Work began in 1717
on a modest project to house
13 Franciscan friars but, as the
wealth began to pour into the
royal coffers from Brazil, the
king and his Italian-trained
architect, Johann Friedrich
Ludwig (1670–1752), made
ever more extravagant plans.

The king's bedroom in the Royal Palace

No expense was spared: 52,000
men were employed and the
finished project eventually
housed not 13, but 330 friars,
a royal palace and one of the
finest libraries in Europe,
decorated with precious
marble, exotic wood and
countless works of art.
The magnificent basilica
was consecrated on
the king's 41st birth-
day, 22 October 1730,
with festivities lasting
for eight days.
The palace was only
popular with those
members of the royal
family who enjoyed
hunting deer and wild
boar. Today, a wolf
conservation project
runs here. Most of the
finest furniture and art
works were taken to
Brazil when the royal
family escaped the French
invasion in 1807. The monastery was abandoned in 1834
following the dis-
solution of all
religious orders, and
the palace itself was
finally abandoned
in 1910, when the
last Portuguese
king, Manuel II, es-
caped from here to
the Royal Yacht an-
chored off Ericeira.
Allow at least an
hour for the lengthy
tour which starts in
the rooms of the
monastery, through
the pharmacy, with

fine old medicine jars and
some alarming medical in-
struments, to the hospital,
where 16 patients in private
cubicles could see and hear
mass in the adjoining chapel
without leaving their beds.
Upstairs, the sumptuous
palace state rooms extend
across the whole of the monumental west façade, with the
King's apartments at one end
and the Queen's apartments
at the other, a staggering
232 m (760 ft) apart. Halfway
between the two, the long,
imposing façade is relieved
by the twin bell towers of the
domed basilica. The interior
of the church is decorated in
contrasting colours of marble
and furnished with six early
19th-century organs. Fine Baroque sculptures, executed by
members of the Mafra School
of Sculpture, adorn the atrium
of the basilica. Begun by José I

in 1754,
many renowned
Portuguese and
foreign artists
trained in the
school under the
directorship of the
Italian sculptor
Alessandro Giusti
(1715–99). Further on,
the Sala da Caça has
a grotesque collection
of hunting trophies
and boars' heads.
Mafra's greatest
treasure, however,
is its magnificent
library, which has
a patterned marble
floor, Rococo-style
wooden bookcases,
and a collection of

**Statue of St Bruno
in the atrium of
Mafra's basilica**

over 40,000 books in gold em-
bossed leather bindings, which
includes a prized first edition
of Os Lusíadas (1572) by the
celebrated Portuguese poet,
Luís de Camões (1524–80).

ENVIRONS: Once a week, on
Thursday mornings, the small
country town of **Malveira**,
10 km (6 miles) east of Mafra,
has the region's biggest market,
selling clothes and household
goods as well as food.
At the village of **Sobreiro**,
6 km (4 miles) west of Mafra,
Zé Franco's model village is
complete with houses, farms,
a waterfall and working wind-
mill, all in minute detail.

Tractor pulling a fishing boat out of the sea at Ericeira

Ericeira ②

🏛 7,500. 🚌 🛈 Rua Mendes Leal (261-86 31 22). 🏪 Apr–Oct daily.

ERICEIRA IS AN OLD fishing village which keeps its traditions despite an ever-increasing influx of summer visitors, from Lisbon and abroad, who enjoy the bracing climate, clean, sandy beaches and fresh seafood. In July and August, when the population leaps to 30,000, pavement cafés, restaurants and bars around the tree-lined Praça da República are buzzing late into the night. Red flags warn when swimming is dangerous: alternative attractions include a crazy golf course in Santa Marta park and a local history museum, the **Museu da Ericeira**, exhibiting model boats and traditional regional fishing equipment.

The unspoilt old town, a maze of whitewashed houses and narrow, cobbled streets, is perched high above the ocean. From Largo das Ribas, at the top of a 30-m (100-ft) stone-faced cliff, there is a bird's-eye view over the busy fishing harbour below, where tractors have replaced the oxen that once hauled the boats out of reach of the tide. On 16 August, the annual fishermen's festival is celebrated with a candlelit procession to the harbour at the foot of the cliffs for the blessing of the boats.

On 5 October 1910, Manuel II, the last king of Portugal *(see p17)*, finally sailed into exile from Ericeira as the Republic was declared in Lisbon; a tiled panel in the fishermen's chapel of Santo António above the harbour records the event. The banished king settled in Twickenham, southwest London, where he died in 1932.

🏛 **Museu da Ericeira**
Largo da Misericórdia. 【 261-86 25 36. 🕐 by appt only. Jun–Sep: Tue–Sun; Oct–May: Mon–Sat (pm only). ⬤ public hols. 🎫

Colares ③

🏛 7,500. 🚌 🛈 Praça da República 23, Sintra, 21-923 11 57.

ON THE LOWER SLOPES of the Serra de Sintra, this lovely village faces towards the sea over a green valley, the Várzea de Colares. A leafy avenue winds its way up to the village, lined with pine and chestnut trees. Small quantities of the famous Colares wine are still made, but current vintages lack the character and ageing potential of classic Colares and growers face a financial struggle to survive. Their hardy old vines grow in sandy soil, with their roots set deep below in clay; these were among the few vines in Europe to survive the disastrous phylloxera epidemic brought from America in the late 19th century with the first viticultural exchanges. The insect, which destroyed vineyards all over Europe by eating the vines' roots, could not penetrate the dense sandy soil of the Atlantic coast. Wine can be sampled at the Adega Regional de Colares on Alameda de Coronel Linhares de Lima.

ENVIRONS: There are several popular beach resorts west of Colares. From the village of Banzão you can ride 3 km (2 miles) to **Praia das Maçãs** on the old tramway, which opened in 1910 and still runs from 1 July to 30 September. Just north of Praia das Maçãs is the picturesque village of **Azenhas do Mar**, clinging to the cliffs; to the south is the larger resort of **Praia Grande**. Both have natural pools in the rocks, which are filled by sea-water at high tide and are now closed to swimmers. The unspoilt **Praia da Adraga**, 1 km (half a mile) further south, has a delightful beach café and restaurant. In the evenings and off-season, fishermen catch bass, bream and flat fish that swim in on the high tide.

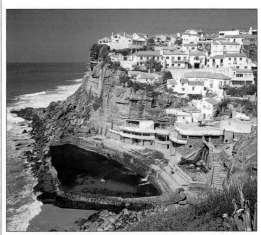

Natural rock pool at Azenhas do Mar, near Colares

Serra de Sintra Tour ❹

THIS ROUND TRIP from Sintra follows a dramatic route over the top of the wooded Serra. The first part is a challenging drive with hazardous hairpin bends on steep, narrow roads that are at times poorly surfaced. It passes through dense forest and a surreal landscape of giant moss-covered boulders, with breathtaking views over the Atlantic coast, the Tagus estuary and beyond. After dropping down to the rugged, windswept coast, the route returns along small country roads passing through hill villages and large estates on the cool, green northern slopes of the Serra de Sintra.

Tiled angels, Peninha chapel

Atlantic coastline seen from Peninha

Colares ⑥
The village of Colares rests on the lower slopes of the wooded Serra, surrounded by gardens and vineyards *(see p93)*.

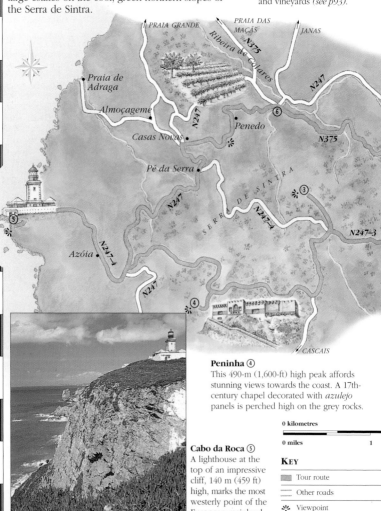

Peninha ④
This 490-m (1,600-ft) high peak affords stunning views towards the coast. A 17th-century chapel decorated with *azulejo* panels is perched high on the grey rocks.

Cabo da Roca ⑤
A lighthouse at the top of an impressive cliff, 140 m (459 ft) high, marks the most westerly point of the European mainland.

0 kilometres

0 miles   1

KEY

▬▬ Tour route

--- Other roads

❊ Viewpoint

TIPS FOR DRIVERS

Length: 36 km (22 miles).
Stopping-off points: There are
wonderful picnic spots in the
forests and in the Parque da Pena,
with cool springs of drinking
water and fountains along the
mountain roads. At Cabo da Roca
you will find a café, restaurant and
souvenir shops; at Colares there
are several delightful restaurants
and bars. (See also p162.)

¿eais ⑧

e elegant, pink palace, now
uxury hotel and restaurant
e p113 & p119), was built in
: 18th century for the Dutch
nsul, Daniel Gildemeester.

Monserrate ⑦
The cool, overgrown forest
park and elaborate 19th-century
palace epitomize the
romanticism
of Sintra.

ERICEIRA
MAFRA

Sintra ①
From the centre of the
old town the road winds
steeply upwards past
magnificent *quintas*
(country estates)
hidden among
the trees.

N247

⑧

①

②

*Palácio
da Pena*

LISBOA

CRUZ ALTA   *N249*

*ESTORIL
CASCAIS*

Parque da Pena ②
This huge, exotic park can be
explored on foot *(see p97)*. It
is also possible to drive as far
as Cruz Alta, the highest point
of the Serra de Sintra.

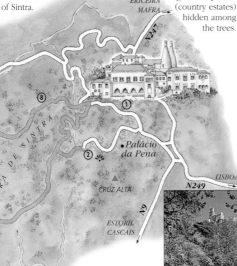

Convento
dos Capuchos ③
Two huge boulders guard
the entrance to this remote
Franciscan monastery,
founded in 1560, where
the monks lived in tiny
rock-hewn cells lined with
cork. There are stunning
views of the coast from
the hill above this austere,
rocky hideaway.

Palace of Monserrate

Monserrate ⑤

Estrada de Monserrate. **[** 21-923
73 00. **[** to Sintra then taxi. **[**
daily; 1 May–14 Jun, 16 Sep–31 Oct:
9am–7pm; 15 Jun–15 Sep: 9am–8pm;
1 Nov–30 Apr: 9am–6pm. **[** 25 Dec.
[**[W]** www.parquesdesintra.pt

THE WILD, ROMANTIC garden
of this once magnificent
estate is a jungle of exotic trees
and flowering shrubs. Among
the sub-tropical foliage and
valley of tree ferns, the visitor
will come across a waterfall, a
small lake and a chapel, built
as a ruin, tangled in the roots
of a giant *Ficus* tree. Its history
dates back to the Moors, but it
takes its name from a small
16th-century chapel dedicated
to Our Lady of Montserrat in
Catalonia, Spain. The gardens
were landscaped in the late
1700s by a wealthy young
Englishman, William
Beckford. They were later
immortalized by Lord
Byron in *Childe Harold's
Pilgrimage* (1812).

In 1856, the abandoned
estate was bought by
another Englishman, Sir
Francis Cook, who built
a fantastic Moorish-style
palace (which now stands
eerily empty) and trans-
formed the gardens with
a large sweeping lawn,
camellias and sub-tropical
trees from all over the
world. These include the giant
Metrosideros (Australian Christmas tree, covered in a blaze of
red flowers in July), the native
Arbutus (known as the strawberry tree because of its juicy
red berries), from which the
medronho firewater drink is
distilled, and cork oak, with
small ferns growing on its bark.

The Friends of Monserrate is
an organization that has been
set up to help restore the sadly
neglected house and gardens
to their former glory.

Sintra ⊙

SINTRA'S STUNNING setting on the north slopes of the granite Serra, among wooded ravines and fresh water springs, made it a favourite summer retreat for the kings of Portugal. The tall conical chimneys of the Palácio Nacional de Sintra *(see pp98–9)* and the fabulous Palácio da Pena *(see pp100–101)*, eerily impressive on its peak when the Serra is blanketed in mist, are unmistakable landmarks.

Today, the town (recognized as a UNESCO World Heritage site in 1995) draws thousands of visitors all through the year. Even so, there are many quiet walks in the wooded hills around the town, especially beautiful in the long, cool evenings of the summer months.

Fonte Mourisca on Volta do Duche

Exploring Sintra

Present-day Sintra is in three parts, Sintra Vila, Estefânia and São Pedro, joined by a confusing maze of winding roads scattered over the surrounding hills. In the pretty cobbled streets of the old town, Sintra Vila, which is centred on the **Palácio Nacional de Sintra**, are the museums and beautifully tiled **post office**. The curving **Volta do Duche** leads from the old town, past the lush **Parque da Liberdade**, north to the Estefânia district and the striking Neo-Gothic **Câmara Municipal** (Town Hall). To the south and east, the hilly village of São Pedro spreads over the slopes of the Serra. The fortnightly Sunday **market** here extends across the broad market square and along Rua 1º de Dezembro.

Exploring Sintra on foot involves a lot of walking and climbing up and down its steep hills. For a more leisurely tour, take one of the horse and carriage rides around the town. The **Miradouro da Vigia** in São Pedro offers impressive views, as does the cosy **Casa de Sapa** café, where you can sample *queijadas*, the local sweet speciality *(see p135)*.

The many fountains dotted around the town are used by locals for their fresh spring drinking water. Two of the most striking are the tiled **Fonte Mourisca** (Arab Fountain), named for its Neo-Moorish decoration, and Fonte da Sabuga, where the water spouts from a pair of breasts.

🏛 Museu do Brinquedo

Rua Visconde de Monserrate. **⌖** 21-924 21 71. **◯** Tue–Sun. ⬛ ♿

This small museum has a fine international collection of toys, ranging from model planes, cars and trains, including 1930s Hornby sets, to battalions of toy soldiers, dolls and dolls' houses, tin toys and curious clockwork models of cars and soldiers. The museum is fun for a rainy day, particularly for nostalgic adults.

Toy Alfa Romeo, Museu do Brinquedo

🏛 Museu de Arte Moderna

Avenida Heliodoro Salgado. **⌖** 21-924 81 70. **◯** Tue–Sun. ⬛ ♿ 🍴 ▢

The Berardo Collection, accumulated by entrepreneur Joe Berardo, is regarded as one of the world's best private collections of 20th-century art and includes such big names as René Magritte, Jackson Pollock, Francis Bacon and Andy Warhol. Located at the north end of Sintra, it is a pedagogic exposé of movements and styles, particularly those of the post-war era.

▦ Quinta da Regaleira

Rua Barbosa du Bocage. **⌖** 21-910 66 50. **◯** daily. **⌗** mandatory; call to book. ⬛ 🍴 ▢

Built during the 1890s, this neo-Manueline palace and extensive gardens are a feast of historical and religious references, occult symbols and mystery. The obsession of the eccentric millionaire António Augusto Carvalho Monteiro, they are an absolute must for anyone interested in freemasonry, alchemy and other esoterica.

Chimneys of the Palácio Nacional de Sintra above the old town

♣ Castelo dos Mouros

Estrada da Pena. 📞 *21-923 73 00.* ⬜ *daily; Nov–Apr: 9:30am–6pm; 15 Jun– 15 Sep: 9am–8pm; May–15 Jun & 15 Sep–Oct: 9am–7pm.* ⬤ *1 Jan, 25 Dec.* Standing above the old town, the ramparts of the 8th-century Moorish castle conquered by Afonso Henriques in 1147, snake over the top of the Serra. On a fine day, there are great views from the castle walls over the old town to Palácio da Pena, on a neighbouring peak, and along the coast. Hidden inside the walls are a ruined chapel and an ancient Moorish cistern. A steep footpath threads up through wooded slopes from the 12th-century church of **Santa Maria**. Follow the signs to a dark green swing gate where the footpath begins. The monogram "DFII" carved on the gateway is a reminder that the castle walls were restored by Fernando II *(see p101)* in the 19th century.

Battlements of the Castelo dos Mouros perched on the slopes of the Serra

VISITORS' CHECKLIST

🏛 *25,000.* 🚉 🚌 *Avenida Dr Miguel Bombarda.* 🛈 *Praça da República 23 (21-923 39 19);* *Cabo de Roca.* 🎪 *2nd & 4th Sun of month in São Pedro.* 🎵 *Festival de Música (Jun–Jul).*

♣ Parque da Pena

Estrada da Pena. 📞 *21-923 73 00.* ⬜ *daily.* ⬤ *1 Jan, 25 Dec.* ♿ A huge park surrounds the Palácio da Pena where footpaths wind among a lush vegetation of exotic trees and shrubs. Hidden among the foliage are gazebos, follies and fountains, and a Romantic chalet built by Fernando II for his mistress in 1869. Cruz Alta, the highest point of the Serra at 530 m (1,740 ft), commands spectacular views of the Serra and surrounding plain. On a nearby crag stands the statue of Baron Von Eschwege, architect of the palace and park.

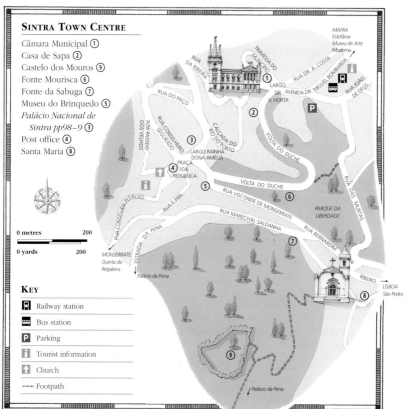

SINTRA TOWN CENTRE

Câmara Municipal ①
Casa de Sapa ②
Castelo dos Mouros ⑨
Fonte Mourisca ⑥
Fonte da Sabuga ⑦
Museu do Brinquedo ⑤
Palácio Nacional de Sintra pp98–9 ③
Post office ④
Santa Maria ⑧

0 metres   200
0 yards   200

KEY

🚉 Railway station
🚌 Bus station
🅿 Parking
🛈 Tourist information
✝ Church
▫▫▫ Footpath

Palácio Nacional de Sintra

**Swan panel,
Sala dos Cisnes**

AT THE HEART of the old town of Sintra (Sintra Vila), a pair of strange conical chimneys rises high above the Royal Palace. The main part of the palace, including the central block with its plain Gothic façade and the large kitchens beneath the chimneys, was built by João I in the late 14th century, on a site once occupied by the Moorish rulers. The Paço Real, as it is also known, became the favourite summer retreat for the court, and continued as a residence for Portuguese royalty until the 1880s. Additions to the building by the wealthy Manuel I, in the early 16th century, echo the Moorish style. Gradual rebuilding of the palace has resulted in a fascinating amalgamation of various different styles.

★ Sala das Pegas
It is said that King João I had the ceiling panels painted as a rebuke to the court women for indulging in idle gossip like chattering magpies (pegas).

The Torre da Meca has dovecotes below the cornice decorated with armillary spheres and nautical rope.

The Sala das Galés (galleons) houses temporary exhibitions.

★ Sala dos Brasões
The domed ceiling of this majestic room is decorated with stags holding the coats of arms (brasões) of 72 noble Portuguese families. The lower walls are lined with 18th-century Delft-like tiled panels.

Jardim da Preta, a walled garden

Sala de Dom Sebastião, the audience chamber

TIMELINE

10th century Palace becomes residence of Moorish governor	**1281** King Dinis orders restoration of the Palácio de Oliva (as it was then known)	**1495–1521** Reign of Manuel I; major restoration and Manueline additions	**1683** Afonso VI dies after being imprisoned here for nine years by brother Pedro II	**1755** Parts of palace damaged in great earthquake *(see pp20–21)*

800	1000	1200	1400	1600	1800

1147 Christian reconquest; Afonso Henriques takes over palace	**1385** João I orders complete rebuilding of central buildings and kitchens		**1880s** Maria Pia (grandmother of Manuel II) is last royal resident
8th century First palace established by Moors	*Siren, Sala das Sereias (c.1660)*		**1910** Palace becomes a national monument

★ Sala dos Cisnes
The magnificent ceiling of the former banqueting hall, painted in the 17th century, is divided into octagonal panels decorated with swans (cisnes).

VISITORS' CHECKLIST

Largo Rainha Dona Amélia. 21-910 68 40. 10am–5:30pm Thu–Tue (last adm: 30 mins before closing). 1 Jan, Easter, 1 May, 29 Jun, 25 Dec. (free 10am–2pm Sun).

Sala das Sereias
Intricate Arabesque designs on 16th-century tiles frame the door of the Room of the Sirens.

The Sala dos Árabes is decorated with fine *azulejos*.

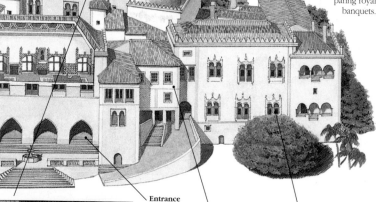

The kitchens, beneath the huge conical chimneys, have spits and utensils once used for preparing royal banquets.

Entrance

Sala dos Archeiros, the entrance hall

Manuel I added the *ajimene* windows, a distinctive Moorish design with a slender column dividing two arches.

Chapel
Symmetrical Moorish patterns decorate the original 15th-century chestnut and oak ceiling and the mosaic floor of the private chapel.

STAR FEATURES

★ **Sala dos Brasões**

★ **Sala dos Cisnes**

★ **Sala das Pegas**

Sintra: Palácio da Pena

Triton Arch

O N THE HIGHEST PEAKS of the Serra de Sintra stands the spectacular palace of Pena, an eclectic medley of architectural styles built in the 19th century for the husband of the young Queen Maria II, Ferdinand Saxe-Coburg-Gotha. It stands over the ruins of a Hieronymite monastery founded here in the 15th century on the site of the chapel of Nossa Senhora da Pena. Ferdinand appointed a German architect, Baron Von Eschwege, to build his summer palace filled with oddities from all over the world and surrounded by a park. With the declaration of the Republic in 1910, the palace became a museum, preserved as it was when the royal family lived here. Allow at least an hour and a half to visit this enchanting place.

Entrance Arch
A studded archway with crenellated turrets greets the visitor at the entrance to the palace. The palace buildings are painted the original daffodil yellow and strawberry pink.

Manuel II's Bedroom
The oval-shaped room is decorated with green walls and stuccoed ceiling. A portrait of Manuel II, the last king of Portugal, hangs above the fireplace.

In the kitchen the copper pots and utensils still hang around the iron stove. The dinner service bears the coat of arms of Ferdinand II.

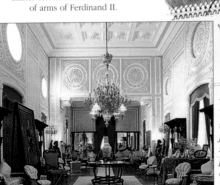

★ Ballroom
The spacious ballroom is sumptuously furnished with German stained-glass windows, precious Oriental porcelain and four lifesize turbaned torch-bearers holding giant candelabra.

★ Arab Room
Marvellous trompe-l'oeil frescoes cover the walls and ceiling of the Arab Room, one of the loveliest in the palace. The Orient was a great inspiration to Romanticism.

VISITORS' CHECKLIST

Estrada da Pena, 5 km (3 mile)
S of Sintra. 21-910 53 40.
434 from Avenida Dr Miguel
Bombarda, Sintra. 10am–5pm
Tue–Sun (to 7pm 1 Jul–15 Sep;
last adm: 30 mins before closing).
1 Jan, Easter, 1 May, 29 Jun,
25 Dec. www.ippar.pt

★ Chapel Altarpiece
The impressive 16th-century alabaster and marble retable was sculpted by Nicolau Chanterène. Each niche portrays a scene of the life of Christ, from the manger to the Ascension.

The Triton Arch is encrusted with Neo-Manueline decoration and is guarded by a fierce sea monster.

The cloister, decorated with colourful patterned tiles, is part of the original monastery buildings.

Entrance

FERDINAND: KING CONSORT

Ferdinand was known in Portugal as Dom Fernando II, the "artist" king. Like his cousin Prince Albert, who married the English Queen Victoria, he loved art, nature and the new inventions of the time. He was himself a watercolour painter. Ferdinand enthusiastically adopted his new country and devoted his life to patronizing the arts. In 1869, 16 years after the death of Maria II, Ferdinand married his mistress, the opera singer Countess Edla. His lifelong dream of building the extravagant palace at Pena was completed in 1885, the year he died.

STAR FEATURES

★ Arab Room

★ Ballroom

★ Chapel Altarpiece

Outdoor café in the popular holiday resort of Cascais

Cascais ❼

🏠 27,800. 🚉 🚌 ℹ️ Rua Visconde da Luz 14 (21-486 82 04). 🔶 1st and 3rd Sun of the month.

HAVING BEEN A holiday resort for well over a century, Cascais possesses a certain illustriousness that younger resorts lack. Its history is most clearly visible in the villas along the coast, built as summer residences by wealthy *Lisboetas* during the late 19th century, after King Luís I had moved his summer activities to the 17th-century fortress here. The military importance of Cascais, now waned, is much older as it sits on the north bank of the mouth of the Tagus.

The sandy, sheltered bay around which the modern suburb has sprawled was a fishing harbour in prehistoric times. Fishing still goes on, and was recently given a municipal boost with the decision to build a new quay for the landing and initial auctioning of the fishermen's catch. But Cascais today is first of all a favoured suburb of Lisbon, a place of apartments with a sea view and pine-studded plots by golf courses. It may sometimes seem more defined by its ceaseless construction boom than by any historic or even touristic qualities, but the beautiful, windswept coastline beyond the town has been left relatively undeveloped.

The Museu do Conde de Castro Guimaraes is perhaps the best place to get a taste of Cascais as it was just over a century ago. A castle-like villa on a small creek by a headland, its grounds are today part of a park. The house and its contents were bequeathed to the municipality.

Across the road from the museum is the new marina, one of the most emblematic new developments in Cascais. With its small shopping centre, restaurants and cafés it is becoming a weekend magnet for today's car-borne Cascais residents and tourists.

🏛 Museu do Conde de Castro Guimarães
Avenida Rei Humberto de Itália. 📞 21-482 54 07. **Museum** ⬜ 10am–5pm Tue–Sun. 🎫 (free 10am–2pm Sun). **Library** Casa da Horta de Santa Clara. ⬜ 10am–7pm Mon–Sat. ● pub hols.

ENVIRONS: At **Boca do Inferno** (Mouth of Hell), about 3 km (2 miles) west on the coast road, the sea rushes into clefts and caves in the rocks making an ominous booming sound and sending up spectacular spray in rough weather. The place is almost obscured by a roadside market and cafés but a small platform gives a good view of the rocky arch with the sea roaring in below.

The magnificent sandy beach of **Guincho**, 10 km (6 miles) further west, is backed by sand dunes with clumps of umbrella pines, and a new cycle path. A small fort (now a luxury hotel) stands perched on the rocks above the sea. Atlantic breakers rolling in make this a paradise for experienced windsurfers and surfers, though beware of the strong currents.

Spectacular view of the weatherbeaten coastline at Boca do Inferno, near Cascais

Estoril ❽

🏠 24,000. 🚉 🚌 ℹ️ Arcadas do Parque (21-466 38 13); Avenida Clotilde 3a (21-467 82 10).

DESPITE ONCE BEING the haunt of exiled royalty fleeing European republicanism, the lovely resort town of Estoril does not rest on its historical laurels. Today it is a tourist and business resort, and a place for comfortable retirement. As such, it relies equally on its historical reputation and on the natural attractiveness it has always possessed. There are also a number of good golf courses.

What separates Estoril from Cascais, besides a pleasant beach promenade of 3 km (2 miles) and a mansion covered ridge known as Monte Estoril, is its sense of place. The heart of Estoril is immediately accessible from the train station. On one side of the tracks, the riviera-like, but

Sandy beach and promenade along the bay of Estoril

relaxed beach, on the other a palm-lined park flanked by grand buildings, stretching up past fountains to what is said to be Europe's biggest casino. Dwarfing the casino is the Estoril Congress Centre, a vast multipurpose edifice that speaks confidently of Estoril's contemporary role.

Palácio de Queluz 9

See pp104–5.

Alcochete 10

🏛 8,000. 🚊 ℹ *Largo da Misericórdia (21-234 86 55).*

THIS DELIGHTFUL old town overlooks the wide Tagus estuary from the southern shore. Salt has long been one of the main industries here, and saltpans can still be seen to the north and south of the town, while in the town centre a large statue of a muscular salt worker has the inscription: "Do Sal a Revolta e a Esperança" (From Salt to Rebellion and Hope). On the outskirts of town, is a statue of Manuel I *(see p16)*, who was born here on 1 June 1469 and granted the town a Royal Charter in 1515.

ENVIRONS: The **Reserva Natural do Estuário do Tejo** covers a vast area of estuary water, salt marshes and small islands around Alcochete and is a very important breeding ground for water birds. Particularly interesting are the flocks of flamingos that gather here during the autumn and spring migration, en route from colonies such as the Camargue in France and Fuente de Piedra in Spain. Ask at the tourist office about boat trips to see the wildlife of the estuary, which includes wild bulls and horses.

🦌 **Reserva Natural do Estuário do Tejo**
Avenida dos Combatentes da Grande Guerra 1. 📞 *21-234 17 42.*

Pilgrims' lodgings, Cabo Espichel

Costa da Caparica 11

🏛 12,000. 🚊 to Cacilhas or Trafaria then bus. 🚉 to Pragal then bus. ℹ *Av. da República 18 (21-290 00 71).*

LONG SANDY beaches, backed by sand dunes, have made this a popular holiday resort for Lisboetas who come here to swim, sunbathe and enjoy the seafood restaurants and beach cafés. A railway, with open carriages, runs for 10 km (6 miles) along the coast during the summer months. The first beaches reached from the town are popular with families with children, while the furthest beaches suit those seeking quiet isolation. Further south, sheltered by pine forests, **Lagoa do Albufeira** is a peaceful windsurfing centre and camp site.

Statue of a salt worker in Alcochete (1985)

Cabo Espichel 12

🚌 *from Sesimbra.*

SHEER CLIFFS DROP straight into the sea at this windswept promontory where the land ends dramatically. The Romans named it Promontorium Barbaricum, alluding to its dangerous location, and a lighthouse warns sailors of the treacherous rocks below. Stunning views of the ocean and the coast can be enjoyed from this bleak outcrop of land but beware of the strong gusts of wind on the cliff edge.

In this desolate setting stands the impressive **Santuário de Nossa Senhora do Cabo**, a late 17th-century church with its back to the sea. On either side of the church a long line of pilgrims' lodgings facing inwards form an open courtyard. Baroque paintings, ex votos and a frescoed ceiling decorate the interior of the church. There are plans to fully restore the building and open it as a hotel. Nearby, a domed chapel has tiled blue and white *azulejo* panels depicting fishing scenes. The site became a popular place of pilgrimage in the 13th century when a local man had a vision of the Madonna rising from the sea on a mule. Legend has it that the tracks of the mule can be seen embedded in the rock. The large footprints, on Praia dos Lagosteiros below the church, are actually believed to be fossilized dinosaur tracks.

Spring flowers by the saltpans of the Tagus estuary near Alcochete

Palácio de Queluz 🟈

In 1747, PEDRO, younger son of João V, commissioned Mateus Vicente to transform his 17th-century hunting lodge into a Rococo summer palace. The central section, including a music room and chapel, was built, but after Pedro's marriage in 1760 to the future Maria I, the palace was again extended. The French architect, Jean-Baptiste Robillion, added the sumptuous Robillion Pavilion and gardens, cleared space for the Throne Room and redesigned the Music Room. During Maria's reign, the royal family kept a menagerie and went boating on the *azulejo*-lined canal.

A sphinx in the gardens

Corridor of the Sleeves
Painted azulejo panels (1784) representing the continents and the seasons, as well as hunting scenes, line the walls of the bright Corridor das Mangas (sleeves).

Neptune's Fountain

★ Sala dos Embaixadores
Built by Robillion, this stately room was used for diplomatic audiences as well as concerts. The trompe l'oeil ceiling shows the royal family attending a concert.

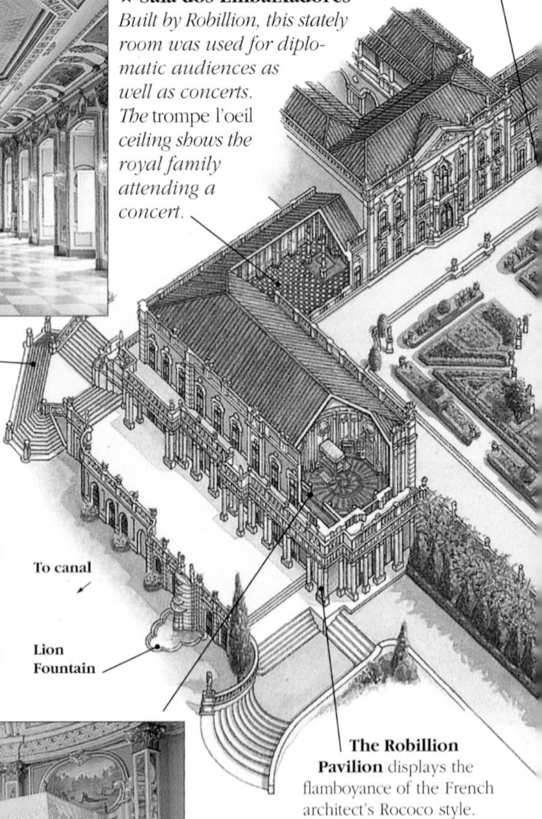

The Lion Staircase is an impressive and graceful link from the lower gardens to the palace.

STAR FEATURES

★ **Throne Room**

★ **Sala dos Embaixadores**

★ **Palace Gardens**

To canal

Lion Fountain

The Robillion Pavilion displays the flamboyance of the French architect's Rococo style.

Don Quixote Chamber
The royal bedroom, where Pedro IV (see p17) was born and died, has a domed ceiling and magnificent floor decoration in exotic woods, giving the square room a circular appearance. Painted scenes by Manuel de Costa (1784) tell the story of Don Quixote.

Music Room
Operas and concerts were performed here by Maria I's orchestra, "the best in Europe" according to English traveller, William Beckford. A portrait of the queen hangs above the grand piano.

Chapel

The royal family's living rooms and bedrooms opened out onto the Malta Gardens.

★ Throne Room
The elegant state room (1770) was the scene of splendid balls and banquets. The gilded statues of Atlas are by Silvestre Faria Lobo.

Entrance

Malta Gardens

The Hanging Gardens, designed by Robillion, were built over arches, raising the ground in front of the palace above the surrounding gardens.

MARIA I (1734–1816)
Maria, the eldest daughter of José I, lived at the palace in Queluz after her marriage to her uncle, Pedro, in 1760. Serious and devout, she conscientiously filled her role as queen, but suffered increasingly from bouts of melancholia. When her son José died from smallpox in 1788, she went hopelessly mad. Visitors to Queluz were dismayed by her agonizing shrieks as she suffered visions and hallucinations. After the French invasion of 1807, her younger son João (declared regent in 1792) took his mad mother to Brazil.

★ Palace Gardens
The formal gardens, adorned with statues, fountains and topiary, were often used for entertaining. Concerts performed in the Music Room would spill out into the Malta Gardens.

Sesimbra ⑬

🏠 42,000. 🚉 🚌 ℹ️ *Largo da Marinha 26–7 (21-228 85 40).* 🗓️ *1st & 3rd Fri of month.*

A STEEP NARROW ROAD leads down to this busy fishing village in a sheltered south-facing bay. Protected from north winds by the slopes of the Serra da Arrábida, the town has become a popular holiday resort with Lisboetas. It was occupied by the Romans and later the Moors until King Sancho II *(see p16)* conquered its heavily defended forts in 1236. The old town is a maze of steep narrow streets, with the **Santiago Fort** (now a customs post) in the centre overlooking the sea. From the terrace, which is open to the public during the day, there are views over the town, the Atlantic and the wide sandy beach that stretches out on either side. Sesimbra is fast developing as a resort, with holiday flats mushrooming on the surrounding hillsides and plentiful pavement cafés and bars that are always busy on sunny days, even in winter.

The fishing fleet of brightly painted boats is moored in the **Porto do Abrigo** to the west of the main town. The harbour is reached by taking Avenida dos Náufragos, a sweeping

Colourful fishing boats in the harbour at Sesimbra

promenade that follows the beach out of town. On the large trawlers *(traineiras)*, the catch is mainly sardines, sea bream, whiting and swordfish; on the smaller boats, octopus and squid. In the late after-noon, when the fishing boats return from a day at sea, a colourful, noisy fish auction takes place on the quayside. The day's catch can be tasted in the town's excellent fish restaurants along the shore.

High above the town is the **Moorish castle**, greatly restored in the 18th century when a church and small flower-filled cemetery were added inside the walls. There are wonderful views from the ramparts, especially at sunset.

Palmela ⑭

🏠 57,000. 🚉 🚌 🚌 ℹ️ *Castelo de Palmela (21-233 21 22).* 🗓️ *every other Tue.*

T HE FORMIDABLE castle at Palmela stands over the small hilltown, high on a north-eastern spur of the wooded Serra da Arrábida. Its strategic position dominates the plain for miles around, especially when floodlit at night. Heavily defended by the Moors, it was finally conquered in the 12th century and given by Sancho I *(see p16)* to the Knights of the Order of Santiago. In 1423, João I transformed the castle into a monastery for the Order, which has now been restored and converted into a splendid *pousada (see p119)*, with a restaurant in the monks' refectory and a swimming pool for residents, hidden inside the castle walls. From the castle terraces, and espe-cially from the top of the 14th-century keep, there are fantastic views all around, over the Serra da Arrábida to the south and on a clear day across the Tagus to Lisbon. In the town square below, the church of **São Pedro** contains 18th-century tiles of scenes from the life of St Peter.

The annual wine festival, the Festa das Vindimas, is held on the first weekend of September in front of the 17th-century Paços do Concelho (town hall). Traditionally dressed villagers press the wine barefoot and on the final day of celebrations there is a spectacular firework display from the castle walls.

The castle at Palmela with views over the wooded Serra da Arrábida

Serra da Arrábida ⑮

🚌 Setúbal. 🛈 Parque Natural da Arrábida, Praça da República, Setúbal (265-54 11 40).

THE PARQUE NATURAL da Arrábida covers the small range of limestone mountains which stretches east-west along the coast between Sesimbra and Setúbal. It was established to protect the wild, beautiful landscape and rich variety of birds and wildlife, including eagles, wildcats and badgers.

The name Arrábida is from Arabic meaning a place of prayer, and the wooded hillsides are indeed a peaceful, secluded retreat. The sheltered, south-facing slopes are thickly covered with aromatic and evergreen shrubs and trees such as pine and cypress, more typical of the Mediterranean. Vineyards also thrive on the sheltered slopes and the town of **Vila Nogueira de Azeitão** is known for its wine, especially the Moscatel de Setúbal.

The **Estrada de Escarpa** (the N379-1) snakes across the top of the ridge and affords astounding views. A narrow road winds down to **Portinho da Arrábida**, a sheltered cove with a beach of fine white sand and crystal clear sea, popular with underwater fishermen. The sandy beaches of **Galapos** and **Figueirinha** are a little further east along the coast road towards Setúbal. Just east of Sesimbra, the Serra da Arrábida drops to the sea in the sheer 380-m (1,250-ft) cliffs of Risco, the highest in mainland Portugal.

Portinho da Arrábida on the dramatic coastline of the Serra da Arrábida

⌂ Convento da Arrábida

Serra da Arrábida. 📞 21-218 05 20. ⏲ by appt only, via Fundação Oriente (phone 21-352 70 02). 🚫

Half-hidden among the trees of the Serra, this 16th-century building was once a Franciscan monastery. The five round towers were probably used for meditation. The building now houses a cultural centre.

KEY

▬▬ Major road

▬▬ Minor road

═══ Other road

0 kilometres 5

0 miles 3

🏛 Museu Oceanográfico

Fortaleza de Santa Maria, Portinho da Arrábida. 📞 21-218 97 91. ⏲ 9am–noon, 2–5pm Tue–Fri. 🚫

This small fort, just above Portinho da Arrábida, was built by Pedro, the Prince Regent, in 1676 to protect local communities from attacks by Moorish pirates. It now houses a Sea Museum and Marine Biology Centre where visitors can see aquaria containing many local sea creatures, including sea urchins, octopus and starfish.

⌘ José Maria da Fonseca

Rua José Augusto Coelho 11, Vila Nogueira de Azeitão. 📞 21-219 75 00. FAX 21-219 75 01. ⏲ 9am–noon, 2:15–4:15pm Mon–Fri; 10am–12:15pm, 2:15–4:30pm Sat. ● 24 Dec–1 Jan. 🚫 ✔ 🅿

The Fonseca winery produces quality table wines and is famous for its fragrant dessert wine, Moscatel de Setúbal (see p125). Tours of the winery explain the process of making moscatel and a visit to a series of old cellars containing huge oak and chestnut vats. Tours last about 45 minutes and include a wine tasting.

Manueline interior of Igreja de Jesus, Setúbal

Setúbal ⑯

🏠 92,000. 🚃 🚌 ⛴ ℹ️ *Casa do Corpo Santo, Praça do Quebedo (265-53 42 22); Travessa Frei Gaspar 10 (265-53 91 20).*

Although this is an important industrial town, and the third largest port in Portugal (after Lisbon and Oporto), Setúbal can be used to explore the area. To the south of the central gardens and fountains are the fishing harbour, marina and ferry port, and a lively covered market. North of the gardens is the old town, with attractive pedestrian streets and squares full of cafés.

The 16th-century **cathedral**, dedicated to Santa Maria da Graça, has glorious tiled panels dating from the 18th century, and gilded altar decoration. Street names commemorate two famous Setúbal residents: Manuel Barbosa du Bocage (1765–1805), whose satirical poetry landed him in prison, and Luísa Todi (1753–1833), a celebrated opera singer.

In Roman times, fish-salting was the most important industry here. Rectangular tanks, carved from stone, can be seen under the glass floor of the Regional Tourist Office on Travessa Frei Gaspar.

🏠 Igreja de Jesus

Praça Miguel Bombarda. 📞 265-52 41 50. 🕐 9am–noon, 2–5pm Tue–Sun. 🎟️ **Museum** 📞 265-52 47 72. 🕐 Tue–Sat. 🔴 public hols.

To the north of the old town, this striking Gothic church is one of Setúbal's architectural treasures. Designed by the

architect Diogo Boitac in 1494, the lofty interior is adorned with twisted columns, carved in three strands from pinkish Arrábida limestone, and rope-like stone ribs decorating the roof, recognized as the earliest examples of the distinctive and ornate Manueline style.

On Rua do Balneário, in the old monastic quarters, a **museum** houses 14 remarkable paintings of the life of Christ. Painted in glowing colours, the works are attributed to the followers of Jorge Afonso (1520–30), influenced by the Flemish school.

🏛️ Museu de Arqueologia e Etnografia

Avenida Luísa Todi 162. 📞 265-23 93 65. 🕐 Tue–Sat. 🔴 public hols.

The archaeological museum displays a wealth of finds from digs around Setúbal, including Bronze Age pots, Roman coins and amphorae made to carry wine and *garum*, a sauce made from fish marinated in salt and herbs considered a great delicacy in Rome. The ethnography display shows local arts, crafts and industries, including the processing of salt and cork over the centuries.

⚓ Castelo de São Filipe

Estrada de São Filipe. 📞 265-55 00 70. 🕐 daily.

The star-shaped fort was built in 1595 by Philip II of Spain during Portugal's period under Spanish rule to keep a wary eye on pirates, English invaders and the local population. A massive gateway and stone tunnel lead to the sheltered interior, which now houses a *pousada (see p119)* and an exquisite small chapel, tiled with scenes from the life of São Filipe by Policarpo de Oliveira Bernardes (1695–1778). A broad terrace offers marvellous views over the city and the Sado estuary.

Environs: Setúbal is an excellent starting point for a tour by car of the unspoilt **Reserva Natural do Estuário do Sado**, a vast stretch of mud flats, shallow

Fisherman's boat on the shallow mud flats of the Reserva Natural do Estuário do Sado

lagoons and salt marshes with patches of pine forest, which has been explored and inhabited since 3500 BC. Otters, water birds (including storks and herons), oysters and a great variety of fish are found in the reserve. The old tidal water mill at Mouriscas, 5 km (3 miles) to the east of Setúbal, uses the different levels of the tide to turn the grinding stones. Rice-growing and fishing are the main occupations today, and pine trees around the lagoon are tapped for resin.

Reserva Natural do Estuário do Sado

Praça da República, Setúbal (265-54 11 40).

Península de Tróia ⑰

Tróia.

Thatched fisherman's cottage in the village of Carrasqueira

HIGH-RISE HOLIDAY apartments dominate the tip of the Tróia peninsula, easily accessible from Setúbal by ferry. The Atlantic coast, stretching south for 18 km (11 miles) of untouched sandy beach, lined with dunes and pine woods, is now the haunt of sunseekers in the summer.

Near Tróia, in the sheltered lagoon, the Roman town of **Cetóbriga** was the site of a thriving fish-salting business; the stone tanks and ruined buildings are open to visit. To the south, smart new holiday villas and golf clubs are springing up along the lagoon.

Further on, **Carrasqueira** is an old fishing community where you can still see traditional reed houses, with walls and roofs made from thatch. The narrow fishing boats

View over Alcácer do Sal and the River Sado from the castle

moored along the mud flats are reached by walkways raised on stilts. From here to Alcácer do Sal, great stretches of pine forest line the road, and there are the first glimpses of the cork oak countryside typical of the Alentejo region.

Cetóbriga

N253-1. 265-49 43 18. daily.

Alcácer do Sal ⑱

14,000. Rua da Republica 76 (265-61 00 70). 1st Sat of month.

BYPASSED by the main road, the ancient town of Alcácer do Sal (*al-kasr* from the Arabic for castle, and *do sal* from its trade in salt) sits peacefully on the north bank of the River Sado. The imposing castle was a hillfort as early as the 6th century BC.

The Phoenicians made an inland trading port here, and the castle later became a Roman stronghold. Rebuilt by the Moors, it was conquered by Afonso II in 1217. The buildings have now taken on a new life as a *pousada (see p118)*, with views over the rooftops and storks' nests on top of trees and buildings.

There are pleasant cafés along the riverside promenade and several historic churches. The small church of Espírito Santo now houses a **Museu Arqueológico** exhibiting local finds and the 18th-century **Santo António** holds a marble Chapel of the 11,000 Virgins. The bullring is a focus for summer events and hosts the agricultural fair in October.

Museu Arqueológico

Igreja do Espírito Santo, Praça Pedro Nunes. 265-61 00 70. 9am–12:30pm, 2–5:30pm daily.

BIRDS OF THE TAGUS AND SADO ESTUARIES

Many waterbirds, including black-winged stilts, avocets, Kentish plovers and pratincoles are found close to areas of open water and mud flats as well as the dried out lagoons of the Tagus and Sado estuaries. Reed-beds also provide shelter for nesting and support good numbers of little bitterns, purple herons and marsh harriers. From September to March, the area around the Tagus estuary is extremely important for wildfowl and wintering waders.

Black-winged stilt, a wader that feeds in the estuaries

TRAVELLERS' NEEDS

WHERE TO STAY

LISBON AND ITS ENVIRONS offer a variety of accommodation, from restored palaces to family-run hostels. The hotels in Lisbon range from modern and luxurious or elegant and old-fashioned to cosy *pensões* and comfortable chain hotels. There are many hotels in and around the main sightseeing areas of the city.

The hotels in Estoril and Cascais along the Lisbon coast are perhaps less varied with fewer characterful options. In the countryside

around Lisbon, hotels are fairly scarce, although Sintra offers a selection of places to stay and is a good base for exploring the area west of Lisbon. *Pousadas*, often historic buildings converted into hotels, are an alternative in the Lisbon Coast area. If you prefer self-catering, farmhouses, villas and apartments usually offer flexibility and good value. The hotels listed on pages 114–19 have been selected from every price category as offering the best value for money in each area.

Porter services are available in Lisbon's top hotels

Bedroom at the York House Hotel in Lisbon, a converted 16th-century convent (see p115)

CHOOSING A HOTEL

THE MAJORITY of the modern, luxury hotels in Lisbon are centrally situated around Parque Eduardo VII, at the north end of Avenida de Liberdade. As an alternative the converted Expo 98 area, Parque das Nações, now has several top-range hotels with easy access to the airport and Oriente railway station.

The Baixa has a number of more modest *pensões* with a wide choice of accommodation located around Rossio square.

Characterful smaller hotels are found in the Lapa district to the west. Most of the city's older districts, including Chiado, Barrio Alto, Graça and Alfama, have small hotels that offer atmosphere if not always top comforts and quiet.

TYPES OF HOTEL

HOTELS IN LISBON vary in quality, price and facilities. There are two main types of lodging, as classified by the

Portuguese tourist authority: hotels and *pensões*. Hotels are distinguished mainly by the fact that they take up an entire building and are often purpose-built. *Pensões* are always housed in shared premises, typically occupying several floors of a residential building. All hotels and *pensões* are meant to provide meals. If they only offer breakfast they must also be called *residencial*.

The *Estalagem* is an inn, usually with a garden, and located outside of city centres. *Albergarias* are *pensãos* that are the equal of 4- or 5-star hotels. *Pousadas* are either country inns or located in historic buildings such as castles or palaces. They are a state-owned chain run by **Enatur**.

HOTEL CHAINS

INTERNATIONAL LUXURY groups are represented in Lisbon by such hotels as the Lapa Palace and the Ritz Four Seasons *(see p116)*. Smaller luxury groups include **Tivoli Hotels**, which has three hotels in Lisbon and two in Sintra, and the **Pestana Group**, which recently opened the Carlton Palace *(see p114)* in Lisbon. **Heritage Hotels** runs four smaller luxury hotels in the city, including the recently opened Solar do Castelo *(see p115)* within the walls of Castelo de Sao Jorge *(see pp38–9)*.

Lower down the scale, **Choice Hotels Portugal** has a number of hotels in its Comfort Inn category in the greater Lisbon area. **Best Western** has two mid-range hotels in central Lisbon and three along the Lisbon coast.

The impressive façade of the luxurious Lapa Palace (see p116)

◁ **Breakfasting beneath the wisteria at the Pousada da Palmela**

View from the Seteais Palace, Sintra, now a luxury hotel *(see p119)*

GRADINGS

THE PORTUGUESE tourist authority grades hotels with one to five stars (five being the top rating) and *pensões* in four categories (albergaria is the top rating, followed by 1st to 3rd category). These ratings are based on a fixed set of criteria which covers most aspects of comfort. They do not take into account more subjective factors such as veiw or atmosphere.

Remember that a one-star hotel will be less comfortable and cheaper than a 1st category *pensão*. All graded establishments should have a sign showing their rating.

PRICES

IN PORTUGAL, establishments are free to set their own prices, but tariffs must be clearly displayed at reception and in the rooms. The cost of the room usually includes all taxes and a continental breakfast. Other meals are charged as extras. It is sometimes possible to bargain for a better rate, especially in low season. As a rule, the cost of a single room is around 60 to 75 per cent of the cost of a double room. Cascais and Estoril can be expensive, but prices drop substantially out of season. *Pousadas* charge two rates for low (Nov–Mar except New Year, carnival and Easter), and high (Apr–Oct) season.

BOOKING

YOU WILL NEED to book in advance for Estoril and Cascais in high season, when much accommodation is taken by tour operators. Book ahead for central Lisbon, which can also get full. Most hoteliers speak English so it should not be a problem to book by phone. Deposits are not usually required but a written confirmation by fax, including a credit card number may be requested.

Pousadas can be booked through **Enatur** or at the *pousadas* website. The Portuguese tourist authority, **Direcção Geral do Turismo** publishes two official guides which are revised regularly, and are available in English, French and Spanish, as well as Portuguese: *Alojamento Túristico* (Tourist Accommodation and *Turismo no Espaço Rural* (Tourism in the Country). These list all of the establishments rated by the authority, but only the latter contains any description of individual settings.

TRAVELLING WITH CHILDREN

THE PORTUGUESE adore children and will welcome them warmly into hotels and restaurants. Travellers who have children with them will find an immediate point of contact with their hosts.

DISABLED TRAVELLERS

THE PORTUGUESE National Tourist Office lists hotels with facilities for the disabled, and produces a general information leaflet. Some youth hostels and campsites provide special facilities and these are listed by the relevant organizations, and in a guide that is published by the **Secretariado Nacional de Reabilitação**.

Choosing a Hotel

THE HOTELS in this guide have been selected across a wide price range for their excellent facilities and locations. Many also have a recommended restaurant. The chart lists the hotels by areas within Lisbon. Hotels in the Lisbon Coast area are listed separately on pages 118–9. For restaurant listings see pp128–133.

LISBON

	CREDIT CARDS	RESTAURANT	GARDEN	SWIMMING POOL	NUMBER OF ROOMS
ALCÂNTARA: *Carlton Palace Hotel* W www.pestana.com €€€€€ Rua Jau 54, 1300-314. **Map** 2 F3. 21-361 56 00. FAX 21-361 56 01. This grand hotel is housed partly in the 19th-century Palácio Valle-Flor and retains the palace's gardens. There is a gym and pool as well as business facilities. 🔧 TV ▤ P	AE DC MC V	●	■	●	190
AVENIDA: *Alegria* € Praça da Alegria 12, 1250-004. **Map** 4 F1. 21-322 06 70. FAX 21-347 80 70. This basic, good-value *pensão* offers clean and homely rooms. It borders on the red-light district, although the police station is next door. 🔧	AE DC MC V				36
AVENIDA: *13 da Sorte* €€ Rua do Salitre 13, 1250-198. **Map** 4 F1. 21-353 18 51. FAX 21-353 18 51. This well located *pensão* is situated close to Avenida da Liberdade and the Jardim Botanico. Breakfast is not included. 🔧 TV ▤	MC V				22
AVENIDA: *Veneza* W www.3khotels.com €€€ Avenida da Liberdade 189, 1250-141. **Map** 5 C5. 21-352 26 18. FAX 21-352 66 78. The ornate staircase decorated with modern murals by Pedro Luiz-Gomes is the highlight of this spacious and comfortable hotel. 🔧 TV ▤ P	AE DC MC V				36
AVENIDA: *Britânia* W www.heritage.pt €€€€ Rua R. Sampaio 17, 1150-278. **Map** 5 C5. 21-315 50 16. FAX 21-315 50 21. Housed in a building designed by the architect Cassiano Branco in 1944, this delightful hotel has a beautiful marble lobby. 🔧 TV ▤ P	AE DC MC V				36
AVENIDA: *Tivoli Jardim* W www.tivolihotels.com €€€€ Rua J. César Machado, 1250-135. **Map** 4 F1. 21-359 10 00. FAX 21-359 12 45. This smart hotel has spacious rooms. A round pool graces the garden behind the hotel and there is use of extensive sports facilities. 🔧 TV ▤ P	AE DC MC V	●	■	●	119
AVENIDA: *Lisboa Plaza* W www.heritage.pt €€€€€ Travessa do Salitre 7, 1250-205. **Map** 4 F1. 21-321 82 18. FAX 21-347 16 30. Built in 1953, and situated off Praça da Alegria and Av. da Liberade, with decor by the Portuguese interior designer, Graça Viterbo. 🔧 TV ▤	AE DC MC V	●			112
AVENIDA: *Sofitel Lisboa* W www.maisturismo.pt €€€€€ Av. da Liberdade 127, 1269-038. **Map** 4 F1. 21-322 83 00. FAX 21-322 83 10. The comfortable, modern Sofitel features an attractive piano bar called the "Molière", situated just off the lobby. 🔧 TV ▤ P ♿	AE DC MC V	●			170
AVENIDA: *Tivoli Lisboa* W www.tivolihotels.com €€€€€ Av. da Liberdade 185, 1269-050. **Map** 4 F1. 21-319 89 00. FAX 21-319 89 50. This large and elegant hotel has modern rooms and a huge two-level central lobby. The suites are particularly spacious. 🔧 TV ▤ P	AE DC MC V	●	■	●	329
BAIRRO ALTO: *Pensão Londres* €€ Rua Dom Pedro V 53, 2º, 1250-092. **Map** 4 F2. 21-346 22 03. FAX 21-346 56 82. One of the better basic *pensões* in the area, avoiding the worst of the Bairro Alto's night-time noise. 🔧 *(13 rooms)*.	DC MC V				40
BAIXA: *Beira Minho* € Praça da Figueira 6, 2º E, 1150. **Map** 7 B3. 21-346 18 46. FAX 21-886 78 11. The central location of this simple but comfortable *pensão* makes up for the lack of facilities. 🔧					24
BAIXA: *Coimbra e Madrid* € Praça da Figueira 3, 3º, 1100-240. **Map** 7 B3. 21-342 17 60. FAX 21-342 32 64. A plain and simple *pensão* with rather sparse decoration. Some of the rooms, however, have magnificent views of the Castelo de São Jorge. 🔧					32

<table>
<tr><td colspan="2">

Price categories in Euros for a standard double room per night, including breakfast:

€ under 50
€€ 50–100
€€€ 100–150
€€€€ 150–200
€€€€€ over 200

</td><td colspan="5">

RESTAURANT
The hotel has one or more restaurants open for lunch and supper, sometimes reserved for residents.

GARDEN
A garden, courtyard or large terrace for the use of hotel guests.

SWIMMING POOL
The hotel has its own indoor or outdoor pool.

CREDIT CARDS
Major credit cards accepted: *AE* American Express, *DC* Diners Club, *MC* MasterCard and *V* Visa.

</td></tr>
</table>

	CREDIT CARDS	RESTAURANT	GARDEN	SWIMMING POOL	NUMBER OF ROOMS
BAIXA: *Norte* € Rua dos Douradores 159, 1100-205. **Map** 7 B3. **(** 21-887 89 41. **FAX** 21-886 84 62. Centrally located near Praça da Figueira, this *pensão* has few facilities and no breakfast but the rooms are neat and comfortable. Good value.	MC V				36
BAIXA: *Duas Nações* €€ Rua da Vitória 41, 1100-618. **Map** 7 B4. **(** 21-346 07 10. **FAX** 21-347 02 06. The "Two Nations" is a friendly place to stay, right in the heart of the Baixa, but the rooms overlooking Rua Augusta can be noisy.	AE DC MC V				69
BAIXA: *Internacional* @ reservas@hotel–internacional.com €€ Rua da Betesga 3, 1100-090. **Map** 7 B3. **(** 21-324 09 90. **FAX** 21-324 09 99. This hotel features modern and spacious rooms. Residents can relax in the hotel's large, comfortable TV lounge and small bar.	AE DC MC V				54
BAIXA: *Portugal* €€ Rua João das Regras 4, 1100-294. **Map** 7 C3. **(** 21-887 75 81. **FAX** 21-886 73 43. Though plain on the outside, this hotel situated off Praça Martim Moniz has a fairly stylish old-fashioned decor.	AE DC MC V				59
BAIXA: *Mundial* @ mundial.hot@mail.telepac.pt €€€€ Rua Dom Duarte 4, 1100-198. **Map** 7 B3. **(** 21-884 20 00. **FAX** 21-884 21 10. This hotel, located centrally off Praça da Figueira, has plain but comfortable rooms. The restaurant offers marvellous views.	AE DC MC V	●			262
CASTELO: *Ninho das Águias* € Costa do Castelo 74, 1100-179. **Map** 7 C3. **(** 21-855 40 70. The simple "Eagle's Nest" *pensão* sits below the castle walls. A stuffed eagle greets visitors on the terrace that has amazing views. No breakfast.				■	16
CASTELO: *Solar do Castelo* w www.heritage.pt €€€€ Rua das Cozinhas 2, 1100-181. **Map** 7 C3. **(** 21-887 09 09. **FAX** 21-887 09 07. This small, luxurious hotel occupies a recently renovated 18th-century mansion located within the castle walls.	AE DC MC V			■	14
CHIADO: *Lisboa Regency Chiado* w www.regency-hotels-resorts.com €€€€€ Rua Nova do Alameda 114, 1200-290. **Map** 7 B4. **(** 21-325 61 00. **FAX** 21-325 61 61. Stylish, small and central, the Regency Chiado has a privileged location and fabulous views over the heart of Lisbon. Car access can be difficult as there are a limited number of parking places.	AE DC MC V				40
ENTRECAMPOS: *Quality Hotel Lisboa* @ quality.lisboa@mail.telepac.pt €€€€ Campo Grande 7, 1700-087. **(** 21-791 76 00. **FAX** 21-795 75 00. A pleasant hotel that caters for the business traveller. Features include a small health club with a jacuzzi.	AE DC MC V	●			84
GRAÇA: *Senhora do Monte* w www.maisturismo.pt/sramonte.html €€€ Calçada do Monte 39, 1170-250. **Map** 7 D1. **(** 21-886 60 02. **FAX** 21-887 77 83. This *albergaria* is somewhat off the beaten track, but it is well worth the effort to find it. The rooms are fairly plain but the views, especially from the rooftop bar and garden, are simply the best in town.	AE DC MC V				28
LAPA: *As Janelas Verdes* w www.heritage.pt €€€€ R. das Janelas Verdes 47, 1200-690. **Map** 4 D3. **(** 21-396 81 43. **FAX** 21-396 81 44. A delightful *pensão* housed in an 18th-century ivy-covered mansion, once owned by the Portuguese novelist Eça de Queirós *(see p55)*. It has Neo-Classical decor and a peaceful, charming patio.	AE DC MC V			■	29
LAPA: *York House* w www.yorkhouselisboa.com €€€€ Rua das Janelas Verdes 32, 1200-691. **Map** 4 D4. **(** 21-396 24 35. **FAX** 21-397 27 93. This enchanting *pensão* is housed in the 17th-century Convento dos Marianos. Set around a shady, plant-filled patio, the luxurious rooms have wooden or terracotta floors and elegant antique furniture.	AE DC MC V	●		■	34

Price categories in Euros for a standard double room per night, including breakfast:
€ under 50
€€ 50–100
€€€ 100–150
€€€€ 150–200
€€€€€ over 200

RESTAURANT
The hotel has one or more restaurants open for lunch and supper, sometimes reserved for residents.
GARDEN
A garden, courtyard or large terrace for the use of hotel guests.
SWIMMING POOL
The hotel has its own indoor or outdoor pool.
CREDIT CARDS
Major credit cards accepted: *AE* American Express, *DC* Diners Club, *MC* MasterCard and *V* Visa.

	Credit Cards	Restaurant	Garden	Swimming Pool	Number of Rooms
LAPA: *Lapa Palace* W www.lapa-palace.com €€€€€ R. do Pau da Bandeira 4, 1249-021. **Map** 3 C3. 21-394 94 94. **FAX** 21-395 06 65. A gracious and charming hotel located in the city's diplomatic area. Each room in the Palace Wing is uniquely decorated in its own Portuguese style – from 18th-century Neo-Classical to Art Deco. 📶 TV 🍽 P ♿	AE DC MC V	●	■	●	109
MARQUÊS POMBAL: *Capitol* W www.sanahotels.com €€ Rua Eça de Queirós 24, 1050-096. **Map** 5 C4. 21-353 68 11. **FAX** 21-352 61 65. A comfortable hotel just off Avenida de Duque de Loulé. All the rooms are equipped with satellite television and mini bars. 📶 TV 🍽 ♿	AE DC MC V	●			57
MARQUÊS POMBAL: *Castilho* €€ Rua Castilho 57 4º, 1250-068. **Map** 4 F1. 21-386 08 22. **FAX** 21-386 29 10. An excellent-value *pensão* on the fourth floor of a building. Good facilities and comfortable rooms, some with three or four beds. 📶 TV ♿	DC MC V				25
MARQUÊS POMBAL: *Nacional* W www.hotel-nacional.com €€ Rua Castilho 34, 1250-070. **Map** 5 B5. 21-355 44 33. **FAX** 21-356 11 22. This interesting glass-fronted hotel has comfortable rooms and extensive facilities. There are also two suites available. 📶 TV 🍽 P ♿	AE DC MC V				61
MARQUÊS POMBAL: *Jorge V* W www.hoteljorgev.com €€€ Rua Mouzinho da Silveira 3, 1250-165. **Map** 5 C5. 21-356 25 25. **FAX** 21-315 03 19. This pleasant, comfortable hotel offers good value for the area, with air conditioning and ensuite bathrooms. Roughly half the rooms have balconies, so request one when checking in. 📶 TV 🍽	AE DC MC V				51
MARQUÊS POMBAL: *Rex* W www.sanahotels.com €€€ Rua Castilho 169, 1070-051. **Map** 5 B4. 21-388 21 61. **FAX** 21-388 75 81. The Rex is located close to the Parque Eduardo VII. The top floor conference room has good views. 📶 TV 🍽	AE DC MC V	●			68
MARQUÊS POMBAL: *Diplomático* W www.viphotels.com €€€€ Rua Castilho 74, 1250-071. **Map** 5 B5. 21-383 90 20. **FAX** 21-386 21 55. The Diplomático has spacious rooms with modern facilities and offers complimentary tea, coffee and chocolate in the rooms. 📶 TV 🍽 P	AE DC MC V	●			90
MARQUÊS POMBAL: *Le Méridien Lisboa* W www.lemeridien.pt €€€€€ Rua Castilho 149, 1099-034. **Map** 5 B4. 21-381 87 00. **FAX** 21-389 05 05. Overlooking the Parque Eduardo VII from one of the city's seven hills, this hotel has comfortable rooms and spectacular views. 📶 TV 🍽 P ♿	AE DC MC V	●			330
MARQUÊS POMBAL: *Ritz Four Seasons* W www.fourseasons.com €€€€€ Rua R. da Fonseca 88, 1099-039. **Map** 5 B5. 21-381 14 00. **FAX** 21-383 17 83. The legendary Ritz is an elegant, comfortable hotel. Many of the rooms have balconies that overlook the Parque Eduardo VII. 📶 TV 🍽 P ♿	AE DC MC V	●	■		283
PARQUE DAS NAÇÕES: *Tivoli Tejo* W www.tivolihotels.com €€€€ Avenida Dom João II, 1990-083. 21-891 51 00. **FAX** 21-891 53 45. This modern hotel caters to conference and trade fair guests. Its location avoids the traffic congestion of central Lisbon. 📶 TV 🍽 P ♿	AE DC MC V	●		●	279
RATO: *Amazónia* W www.amazoniahoteis.com €€€ T. da Fábrica dos Pentes 12–20, 1250-106. **Map** 5 B5. 21-387 70 06. **FAX** 21-387 90 90. Conveniently close to the city centre, this mid-range hotel has elegant public rooms, large bedrooms and a piano bar. 📶 TV 🍽 P ♿	AE DC MC V			●	192
RATO: *Altis* W www.hotel-altis.pt €€€€€ Rua Castilho 11, 1269-072. **Map** 4 F1. 21-310 60 00. **FAX** 21-310 62 62. This huge hotel has every expected facility, including a rooftop grill and well-equipped health club with an indoor pool. 📶 TV 🍽 P ♿	AE DC MC V	●		●	303

RESTAURADORES: *Restauradores* € 30
Praça dos Restauradores 13, 4°, 1250-187. **Map** 7 A2. **(** *21-347 56 60.*
A very small and fairly basic *pensão* on the fourth floor of a building with a great location in the busy centre of the city. No breakfast. 🛗

RESTAURADORES: *Florescente* W www.residencialflorescente.com €€ AE MC V 68
Rua das Portas de S. Antão 99, 1150-266. **Map** 7 A2. **(** *21-342 66 09.* **FAX** *21-342 77 33.*
For a *pensão* the rooms of the Florescente are extremely well equipped. The street is known for its many fine restaurants. No breakfast. 🛗 📺 ▤

RESTAURADORES: *Suíço Atlântico* €€ AE DC MC V 90
Rua da Glória 3–19, 1250-114. **Map** 7 A2. **(** *21-346 17 13.* **FAX** *21-346 90 13.*
In a small side street by the Elevador da Glória, this hotel has large old-fashioned rooms and public areas with stone arches and wooden beams. 🛗

RESTAURADORES: *Nova Goa* €€€ 42
Rua do Arco do Marquês de Alegrete 13, 1100-034. **Map** 7 C3. **(** *21-888 11 37.*
FAX *21-886 78 11.* Just around the corner from Praça da Figueira, this *pensão* is like many in the vicinity: clean, comfortable and fairly basic. 🛗 📺

RESTAURADORES: *Roma* W www.residenciaroma.com €€€€ AE DC MC V 24
Travessa da Glória 22a, 1°, 1250-118. **Map** 7 A2. **(** *21-346 05 57.* **FAX** *21-346 05 57.*
This simple *pensão* has a fine location just off Avenida da Liberdade, convenient for shops and sightseeing. There is a 24-hour bar service. 🛗 📺 ▤

RESTAURADORES: *VIP Eden* W www.viphotels.com €€€€ AE DC MC V ● 134
Praça dos Restauradores 24, 1250-187. **Map** 7 A2. **(** *21-321 66 00.* **FAX** *21-321 66 66.*
The modern VIP Eden offers apartments and studios, all with a private kitchen. Three studios have been adapted for the disabled. 🛗 📺 ▤ ♿

RESTAURADORES: *Avenida Palace* W www.hotel-avenida-palace.com €€€€€ AE DC MC V 82
Rua 1° de Dezembro 123, 1200-359. **Map** 7 B3. **(** *21-321 81 00.* **FAX** *21-342 28 84.*
Elegant and luxurious, the Avenida Palace hotel, with its Neo-Classical façade and enviable location, retains many charming original details. 🛗 📺 ▤ 🅿

ROSSIO: *Metrópole* @ sales@almeidahotels.com €€€€ AE DC MC V 36
Praça Dom Pedro IV 30, 1100-200. **Map** 7 B3. **(** *21-321 90 30.* **FAX** *21-346 91 66.*
This charming and elegant hotel has been renovated in a style reminiscent of the 1920s. Buçaco wines *(see p210)* are sold here. 🛗 📺 ▤

SALDANHA: *Marisela* W www.residencialmarisela.com €€ AE MC V 19
Rua Filipe Folque 19, 1050-111. **Map** 5 C3. **(** *21-353 32 05.* **FAX** *21-316 04 23.*
A good-value *pensão* with rather basic rooms, in a quiet street between the gardens of Parque Eduardo VII and Praça do Duque de Saldanha. 🛗 📺

SALDANHA: *Príncipe* @ confortprincipe@mail.telepac.pt €€ AE DC MC V ● 67
Avenida Duque de Ávila 201, 1050-082. **Map** 5 B3. **(** *21-353 61 51.* **FAX** *21-353 43 14.*
Most of the rooms in this modern hotel have their own balcony. There is a small bar and lounge just off the lobby. 🛗 📺 ▤ 🅿 ♿

SALDANHA: *VIP* €€ AE DC MC V 54
Rua Fernão Lopes 25, 1000-132. **Map** 5 C3. **(** *21-356 86 00.* **FAX** *21-315 87 73.*
A simple hotel built over shops in a busy part of the city, the VIP is neat and tidy, although the decor is somewhat old-fashioned. 🛗 📺 ▤

SALDANHA: *Horizonte* €€€ AE DC MC V 61
Av. António A. de Aguiar 42, 1050-017. **Map** 5 B4. **(** *21-353 95 26.* **FAX** *21-353 84 74.*
This large *pensão* offers good value for money for this area. The rooms at the front can be noisy. 🛗 📺 ▤

SALDANHA: *Hotel Marquês de Sá* W www.olissippohotels.com €€€ AE DC MC V 164
Av. Miguel Bombarda 130, 1050-167. **Map** 6 B2. **(** *21-791 10 14.* **FAX** *21-793 69 86.*
A pleasant hotel located in one of the most elegant areas of Lisbon, and a short walk from the Museu Calouste Gulbenkian *(see p76–9).* 🛗 📺 ▤ 🅿

SALDANHA: *Real Parque* W www.hoteisreal.com €€€ AE DC MC V ● 153
Avenida L. Bivar 67, 1069-146. **Map** 5 C3. **(** *21-319 90 00.* **FAX** *21-382 29 30.*
This impressive modern hotel, located on a quiet side street, has six rooms specially designed for the disabled. 🛗 📺 ▤ 🅿 ♿

SALDANHA: *Sheraton Lisboa* W www.sheraton.com/lisboa €€€ AE DC MC V ● ● 375
Rua L. Coelho 1, 1069-025. **Map** 5 C3. **(** *21-312 00 00.* **FAX** *21-354 71 64.*
Lisbon's Sheraton offers spacious rooms, a top-floor restaurant and bar with fine views, a communications centre and a health club. 🛗 📺 ▤ 🅿 ♿

Price categories in Euros for a standard double room per night, including breakfast: ·
€ under 50
€€ 50–100
€€€ 100–150
€€€€ 150–200
€€€€€ over 200

RESTAURANT
The hotel has one or more restaurants open for lunch and supper, sometimes reserved for residents.
GARDEN
A garden, courtyard or large terrace for the use of hotel guests.
SWIMMING POOL
The hotel has its own indoor or outdoor pool.
CREDIT CARDS
Major credit cards accepted: *AE* American Express, *DC* Diners Club, *MC* MasterCard and *V* Visa.

	CREDIT CARDS	RESTAURANT	GARDEN	SWIMMING POOL	NUMBER OF ROOMS

THE LISBON COAST

	CREDIT CARDS	RESTAURANT	GARDEN	SWIMMING POOL	NUMBER OF ROOMS
ALCÁCER DO SAL: *Pousada Dom Alfonso II* W www.pousadas.pt €€€€ Alcácer do Sal, 7850. (265-61 30 70. FAX 265-61 30 74. This atmospheric and historic *pousada* occupies a converted castle on a hilltop, overlooking the town and surrounding countryside.	AE DC MC V	●	■	●	35
CARCAVELOS: *Praia-Mar* W www.almeidahotels.com €€€ Rua do Gurué 16, 2775-581. (21-458 51 00. FAX 21-457 31 30. This delightful hotel overlooks the Estoril coast's largest sandy beach. Modern and elegant throughout, the rooms are spacious and comfortable. The famed wines from Buçaco *(see p210)* are also available.	AE DC MC V	●	■	●	158
CASCAIS: *Casa da Pérgola* W www.maisturismo.pt/cpergola €€€ Avenida Valbom 13, 2750-508. (21-484 00 40. FAX 21-483 47 91. This grand 19th century house has rooms with stucco ceilings and ornate furniture. It is closed from 15 Dec-1 Mar.			■		6
CASCAIS: *Solar Dom Carlos* W www.solardomcarlos.com €€€ Rua Latino Coelho 8, 2750-408. (21-482 81 15. FAX 21-486 51 55. This delightful hotel, the former summer residence of King Carlos I, has a garden, historic chapel and comfortable rooms.	AE DC MC V		■		18
CASCAIS: *Cidadela* €€€€ Avenida 25 de Abril, 2750. (21-482 76 00. FAX 21-486 72 26. A short walk from the town centre, the Cidadela is surrounded by gardens. Most of the rooms have spectacular views over the bay.	AE DC MC V	●	■	●	113
CASCAIS: *Albatroz* W www.albatrozhotels.com €€€€€€ Rua F. Arouca 100, 2750-353. (21-484 73 80. FAX 21-484 48 27. Built in the 19th century as a retreat for the Portuguese royal family, the Albatroz sits perched on the rocks directly overlooking the ocean. Inside, the luxurious decoration is matched by excellent service.	AE DC MC V	●	■	●	53
COSTA DA CAPARICA: *Praia do Sol* €€ Rua dos Pescadores 12, 2825-386. (21-290 00 12. FAX 21-290 25 41. W www.viphotels.com A small hotel, the Praia do Sol offers well-appointed rooms conveniently located close to the beach in this popular resort town.	AE DC MC V				54
COSTA DA CAPARICA: *Costa da Caparica* W www.hotelcostacaparica.pt €€€€ Av. Gen. Delgado 47, 2829-506. (21-291 89 00. FAX 21-291 06 87. This hotel, with an unusual semi-circular entrance, overlooks the beach. It has seven rooms adapted for the disabled.	AE DC MC V	●	■	●	353
ERICEIRA: *Vilazul* W www.hotelvilazul.net €€ Calçada da Baleia 10, 2655-238. (261-86 00 00. FAX 261-86 29 27. Only 500 m (550 yds) from the sea, this bright and airy hotel has panoramic views from the terrace and some of the bedrooms.	AE DC MC V	●			21
ESTORIL: *Hotel Alvorada* €€€ Rua de Lisboa 3, 2765-240. (21-464 98 60. FAX 21-468 72 50. W www.hotelalvorada.com Only a few minutes' walk from the beach and opposite the casino, this hotel offers friendly service and bright, well-appointed rooms.	AE DC MC V				52
ESTORIL: *Hotel da Inglaterra* €€€ Rua do Porto 1, 2765-271. (21-468 44 61. FAX 21-468 21 08. Some rooms in this impressive early 20th-century mansion have lovely views over the bay of Cascais or the Sintra hills.	AE DC MC V	●	■	●	55
ESTORIL: *São Cristóvão* W www.residencial-saocristovao.com €€€ Av. Marginal 7079, 2765-480. (21-468 09 13. FAX 21-468 09 13. This charming *pensão* is housed in an interesting old villa. Located on the ocean side of the Avenida Marginal, it offers spectacular views.			■		14

ESTORIL: *Palácio* w www.hotel-estoril-palacio.com €€€€€ — AE DC MC V — 161
Rua do Parque, 2769-504. (21-464 80 00. FAX 21-468 48 67.
An elegant hotel located between the sea and the casino. Guests have access to an 18-hole golf course and tennis courts. 🔼 TV P &

GUINCHO: *Fortaleza do Guincho* w www.guinchotel.pt €€€€€ — AE DC MC V — 29
Estrada do Guincho, 2750-642. (21-487 04 91. FAX 21-487 04 31.
Perched on a clifftop overlooking the ocean, this atmospheric hotel with arched ceilings and medieval decor was once a fortress. 🔼 TV ▤ P &

GUINCHO: *Senhora da Guia* w www.senhoradaguia.com €€€€€ — AE DC MC V — 41
Estrada do Guincho, 2750-374. (21-486 92 39. FAX 21-486 92 27.
Set in its own grounds with a sea-water pool, this charming *estalagem* is housed in a comfortable and relaxing manor house. 🔼 TV ▤ P

MAFRA: *Castelão* w www.hotelcastelao.com €€ — AE DC MC V — 24
Avenida 25 de Abril, 2640-456. (261-81 60 50. FAX 261-81 60 59.
Convenient as a base when visiting the fabulous monastery in Mafra, this hotel is comfortable and clean. 🔼 TV P

PALMELA: *Pousada do Castelo de Palmela* w www.pousadas.pt €€€€€ — AE DC MC V — 28
Castelo de Palmela, 2950-997. (21-235 12 26. FAX 21-233 04 40.
The fortified walls of this 12th-century castle now enclose a tranquil *pousada* with whitewashed rooms and many plants. 🔼 TV ▤ P

QUELUZ: *Pousada Dona Maria I* w www.pousadas.pt €€€€€ — AE DC MC V — 26
L. do Palácio Nacional, 2745-191. (21-435 61 58. FAX 21-435 61 89.
Once used by staff of the marvellous 18th-century Palácio de Queluz, today the "Clock Tower" is an impressive *pousada*. 🔼 TV ▤ P &

SESIMBRA: *Hotel do Mar* w www.hoteldomar.pt €€€€ — AE DC MC V — 168
R. Gen. Humberto Delgado 10, 2970-628. (21-228 83 00. FAX 21-223 38 88.
This hotel, built on different levels on the cliffside, is surrounded by lush gardens. The presidential suite has a private pool. 🔼 TV ▤ P &

SETÚBAL: *IBIS Setúbal* €€ — AE DC MC V — 102
Estrada Nacional 10, Vale da Rosa, 2914-518. (265-77 22 00. FAX 265-77 24 47.
Featuring the usual combination of IBIS comforts and economy, this hotel is surrounded by its own peaceful gardens. 🔼 TV ▤ P &

SETÚBAL: *Pousada de São Filipe* w www.pousadas.pt €€€€ — AE DC MC V — 16
Castelo de São Filipe, 2900-300. (265-55 00 70. FAX 265-53 25 38.
This historic castle, built by Philip II of Spain *(see p50)* in 1590, is an friendly pousada with fine views over the estuary. 🔼 TV ▤ P

SINTRA: *Central* €€ — AE DC MC V — 10
Praça da República 35, 2710-625. (21-923 09 63.
Heavy furniture and peeling paint give this hotel an old-fashioned atmosphere. It has an excellent position opposite the Palácio Nacional. 🔼

SINTRA: *Residencial Sintra* @ pensao.residencial.sintra@clix.pt €€€ — MC V — 15
T. dos Avelares 12, 2710-506. (21-923 07 38. FAX 21-923 07 38.
Located just east of Sintra town centre, in the residential area of São Pedro, this rambling old *pensão* is friendly and full of character. 🔼 P

SINTRA: *Tivoli Sintra* w www.tivolihotels.com €€€€ — AE DC MC V — 77
Praça da República, 2710-616. (21-923 35 05. FAX 21-923 15 72.
The modern Tivoli Sintra, tucked away in a corner of Sintra's main square, has wonderful views across the valley, a bar and a boutique. 🔼 TV ▤ P &

SINTRA: *Caesar Park* w www.caesarparkpenhalonga.com €€€€€ — AE DC MC V — 194
Estr. da Lagoa Azul, Linhó 2714-511. (21-924 90 11. FAX 21-924 90 07.
This huge, luxurious complex in the Sintra hills has a 9 and an 18-hole golf course, designed by Robert Trent Jones Jr, and a health club. 🔼 TV ▤ P &

SINTRA: *Lawrence's* w www.lawrenceshotel.com €€€€€ — AE DC MC V — 16
Rua Consiglieri Pedroso 38-40, 2710-550 Sintra. (21-910 55 00. FAX 21-910 55 05.
A cosy, family-run luxury hotel that dates back to the 18th century. Lord Byron is said to have stayed here in 1809. 🔼 TV ▤ P &

SINTRA: *Palácio de Seteais* w www.tivolihotels.com €€€€€ — AE DC MC V — 30
Av. B. du Bocage 8, 2710-517. (21-923 32 00. FAX 21-923 42 77.
Just outside town, this elegant hotel occupies a delightful 18th-century palace with tastefully decorated interiors and a topiary garden. 🔼 TV P

RESTAURANTS, CAFÉS AND BARS

PARTICULARLY IN Lisbon and along the coast, there are many restaurants dedicated to cooking all manner of freshly caught fish and seafood. It may be grilled, pan-fried or turned into soup or a stew. However, meat dishes are also plentiful, some of the most popular being made of pork and lamb. Lisbon has an abundance of cheap restaurants and cafés, as well as more expensive ones. There are not

Drinks waiter at the Palácio de Seteais *(see p133)*

only typically Portuguese restaurants in Lisbon, but also Chinese, Indian, Brazilian and African, all of which reflect Portugal's colonial past. This section gives tips on the different types of restaurants and cafés, as well as advice on menus, drinks and ordering your meal. The listings found on pages 128–33 are a selection of the best restaurants in all price ranges that are to be found throughout the capital and in the Lisbon Coast area.

TYPES OF RESTAURANT

EATING VENUES in Lisbon come in all shapes and sizes and at all price levels. Among the most reasonable is the local *tasca* or tavern, often just a room with half-a-dozen tables presided over by a husband-and-wife team. *Tascas* are often frequented by locals and professionals at lunchtime, which is a good indication of quality food. The *casa de pasto* offers a budget three-course meal in a large dining room, while a *restaurante* is more formal and offers a wider choice of dishes. At a typical *marisqueira*, the emphasis is on seafood and fresh fish. A *churrasqueira*, originally Brazilian, specializes in spit-roasted foods. A *cervejaria* is the ideal place to go for a beer and snack, maybe of delicious seafood. The restaurants in better hotels are generally of good quality. *Pousadas (see p112)*, found mainly in country areas, offer a network of traditional restaurants, with the focus on local gastronomic specialities.

The pleasant courtyard of Lautasco *(p128)* along Beco do Azinhal in the Alfama

EATING HOURS

LUNCH is usually served between 1 and 3pm, when many restaurants get very crowded. Dinner is served from 7pm until at least 10pm in most places, and can often be later. An alternative for a late dinner would be a *fado* house *(see pp142–3)*, usually open from about 9:30pm to 3 or 4am. However, a meal here will be somewhat more expensive as the price includes a show.

RESERVATIONS

IT IS A GOOD IDEA to book ahead for expensive restaurants, and for those in popular locations in high season. Disabled people should certainly check in advance on facilities and access. Special facilities are generally lacking but most places will try to be helpful.

THE MENU

SOME restaurants, in tourist areas particularly, offer an *ementa turística*, a cheap, daily-changing menu. This is served with coffee and a drink (a glass of wine or beer, a soft drink or water) and provides a full meal at a good price with no hidden costs. Lunch

The impressive interior of Cozinha Velha *(see p133)* at Queluz

Eating outside in Cascais along the Lisbon coast

(almoço) generally consists of a soup or starter and a fish or meat dish with potatoes or rice. To sample a local speciality, you should ask for the *prato do dia* – dish of the day. The choice of sweets can be limited, but there is usually a good selection of fresh fruits in season or you can try a pastry such as a *pastel de nata*.

Dinner *(jantar)* may be two or more courses, perhaps rounded off with ice cream, fruit, a simple dessert or cheese. Casserole-style dishes, such as *cataplana* (a kind of tightly sealed wok in which the food is steamed, often used for fish and seafood) or *porco à alentejana* (pork with clams), are brought to the table in a pot for diners to share. This is similarly done with large fish, such as sea bass, which are sold by weight. One serving is large and can easily be shared by two people, and it is perfectly acceptable to ask for a *meia dose* or half-portion. If requested, Portuguese restaurants will be more than happy to supply these half-portions for adults as well as for any children present.

Pasteís de nata (custard pastries)

Peculiar to Portugal is the plate of assorted appetizers – perhaps olives, cheese and sardine pâté – which are served with bread at the start of a meal. However, these are not usually included in the price of the meal and an extra charge will be made for each item consumed.

VEGETARIANS

VEGETARIANS WILL not eat as well as fish lovers, although local cheeses and breads can be excellent. Chefs are usually happy to provide something meatless, although this will probably mean just a salad or omelette. A greater variety of vegetarian dishes can be found in ethnic restaurants.

WHAT TO DRINK

IT WOULD BE a pity to visit Portugal without sampling port *(see pp124–5)* and Madeira, the country's two most famous drinks. Some restaurants may suggest a glass of white port as an aperitif while you wait for your meal. As far as house wine is concerned, it is usually of an acceptable quality to wash down your meal whatever the standard of the restaurant. Otherwise, ask for the wine list *(carta de vinhos)* and choose one of the Portuguese wines *(see pp124–5)*. As a complement to the wine, mineral water is recommended. This is either *com gás* (sparkling) or *sem gás* (still). If you prefer to drink beer, Sagres and Super Bock are both good lagers. *Cervejarias*, such as the lively Cervejaria Trindade in the Bairro Alto *(see pp48–59)*, are ideal places to get a snack late at night and enjoy an excellent range of beers, from lagers to dark beers, many of which are draught.

PAYING

IT IS COMMON PRACTICE to add a five or ten per cent tip to bills. Although service is included, it provides a low wage which the tip is meant to supplement. Note that not all restaurants accept credit cards.

CHILDREN

THE PORTUGUESE view children as a blessing rather than a nuisance, so Lisbon is an ideal city for families to eat out together. Half portions *(meia dose)* at reduced prices are advertised in restaurants or are provided on request.

SMOKING

SMOKING IS COMMON and permitted in all public places in Portugal, unless there is a sign saying *proibido fumar*. No-smoking areas in restaurants are fairly rare.

DRINKING COFFEE IN LISBON

Coffee is widely drunk in Lisbon and served in many forms. The most popular, *uma bica*, is a small cup of strong black coffee like an espresso. For a weaker version, ask for *uma carioca de café*. A strong *bica* is called *uma italiana*. *Uma meia de leite* is half coffee, half milk. Strong coffee with a dash of milk is known as *um garoto escuro* (*um garoto claro* is quite milky). If you like coffee with plenty of milk, ask for *um galão* (a gallon). It is served in a glass, and again you can order *um galão claro* (very milky) or *escuro* (strong).

Uma bica **Um galão**

What to Eat in Lisbon

Serra cheese

Gastronomically, the Lisbon region is immensely varied, incorporating many different foods from all over Portugal. Situated near the Atlantic, Lisbon and its coast enjoy a proliferation of excellent seafood, in particular shellfish, dried cod *(bacalhau)* and grilled sardines. A popular dish is *porco à alentejana*, a mixture of pork and clams, originating from southern Portugal. Milk from sheep and goats is turned into a variety of cheeses, one of the most popular being the buttery Serra, which becomes harder as it ages. Sweet dishes include a vanilla flavoured rice pudding and a rich, dark chocolate mousse.

***Fresh fruit** is plentiful in Lisbon and grapes and oranges from the Algarve are delicious when in season.*

Pastéis de bacalhau *are a national addiction. These little salt-cod cakes are eaten cold as a snack or hot as a main dish.*

Caldo verde, *Portugal's most famous soup, gets its vibrant colour from its main ingredient, couve galega, a type of kale.*

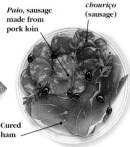
Paio, sausage made from pork loin

Spiced chouriço (sausage)

Cured ham

Cured meats *play an important role in Portuguese cuisine. The chouriços are flavoured with paprika and often wine.*

Leitão à Bairrada, *roasted sucking pig with crisp crackling, is relished hot or cold, and can be bought in good delicatessens.*

Frango à piri-piri, *a great favourite from Portugal's former colonies in Africa, is barbecued chicken with chilli.*

Bife à café, *café-style steak, is tender steak with a creamy sauce, served with chips and topped with a fried egg.*

Bacalhau à Gomes de Sá *is a creation from Oporto, in northern Portugal, made of layers of salt cod, potato and onion, and garnished with egg and olives.*

Porco à alentejana, *a curious marriage of pork and clams, is usually cooked with white wine, garlic and parsley, as well as spices such as paprika.*

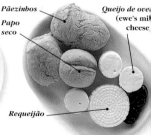
Pãezinhos

Papo seco

Queijo de ove (ewe's mil cheese

Requeijão

Fresh cheeses *made from ewe's or goat's milk are enjoyed with a variety of fresh rolls. Especially prized is* Requeijão.

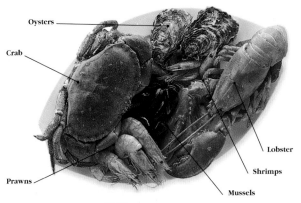

Shellfish is plentiful and much enjoyed in Portugal. Lisbon is full of specialist seafood restaurants artfully displaying lobsters, crayfish, oysters, prawns of all sizes, crabs and other lesser known delicacies. Cockles and clams find their way into many dishes, such as the rich seafood rice, arroz de marisco.

Oysters

Crab

Lobster

Shrimps

Prawns

Mussels

Açorda de marisco is a special and unusual dish: shellfish are added to a thick soup of mashed bread, oil, garlic and coriander.

Sardinhas assadas, charcoal-grilled sardines, are a seaside tradition – a feast in summer when they are at their best.

Mousse de chocolate can be spectacular when made with really good dark chocolate.

Arroz doce, creamy rice pudding rich with egg, is flavoured with lemon rind and vanilla.

DRINKS

Portugal produces many fine wines *(see pp124–5)*, from which houses such as JM da Fonseca distil *aguardente* (brandy). Mineral waters, such as Luso, from the spa in central Portugal, are widely available. A tradition of beer-making thrives in the Lisbon area, with many *cervejarias* (beer houses) in the city. *Licor de Amêndoa Amarga* is a bitter almond liqueur.

Aguardente Velha Reserva

Mineral water from Luso

Licor de Amêndoa Amarga

Sagres beer

Queijadas de Sintra (cheese tarts spiced with cinnamon)

Pastéis de nata (custard-cream tartlets)

Pastel de feijão (almonds, eggs and beans)

Broas (cornflour and honey)

Tartlets such as pastéis de nata *epitomize the region's infinite variety of cakes, many based on egg yolks, almonds and spices.*

The Wines of Portugal

ALTHOUGH STILL overshadowed by the excellence and fame of port, Portuguese table wine deserves to be taken seriously. After years of investment in the industry, many of the reds, such as the full-bodied wines from the Douro (made with some of the same grapes as port), have established an attractive style all their own. Great whites are fewer, but most regions have some. And of course there is *vinho verde*, the usually white, light, slightly carbonated wine from the north.

Sparkling rosés, such as Mateus and Lancers, have been Portugal's great export success. But the country now has many excellent wines that reach beyond the easy-drinking charms of these.

WINE REGIONS

Many of Portugal's wine regions maintain their individual style by specializing in particular Portuguese grape varieties. The introduction of modern wine-making techniques has improved overall quality, and as yet the increasing use of imported grape varieties seems no threat to Portuguese individuality.

KEY

☐	Vinhos Verdes
☐	Douro
☐	Dão
☐	Bairrada
☐	Estremadura
☐	Ribatejo
☐	Setúbal
☐	Alentejo

0 kilometres 50
0 miles 25

Vinho verde vineyards in the village of Lapela, near Monção in the Minho

Cellar of the Buçaco Palace Hotel, near Mealhada, famous for its red wine

HOW TO READ A WINE LABEL

Tinto is red, *branco* is white, *seco* is dry and *doce* is sweet. Beyond that, the essential information concerns the producer, the region and the year. Wines made to at least 80 per cent from a single grape variety may give the name of that grape on the front label. *Denominação de Origem Controlada* (DOC) indicates that the wine has been made according to the strictest regulations of a given region, but, as elsewhere, this need not mean higher quality than the nominally simpler *Vinho Regional* appellation. The back label often describes grape varieties and wine-making techniques.

The Sociedade Agrícola e Comercial dos Vinhos Vale da Corça, Lda, produced and bottled this wine.

This wine is from the Douro and is made according to DOC regulations for the region.

The name of this wine means "banks of the River Tua", further specifying its geographical origin.

Reserva means that the wine has been aged, probably in oak casks. It also implies that the wine is of higher quality than non-reserva wine from the same producer.

DOURO
DENOMINAÇÃO DE ORIGEM CONTROLADA
ENCOSTAS DO TUA
Reserva de 2000
VINHO TINTO

Vinho verde, *"green wine" from the Minho region, can be either red or white, but the fizzy, dry reds are generally consumed locally. Typical white* vinho verde *is bone dry, slightly fizzy, low in alcohol and high in acidity. A weightier style of white* vinho verde *is made from the Alvarinho grape, near the Spanish border. Among the best brands are Soalheiro and Palácio da Brejoeira.*

Bairrada is a region where the small and thick-skinned Baga grape dominates. It makes big, tannic wines, sometimes with smoky or pine-needle overtones and like the older Dão wines, they need time to soften. Modern winemaking and occasional disregard for regional regulations have meant more approachable reds (often classified as Vinho Regional das Beiras) and crisper whites. Quality producers include Luís Pato and Caves Aliança.

Ribatejo *is the fertile valley of the Tagus to the north and east of Lisbon. After Estremadura, it is Portugal's biggest wine region measured by volume, but its potential for quality wines has only just begun to be realized. As in Estremadura, Vinho Regional bottlings are frequently better than DOC ones. Producers to look for include Quinta da Alorna, Casa Branco and Fiuza & Bright.*

The Douro *region is best known as the source of port wine, but in most years about half of the wine produced is fermented dry to make table wine, and these wines are now at the forefront of Portuguese wine-making. The pioneer, Barca Velha, was launched half a century ago and is both highly regarded and among the most expensive. Other quality producers include Calheiros Cruz, Domingos Alves de Sousa, Quinta do Crasto, Niepoort and Ramos-Pinto.*

Picking grapes for *vinho verde*

Setúbal, *to the south of Lisbon, is best known for its sweet, fortified Muscat wine, Moscatel de Setúbal. In addition, the region also produces excellent, mostly red, table wine. Two big quality producers dominate the region: José Maria da Fonseca (see p107) and J.P. Vinhos. The co-operative at Santo Isidro de Pegões makes good-value wines, while interesting smaller producers include Venâncio Costa Lima, Hero do Castanheiro and Ermelinda Freitas.*

The Dão region *now offers some of Portugal's best wines. Small producers, such as Quinta dos Roques, Quinta da Pellada and Quinta de Cabriz, and the large Sogrape company make fruity reds for younger drinking, fresh, dry whites and deeper, richer reds which retain their fruit with age – a far cry from the heavy, hard-edged, and often oxidized wines of the past.*

Estremadura *is Portugal's westernmost wine area and has only recently emerged as a region in its own right. Several producers now make modern Vinho Regional wines with character; look for wines by DFJ, Casa Santos Lima, Quinta de Pancas and Quinta do Monte d'Oiro. The most interesting DOC is Alenquer. Bucelas, to the south of the region, produces characterful white wines.*

Alentejo *wine has possibly made the biggest leap in quality in the last decade. Long dismissed by experts as a region of easy-drinking house reds for restaurants, this area now produces some of Portugal's most serious red wines and a surprising number of excellent whites. Among the best producers are Herdade do Esporão, Herdade dos Coelheiros, Cortes de Cima and João Portugal Ramos.*

The Story of Port

T HE "DISCOVERY" OF PORT dates from the 17th century when British merchants added brandy to the wine of the northern Douro region to prevent it souring in transit. They found that the stronger and sweeter the wine, the better flavour it acquired. Methods of maturing and blending continue to be refined by the main port producers. Croft was one of the first big shippers, followed by other English and Scottish firms. Despite the consolidation of the global drinks industry, much of the port trade is still in British hands, and some firms are still family-run.

Barco rabelo ferrying port down the Douro river

THE PORT REGION

Port comes only from a demarcated region of the upper Douro valley, stretching 100 km (62 miles) to the Spanish border. Régua and Pinhão are the main centres of production, but most top-quality vineyards lie on estates or *quintas* in the harsh eastern terrain.

STYLES OF PORT

There are essentially two categories of red port: bottle-aged and wood-aged. The former are deeper in colour and will develop after bottling; the latter, which include tawny ports, are ready to drink when they are bottled. White port is in a category of its own.

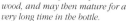

Vintage, the star of any shipper's range, is made from wines of a single year, from the best vineyards. It is blended and bottled after two years in wood, and may then mature for a very long time in the bottle.

Vintage

Late Bottled Vintage (LBV) is wine of a single year, bottled between four and six years after the harvest. Filtered LBV does not require decanting but may have less flavour than unfiltered, "traditional" LBV.

LBV

Aged tawny port is blended from top-quality wines that have been aged in wood for a long time. The age on the label is not precise, but the older it is, the paler, more delicate, less fruity and more expensive the port is likely to be.

Aged Tawny

Tawny port without indication of age may not have been in wood for long enough to develop the complex flavours of aged tawny; its style is light and its price fairly low. It may be a blend of red and white ports.

Tawny

Ruby port is deep red and should be full of lively fruit flavour. It has been aged for two or three years, sometimes in wood, sometimes not. It is less complex than either LBV or Vintage, but costs considerably less.

Ruby

White port is made from white grapes and may be dry, sweet or very sweet. It is mainly drunk chilled as an aperitif. Some types of white port have a slightly lower alcohol content than the normal 20% for port.

White

lecting grapes in tall wicker baskets for transport to the wineries

OW PORT IS MADE

e climax of the Douro farmers' year comes in late Septem-
r when bands of pickers congregate to harvest the grapes.
More than 40 varieties are used for
making port, but there are five
recommended top varieties.

*eading the grapes in stone
aks or lagares to extract the
ce is a feature of very tradi-
nal quintas. Some shippers
ieve it adds a special quality.*

*Fermentation in cement or
steel tanks is a more common
method. Carbon dioxide builds
up within the tank, forcing the
fermenting must (juice from
the grapes) up a tube into an
open trough at the top. The gas
is released and the must sprays
back over the pips and skins, in
a process similar to treading.*

*In the fortification process,
the semi-fermented must is run
into a second vat where brandy
– actually grape spirit – is
added. This arrests the fermentation, leaving the wine sweet
from natural grape sugar.*

*bousands of bottles of
raham's vintage port from
?77 await full maturation in
e cellars of the Vila Nova de
aia lodge.*

*Quality tawny port is
matured in oak casks in the
port lodges. Once bottled, it is
ready for drinking and does
not require decanting.*

VINTAGE PORT

In the interests of
maintaining the
highest standards of
quality – and of not
saturating the market
– port producers do not
"declare" a vintage every year.
Each year, the wine from the
best vineyards is closely moni-
tored for 18 months, other
producers are consulted about
their quality, and then a decision is taken. If a vintage is
not declared, the wine may
remain in wood to be blended
as tawny or LBV in future, or
it may be bottled as a "single
quinta" port – a kind of
second-label vintage. On
average, producers declare
a vintage three times in a
decade, though not always
in the same years.

A good vintage needs time in
bottle to reveal itself. Fifteen
years is regarded as a mini-
mum, although many impatient
drinkers do not actually wait
that long; there is even a fashion for drinking young vintage
port. The nature of vintage
port's aging process results in a
continuously evolving list of
truly great vintages. Most con-
noisseurs agree, however, that
no recent vintage has yet
equalled that produced in 1963.

Pre-war vintages
1927, 1931, 1935:
All great and now very rare.

Post-war vintages
1945, 1947, 1948, 1955:
For the very rich and
extremely lucky.
1963 Perhaps the greatest
post-war vintage.
1970 Its reputation has been
rising and is now on
par with 1963.
1994 A fine vintage,
particularly
from producers
Dow, Taylor
and Quinta do
Noval.
1997 Another fine
vintage.
2000 A very pro-
mising year.

Taylor's 1994 vintage

Choosing a Restaurant

THE RESTAURANTS in this guide have been selected for their good value, exceptional food or interesting location. This chart highlights some of the factors which may influence your choice. This chart lists the restaurants by areas within Lisbon. Restaurants in the Lisbon Coast area are listed separately on pages 132–33.

		CREDIT CARDS	LATE OPENING	OUTDOOR TABLES	GOOD WINE LIST
LISBON					
AJUDA: *O Nobre* €€€€ Rua das Mercês 71a–b. **Map 2 D3.** 【 21-893 16 04. Worth searching out on a day trip to Belém, O Nobre serves crab soup, game stew, partridge, fish with olives and roast pork with grapes. ● *Sun eve.* 🍴 🔵		AE MC V	■		■
ALCÂNTARA: *Alcântara Café* €€€€€ Rua Maria Luísa Holstein 15. **Map 3 A4.** 【 21-362 12 26. Long the only contemporary restaurant in Lisbon, Alcântara Café is now a "classic". The 1980's interior is still impressive. ● *lunch.* 🍴 🔵		AE DC MC V	■		■
ALFAMA: *Hua-Ta-Li* €€ Rua dos Bacalhoeiros 109–115. **Map 7 C4.** 【 21-887 91 70. This is a large Chinese restaurant close to the docks that serves all the regular rice and noodle favourites. Fast and efficient service. 🍴					
ALFAMA: *Lautasco* €€ Beco do Azinhal 7a (off Rua de São Pedro). **Map 8 E4.** 【 21-886 01 73. Rustically decorated with wooden panelling and wagon-wheel chandeliers, Lautasco specializes in typical Portuguese cuisine. ● *Sun; 20 Dec –15 Jan.*		AE DC MC V	■	●	
ALFAMA: *Mestre André* €€€ Calçadinha de Santo Estevão 6. **Map 8 E3.** 【 21-887 14 87. Lively Portuguese restaurant offering delicious pork and fish dishes as well as excellent *churrasco* (spit-roasted meat) *(see p120).* ● *Sun.*		AE	■	●	
ALFAMA: *Viagem de Sabores* €€€ Rua de São João da Praça 103. **Map 8 D4.** 【 21-887 01 89. Located in a converted fish shop close to the cathedral, this restaurant serves an eclectic mix of eastern and western cuisines. Great starters. ● *Lunch, Sun.* 🍴		DC MC V			
ALFAMA: *Faz Figura* €€€€ Rua do Paraíso 15b. **Map 8 F2.** 【 21-886 89 81. A smart restaurant, where panoramic views of the river and city can be enjoyed from the covered terrace. Specialities include *cataplana* dishes *(see p121)* and *picanha* (steak grilled over an open fire). ● *Sat lunch; Sun.* 🍴		AE DC MC V		●	■
BAIRRO ALTO: *Bota Alta* €€€ Travessa da Queimada 35-37. **Map 7 A3.** 【 21-342 79 59. The "High Boot" is an attractive restaurant with original paintings on the walls. The menu consists of traditional Portuguese dishes. ● *Sat lunch; Sun.*		AE DC MC V			
BAIRRO ALTO: *Casanostra* €€€€ Travessa do Poço da Cidade 60. **Map 7 A3.** 【 21-342 59 31. Within the green, white and black interior of this Italian restaurant you can choose from a six-page menu full of delicacies. ● *Mon, Sat lunch.* 🍴		AE MC V			
BAIRRO ALTO: *Imperio dos Sentidos* €€€€ Rua da Atalaia 35-7. **Map 4 F2.** 【 21-343 18 22. Located in an early 20th-century building, this restaurant offers dishes such as pasta with creamed spinach sauce and shrimp. ● *lunch; Mon.* 🍴		MC V	■		
BAIRRO ALTO: *Pap'Açorda* €€€€ ...47. 【 21-346 48 11. ...is come here for the *açorda de mariscos* (bread ...menu is traditional Portuguese with some novel ...n; 2 weeks in Jul; 2 weeks in Oct. 🍴		AE DC MC V			■
...fé €€€€ ...275. **Map 4 E1.** 【 21-342 22 81. ...t you will find traditional Portuguese cuisine with ...y the crab soup or the oven-roasted lamb. 🍴 🔵		MC V	■		■

					CREDIT CARDS	LATE OPENING	OUTDOOR TABLES	GOOD WINE LIST

Price categories are for a three-course meal for one with half a bottle of wine, including cover charge, service and VAT:

€ under 10
€€ 10–15
€€€ 15–20.5
€€€€ 20.5–30
€€€€€ over 30

LATE OPENING
The kitchen stays open after 10pm, and you can usually have a meal up until at least 11pm.

OUTDOOR TABLES
Tables for eating outdoors, in a garden or on a balcony, often with a pleasant view.

GOOD WINE LIST
The restaurant will have a good selection of quality wines.

CREDIT CARDS
This indicates which of the major credit cards are accepted: AE American Express, DC Diners Club, MC MasterCard and V Visa.

BAIRRO ALTO: *Tavares*   €€€€€   AE DC MC V   ■
Rua da Misericórdia 35-37. **Map** 7 A4. **℡** 21-342 11 12. **W** www.tavaresrico.pt
Lisbon's oldest restaurant, Tavares, dates from 1784. Its reputation is maintained with dishes such as breast of partridge on toast with *foie gras* and fillets of sea bass *au gratin* with prawn sauce. ● Sat; Sun lunch. 🍴 ♿

BAIXA: *Paris*   €€€   AE DC MC V
Rua dos Sapateiros 126. **Map** 7 B4. **℡** 21-346 97 97.
Open for nearly half a century, Paris offers a mixture of Portuguese and Galician cuisine. Try the swordfish steak or the Alentejan pork. ● 1 Jan, 25 & 31 Dec. 🍴 ♿

BELÉM: *Já Sei*   €€€€   AE DE MC V   ● ■
Avda Brasilia 202. **Map** 1 A5. **℡** 21-301 59 69.
This has a beautiful location, right on the river, so it is pleasant in the summer; the seafood-based menu is good all-year-round. ● Sun dinner; Mon. 🍴 🎵

BELÉM: *São Jerónimo*   €€€€   AE DC MC V   ■
Rua dos Jerónimos 12. **Map** 1 C4. **℡** 21-364 87 97.
An elegant, spacious restaurant with 1930s decor. The excellent mixed menu of Portuguese and French cuisine includes skate in peach sauce and duck with nuts in wine sauce. ● Sat lunch; Sun; public hols (exc. 1 Jan & 31 Dec). 🍴

BELÉM: *Vela Latina*   €€€€   AE DC MC V   ■
Doca do Bom Sucesso. **Map** 1 B5. **℡** 21-301 71 18.
On the waterfront, this restaurant has a bar and terrace overlooking the Torre de Belém. The speciality is *cataplana rica do mar* (seafood). ● Sun. 🍴 ♿

CACILHAS: *Atira-te ao Rio*   €€€   ■ ●
Cais do Ginjal 69–70. **℡** 21-272 17 76.
View Lisbon from the other bank of the Tagus and enjoy the restaurant's Brazilian specialities, including *feijoada à Brasileira* (bean stew). ● Mon.

CAMPO DE OURIQUE: *Tasquinha d'Adelaide*   €€€€   AE DC MC V   ■
Rua do Patrocínio 72–4. **Map** 3 C2. **℡** 21-396 22 39.
Popular with locals, this small restaurant serves inspired interpretations of classic Portuguese regional dishes. Booking essential. ● Sun. 🍴

CAMPO PEQUENO: *Chimarrão*   €€   AE DC MC V   ■   ■
Campo Pequeno 79. **Map** 5 C1. **℡** 21-793 97 60.
One of a small restaurant chain specializing in Brazilian food. Try *rodízio* (unlimited amount of grilled meat) with salad, rice and black beans. 🍴 🎵

CAMPO PEQUENO: *A Gôndola*   €€€   AE MC V   ● ■
Avenida de Berna 64. **Map** 5 B2. **℡** 21-797 04 26.
A Gôndola is a charming restaurant offering a wide choice of dishes including Italian as well as Portuguese specialities. In the summer enjoy your meal in the pleasant surrounding gardens. ● Sun. 🍴

CAMPO PEQUENO: *António Clara – Clube dos Empresários*   €€€€   AE DC MC V   ■
Avenida da República 38. **Map** 5 C1. **℡** 21-799 42 80.
This wonderful old mansion offers a French-influenced menu in dining areas that were once individual rooms in the house. ● Sun; public hols. 🍴

CASTELO: *Restô do Chapitô*   €€€   ■ ● ■
Costa do Castelo 7. **Map** 7 C3. **℡** 21-886 73 34.
The extensive menu includes a wide range of international dishes. A cheerful restaurant with a bar and fine views over the harbour. 🎵 irregularly.

CASTELO: *Casa do Leão*   €€€€   AE DC MC V   ● ■
Castelo de São Jorge. **Map** 8 D3. **℡** 21-887 59 62.
Beneath arched brick ceilings, inside part of Castelo de São Jorge (see pp78–9), this restaurant offers superb service and excellent traditional Portuguese cuisine. Sit outside to enjoy the magnificent views. 🍴 🎵 Wed–Fri.

Price categories are for a three-course meal for one with half a bottle of wine, including cover charge, service and VAT:

€ under 10
€€ 10–15
€€€ 15–20.5
€€€€ 20.5–30
€€€€€ over 30

LATE OPENING
The kitchen stays open after 10pm, and you can usually have a meal up until at least 11pm.

OUTDOOR TABLES
Tables for eating outdoors, in a garden or on a balcony, often with a pleasant view.

GOOD WINE LIST
The restaurant will have a good selection of quality wines.

CREDIT CARDS
This indicates which of the major credit cards are accepted: *AE* American Express, *DC* Diners Club, *MC* MasterCard and *V* Visa.

	CREDIT CARDS	LATE OPENING	OUTDOOR TABLES	GOOD WINE LIST
CHIADO: *Tágide* €€€€€ Largo da Academia Nacional de Belas Artes 18–20. **Map 7 B5.** 21-347 18 80. An elegant restaurant with 18th-century tiles, a 17th-century fountain and a superb view over the Tagus. Luxurious dishes include marinated salmon, baby octopus in red wine sauce and partridge in port sauce. ● *Sat lunch; Sun.*	AE DC MC V			▪
GRAÇA: *Via Graça* €€€€ Rua Damasceno Monteiro 9b. **Map 8 D1.** 21-887 08 30. Via Graça offers some fine views of the castle and the Baixa, and well-presented Portuguese cuisine. ● *Sat & public hols lunch; Sun.*	AE DC MC V			
LAPA: *Café d'Arte* €€ Rua das Janelas Verdes, Museu de Arte Antiga. **Map 4 D4.** 21-391 28 00. An excellent opportunity to combine lunch with a museum trip in a fantastic riverside setting. ● *Mon; Tue & evenings (closes with museum).*	AE MC V		●	
LAPA: *Picanha* €€€ Rua das Janelas Verdes 96. **Map 4 D4.** 21-397 54 01. Picanha sells one dish: *picanha*, which is rump steak grilled on an open fire, served with potatoes, rice, salad and beans. ● *Sat & Sun lunch; public hols (lunch); 1 Jan, Good Friday, 24 & 25 Dec.*		▪		▪
LAPA: *A Confraria* €€€€ Pensão York House, Rua das Janelas Verdes 32. **Map 4 D4.** 21-396 24 35. This delightful hotel restaurant has a varied menu. Sit inside and admire the tiled walls, or outside below a palm in the flower-laden courtyard.	AE DC MC V		●	▪
LAPA: *Sua Excelência* €€€€ Rua do Conde 34. **Map 4 D3.** 21-390 36 14. The owner here can recite the menu in five languages. Classical Portuguese dishes served in a relaxed atmosphere. ● *Sat lunch.*	AE DC MC V		●	
LAPA: *Ristorante Hotel Cipriani* €€€€€ Lapa Palace, Rua do Pau da Bandeira 4. **Map 3 C3.** 21-394 94 34. This restaurant offers modern Italian and Mediterranean food in an elegant setting. There is a non-smoking section.	AE DC MC V			▪
MARQUÊS POMBAL: *Esplanada Santa Marta* €€€€ Travassa do Enviado de Inglaterra 1d, e, f. 21-352 11 94. Known for its wide range of fish and shellfish dishes, as well as for a good choice of traditional Portuguese fare. During the summer the food is also served outside on a small terrace overlooking the sea.	AE MC V	▪	●	▪
MARQUÊS POMBAL: *Restaurante 33A* €€€€ Rua Alexandre Herculano 33a. **Map 5 C5.** 21-354 60 79. Offering traditional Portuguese cuisine, this restaurant has a small lounge with a country ambience and decor to match. ● *Sat lunch; Sun; public hols.*	AE DC MC V		●	▪
MARQUÊS POMBAL: *Pabe* €€€€€ Rua Duque de Palmela 27a. **Map 5 C5.** 21-353 74 84. Pabe looks like a Tudor house and serves Portuguese food. A medieval atmosphere is accentuated by wooden beams and copper tables. ● *1 May.*	AE DC MC V	▪		▪
PRAÇA DO CHILE: *Cervejaria Portugalia* €€€ Avenida Almirante Reis 117. **Map 6 E5.** 21-314 00 02. This atmospheric beer hall is the original of a small chain (*see p135*), the restaurant serves excellent shellfish and steaks. ● *public hols (lunch).*	AE DC MC V			
PRAÇA ESPANHA: *Adega da Tia Matilde* €€€ Rua da Beneficiência 77. **Map 5 A1.** 21-797 21 72. Known for its hearty Portuguese cuisine and good regional food. Specialities include *arroz frango* (rice with chicken). ● *Dinner Sat, Sun & public hols.*	AE MC V			

PRAÇA ESPANHA: *O Polícia* €€€

Rua Marquês Sá da Bandeira 112a. **Map 5 B3.** 21-796 35 05.

A restaurant with an attractive bar, so named because the owner's grandfather was a policeman. The menu changes daily. Sat eve; Sun; public hols.

	AE
	MC
	V

RATO: *Os Tibetanos* €€

Rua do Salitre 117. **Map 4 F1.** 21-314 20 38.

This vegetarian restaurant, in a Tibetan Buddhist centre, offers a tasty and inexpensive Tibetan menu. No smoking. Sat, Sun; public hols.

	AE	●	
	MC		
	V		

RATO: *Casa da Comida* €€€€

Travessa das Amoreiras 1. **Map 5 B5.** 21-388 53 76.

A refined Lisbon restaurant with a charming patio and a menu offering caviar, frogs' legs, goat, duck and pheasant. Mon & Sat lunch; Sun; public hols.

	AE	■	●	■
	DC			
	MC			
	V			

RESTAURADORES: *Casa do Alentejo* €€

Rua das Portas de Santo Antão 58. **Map 7 A2.** 21-340 51 40.

Set in a fine 19th-century house, this restaurant specializes entirely in Alentejan food such as *açorda alentejana* (coriander and bread soup). 1–19 Aug.

	MC
	V

RESTAURADORES: *Ribadouro* €€€

Rua do Salitre 2–12. **Map 4 F1.** 21-354 94 11.

On the corner of the Avenida da Liberdade in a long, pointed building. Like most, this cervejaria specializes in seafood.

	AE	■
	DC	
	MC	
	V	

RESTAURADORES: *Lagosta Real* €€€€

Rua das Portas de Santo Antão 37. **Map 7 A2.** 21-342 39 95.

Fish, and particularly shellfish, is the order of the day here. Shellfish casserole, lobster stew and a grilled seafood platter are house specialities.

	AE	■	●	■
	DC			
	MC			
	V			

RESTAURADORES: *Solar dos Presuntos* €€€€

Rua das Portas de Santo Antão 150. **Map 7 A2.** 21-342 42 53.

An enticing window display of fish and shellfish draws diners inside. Caricatures of famous footballers adorn the walls. Sun; 15–31 Aug; 1 week at Christmas.

	AE
	DC
	MC
	V

RESTAURADORES: *Gambrinus* €€€€€

Rua das Portas de Santo Antão 23. **Map 7 A2.** 21-342 14 66.

Renowned throughout Portugal, Gambrinus is exceptional and expensive. The extensive wine list includes an array of vintage ports. 1 May, 24 Dec (eve).

	AE	■		■
	V			

SALDANHA: *António* €€

Rua Tomás Ribeiro 63. **Map 5 C3.** 21-353 87 80.

This restaurant is a good stop for lunch. The cooking is straightforward, and includes steak and fries and roast chicken. Sun.

	V	●

SALDANHA: *Isaura* €€€€

Avenida de Paris 4b. **Map 6 E2.** 21-848 08 38.

This 52-year-old restaurant in a red building specializes in fish, with many dishes on the menu based on salt cod. Sat.

	AE			■
	DC			
	MC			
	V			

SALDANHA: *Mezzaluna* €€€€€

Rua Arlilharia 16. **Map 5 A4.** 21-387 99 44.

An attractive, elegant Italian restaurant serving classics like *spaghetti alla carbonara*, as well as pasta with shrimp and lobster. 1 Jan, 25 Dec.

	AE
	DC
	MC
	V

SANTA APOLÓNIA: *Casanova* €€€

Avenida Infante Dom Henrique. **Map 8 D5.** 21-887 75 32.

Housed in a converted warehouse, this is said to be Lisbon's best pizzeria. Italian standards including pastas and salads are also served. Mon, Sat lunch.

	AE	■	●
	MC		
	V		

SANTA APOLÓNIA: *Bica do Sapato* €€€€€

Avenida Infante Dom Henrique, at Cais de Pedra. **Map 8 D5.** 21-881 03 20.

Lisbon's trendiest restaurant serves excellent modern fish dishes. Housed in a converted warehouse, the interior is 1970's retro. Mon lunch, Sun.

	AE	■	●	■
	MC			
	V			

SANTOS: *Kais* €€€€

Cais da Viscondessa, Rua da Cintura do Porto de Lisboa. **Map 4 D4.** 21-342 37 40.

Modern Portuguese and Mediterranean cooking served in a converted engine shed. The interior would not look out of place in a Batman film. Mon.

	AE	■	●	■
	DC			
	MC			
	V			

SÃO BENTO: *Conventual* €€€€

Praça das Flores 44-45. **Map 4 E2.** 21-390 91 96.

Decorated with religious antiques, this restaurant has a menu that includes duck in a rich champagne sauce. Book ahead. Sat lunch; Sun; Aug.

	AE			■
	DC			
	MC			
	V			

Price categories are for a three-course meal for one with half a bottle of wine, including cover charge, service and VAT: €€ under 10 €€ 10–15 €€€ 15–20.5 €€€€ 20.5–30 €€€€€ over 30	**LATE OPENING** The kitchen stays open after 10pm, and you can usually have a meal up until at least 11pm. **OUTDOOR TABLES** Tables for eating outdoors, in a garden or on a balcony, often with a pleasant view. **GOOD WINE LIST** The restaurant will have a good selection of quality wines. **CREDIT CARDS** This indicates which of the major credit cards are accepted: *AE* American Express, *DC* Diners Club, *MC* MasterCard and *V* Visa.		

	CREDIT CARDS	**LATE OPENING**	**OUTDOOR TABLES**	**GOOD WINE LIST**
XABREGAS: *D'Avis* €€€€ Rua do Grilo 96-98. 21-868 13 54. Specialities at this restaurant, located east of the city centre, include cod with coriander and *migas* (bread dish with spare ribs). ● *Sun.* ▤ ♿	AE DC MC V			▨

THE LISBON COAST

	CREDIT CARDS	**LATE OPENING**	**OUTDOOR TABLES**	**GOOD WINE LIST**
CASCAIS: *Dom Manolo* €€ Avenida Marginal 11. 21-483 11 26. A good-value mixed menu; the house speciality is *frango no churrasco* (spit-roast chicken). *Pastéis de bacalhau* (cod croquettes) are also good. ● *Jan.* ▤			●	
CASCAIS: *Estrela da India* €€ Rua Freitas Reis 15b. 21-484 65 40. Some distance from the waterfront, this unpretentious Indian restaurant has a good choice of vegetarian dishes and a takeaway service. ● *25 Dec.* ▤	AE MC V			
CASCAIS: *Os Navegantes* €€€ Travassa dos Navegantes 13. 21-483 23 31. This Portuguese restaurant is very popular with locals and is famous for its fresh fish and spit-roasted meats. ● *Sun.*	AE V	▨		▨
CASCAIS: *Buchanan's Café, Bar and Restaurant* €€€€ Travessa da Alfarrobeira 2. 21-484 75 90. Located on the top floor of a building with stunning views over the new marina. High-quality modern European cuisine is served, with a choice of vegetarian dishes and fine wines. The café/bar has a fireplace. ▤	AE MC V	▨	●	▨
CASCAIS: *Casa Velha* €€€€ Avenida Valbom 1. 21-483 25 86. With a recommended regional menu and charming rustic decor, Casa Velha also boasts a table always reserved for the president. ● *Wed.* ▤ ♿	AE MC V	▨		
CASCAIS: *Eduardo's* €€€€ Largo das Grutas 3. 21-483 19 01. Tucked away in a quiet corner, Eduardo's serves a mix of Belgian cuisine and Portuguese dishes, many of which are flambéed at the table. ● *Wed.*	AE MC V		●	▨
CASCAIS: *O Pescador* €€€€€ Rua das Flores 10b. 21-483 20 54. A well-known seaside restaurant, decorated with old boats, nets and pictures of famous people who have eaten here. Specializes in seafood. ● *Sun.* ▤	AE DC MC V	▨	●	▨
ERICEIRA: *O Barco* €€€ Rua Capitão João Lopes 14. 261-86 27 59. The fish specialities here include *feijoada de marisco* (seafood and bean stew) and seafood curry. ● *Thu; last wk in Jun, 1st wk in Jul & 2 wks before Christmas.* ▤	AE DC MC V			
ESTORIL: *Pinto's* €€€ Arcadas do Parque 18b. 21-468 72 47. Close to the Palácio Hotel, Pinto's is a mix of bar, cafeteria and restaurant. It serves pizzas and pastas, as well as a large selection of shellfish. ● *Thu; 2 weeks before Christmas.* ▤	AE DC MC V	▨	●	
ESTORIL: *Four Seasons* €€€€€ Hotel Palácio Estoril, Rua do Parque. 21-464 80 00. Exposed beams and leather seats furnish this luxurious restaurant. Try the flambéed prawns with Pernod, cream and hollandaise sauce. ▤ ♫ ♿	AE DC MC V			▨
GUINCHO: *Estalagem Muchaxo* €€€€€ Praia do Guincho. 21-487 02 21. Overlooking Cabo da Roca, Muchaxo offers a good seafood menu. A popular dish is lobster in a tomato, cream and port sauce. ▤ ♫ *Sat & Sun lunch.* ♿	AE DC MC V	▨	●	▨

GUINCHO: *Porto de Santa Maria*   €€€€€   AE MC DC V
Estrada do Guincho. **【** 21-487 94 50.
One of the best seafood restaurants in the area. Choose your meal from the fish
tanks and marble table where the best fish is displayed. ● *Mon; 25 Dec.* 🍽 ♿

MONTE ESTORIL: *O Sinaleiro*   €€€   AE MC DC V
Avenida de Sabóia 595. **【** 21-468 54 39.
O Sinaleiro serves excellent food and is popular with locals. Try *escalopes à
Zíngara* (in Madeira wine sauce with cream). ● *Wed; 2 weeks in Apr & Oct.* ♿ 🍽

MONTE ESTORIL: *O Festival*   €€€€   AE MC DC V
Avenida de Sabóia 515d. **【** 21-468 85 63.
This delightful restaurant serves an essentially French menu. Try the duck
à l'orange or the sole filled with salmon mousseline. ● *Sun; Tue lunch.* 🍽

PAÇO D'ARCOS: *La Cocagne*   €€€€€   AE DC MC V
Avenida Marginal (Curva dos Pinheiros). **【** 21-441 42 31.
One of the best French restaurants in Portugal, La Cocagne has refined decor,
impeccable service, exquisite dishes and great views of the ocean. ● *25 Dec.* 🍽

PALMELA: *Pousada de Palmela*   €€€€   AE DC MC V
Pousada de Palmela, Castelo de Palmela. **【** 21-235 12 26.
The converted refectory of the 15th-century monastery offers such delicacies as
oyster soup or salt cod filled with bacon and coated in corn bread. 🎵 *Fri & Sat.*

PORTINHO DA ARRÁBIDA: *Beira-Mar*   €€€€   AE DC MC V
Portinho da Arrábida. **【** 21-218 05 44.
Enjoy specials such as *arroz de tamboril* (monkfish rice) and *arroz de marisco*
(seafood rice) in this stunning seaside setting. ● *Wed (Oct–Mar); 15 Dec–15 Jan.*

QUELUZ: *Cozinha Velha*   €€€€   AE DC MC V
Largo Palácio Nacional de Queluz. **【** 21-435 61 58.
Set in the old kitchens of the Queluz Royal Palace, this spacious restaurant
is famous for its typical Portuguese fare, such as pork with clams. 🍽 🎵

SESIMBRA: *Ribamar*   €€€€   AE MC V
Avenida dos Náufragos 29. **【** 21-223 48 53.
Right next to the sea and offering fantastic views, Ribamar serves some
unusual specialities; try fish with seaweed, or cream of sea-urchin soup. 🍽 ♿

SETÚBAL: *Copa d'Ouro*   €€€€   AE MC V
Rua João Soveral 17. **【** 265-52 37 55.
A superb fish menu here features *caldeirada à Setubalense* (seafood stew)
and *cataplana de tamboril* (monkfish steamed *a cataplana*). ● *Tue; Sep.* 🍽

SETÚBAL: *Pousada de São Filipe*   €€€€   AE DC MC V
Pousada de São Filipe, Castelo de São Filipe. **【** 265-55 00 70.
This restaurant is part of a *pousada* that overlooks Setúbal and the Sado estuary.
Its regional dishes include pumpkin cream soup and fried red mullet. 🍽

SINTRA: *Tulhas*   €€€   AE DC MC V
Rua Gil Vicente 4–6. **【** 21-923 23 78.
This rustic restaurant, decorated with blue and yellow Sintra *azulejos*, serves
superb traditional dishes such as veal steaks in Madeira sauce. ● *Wed.* 🍽

SINTRA: *Lawrence's*   €€€€   AE V
Rua Consiglieri Pedroso 39–40, Sintra. **【** 21-910 55 00.
Set in the Lawrence's Hotel, this restaurant has a wide-ranging international
and Portuguese menu that changes daily. 🍽 ♿

SINTRA: *Panorâmico*   €€€€   AE DC MC V
Hotel Tivoli Sintra, Praça da República. **【** 21-923 35 05.
Overlooking the lush, verdant Sintra valley, this restaurant offers a different
speciality as a main dish each evening, as well as a regular menu. 🍽 ♿

SINTRA: *Restaurante Palácio de Seteais*   €€€€€   AE DC MC V
Avenida Barbosa du Bocage 8, Seteais. **【** 21-923 32 00.
Set in an 18th-century palace, which is now a hotel, this restaurant has a daily-
changing menu of international and traditional Portuguese cuisine. 🎵 ♿

VILA FRESCA DE AZEITÃO: *O Manel*   €€€   AE MC V
Largo Dr Teixeira 6a. **【** 21-219 03 36.
A family-run restaurant with a good-value menu. Specialities here are cod in
cream sauce and *feijoada de gambas* (seafood and bean stew). ● *Sun; Oct.* 🍽

Cafés and Bars

THE PORTUGUESE LOVE COFFEE, and an entire culture has developed around it (see p121). Relaxing over a coffee and a pastry in a café is a way of life in Lisbon.

Some of the most famous and delicious pastries served include *travesseiros* (almond pastries) and *bolos de arroz* (rice cakes). Belém is famous for its *pastéis de nata*, custard pastries, while Sintra is renowned for its *queijadas*, cinnamon cheesecakes (see p123). There is a good selection of bars and restaurants in Bairro Alto and along the riverfront, many with pleasant views.

Evening drinking is equally popular, and Lisbon and its coast offer a range of night-time venues, from sophisticated bars serving wine and cocktails to brasher venues pumping out beer and live music.

On the Lisbon Coast, there are many bars in central Cascais and plenty of cafés along the seafront promenade. Sintra's cafés are rightly famous for their fine selection of mouthwatering pastries.

LISBON

ALFAMA: *Bar Cerca Moura*
Largo das Portas do Sol 4.
Map 8 D3. 21-887 48 59.
A pleasant place for a drink, the bar has a wonderful panoramic view of Alfama and the river below. Mainly serves snacks such as salads and finger food.

ALFAMA: *Bar das Imagens*
Calçada Marquês de Tancos 1b.
Map 7 C3. 21-888 46 36.
This bar, with tables on the sloping pavement outside, has a great view over downtown Lisbon. The atmosphere is trendy but pleasurably relaxed.

ALFAMA: *Restô do Chapitô*
Costa do Castelo 7. **Map** 7 C3.
21-886 73 34.
With superb views of the Alfama and the river, this lively bar also has a restaurant that serves exciting and innovative cuisine.

BAIRRO ALTO: *Frágil*
Rua Atalaia 126. **Map** 4 F2.
21-346 95 78.
A cutting-edge dance club that attracts international DJs and musical acts. Closed Sun & Mon.

BAIRRO ALTO: *Mesón El Gordo Tapas Bar*
Rua São Boaventura 16–18.
Map 4 F2. 21-342 42 66.
This tastefully decorated bar and restaurant has a selection of 73 different *tapas*. Portuguese and Spanish wines are served by the glass.

BAIRRO ALTO: *Pavilhão Chinês*
Rua Dom Pedro V 89. **Map** 4 F2.
21-342 47 29.
One of Lisbon's best-known bars is decorated with collections of both mundane and curious artefacts from all over the world.

BAIRRO ALTO: *Bar Pintaí*
Largo da Trindade 22. **Map** 7 A3.
21-342 48 02.
There is live Brazilian music daily in this large cavernous bar and plentiful *caipirinha*, a drink made of *cachaça* (sugar cane spirit), lime, sugar and crushed ice.

BAIRRO ALTO: *Solar do Vinho do Porto*
Rua de São Pedro de Alcântara 45.
Map 4 F2. 21-347 57 07.
Set in an old mansion (see p54), this establishment serves a wide range of different ports, including some fine vintages.

BAIRRO ALTO: *Tertúlia*
Rua do Diário de Notícias 60.
Map 7 A4. 21-346 27 04.
This tranquil café and bar has reasonably priced drinks and offers a selection of newspapers and magazines. Art exhibitions are also held here.

BAIXA: *A Ginjinha*
Largo de São Domingos 8.
Map 7 B3. 21-388 08 50.
The smallest bar in Lisbon, off Rossio, is dedicated entirely to serving shots of a *ginjinha* (cherry liqueur) and nothing else.

BAIXA: *Café Martinho da Arcada*
Praça do Comércio 3. **Map** 7 C5.
21-886 62 13.

A traditional Lisbon café under the arches of Praça do Comércio, it was once frequented by Fernando Pessoa (see p53).

BAIXA: *Café Nicola*
Praça Dom Pedro IV 24–25.
Map 7 B3. 21-346 05 79.
One of Lisbon's oldest and most famous terraced cafés, this is a charming spot for breakfast, served by smart waiters. It is famous as the haunt of the satirical poet Manuel du Bocage (1765–1805). Wall paintings inside the café illustrate his life.

BAIXA: *Cén de Lisboa*
Alto do Elevador de Santa Justa.
Map 7 B3. 966 584 983.
Situated at the top of the Santa Justa lift, the Chiadomel serves drinks and rather pricey snacks.

BAIXA: *Confeitaria Nacional*
Praça da Figueira 18b. **Map** 7 B3.
21-342 44 70.
This classic café has wonderful Art Nouveau decor. Pastries and cakes baked on the premises include good *pastéis de nata* and *bolo rei*.

BAIXA: *Pastelaria Suiça*
Praça Dom Pedro IV 96–101.
Map 7 B3. 21-321 40 90.
A good place to have breakfast outdoors before a day of sight-seeing, this café serves a wide variety of pastries. Overlooking the square, it is popular with Lisboetas stopping off on their way to work.

BELÉM: *Antiga Casa dos Pastéis de Belém*
Rua de Belém 84–88. **Map** 1 C4.
21-363 74 23.
A trip to Belém is not complete without visiting this charming tiled café to sample its delicious *pastéis de nata* and excellent coffees.

CAIS DO SODRE: *O'Gilins*
Rua dos Remolares 8.
Map 7 A5. 21-342 18 99.
This Irish-style pub has a wooden interior. The atmosphere is lively, especially on band nights. Irish stouts and other beers are available.

CAMPO PEQUENO: *Galeto*
Avenida da República 14.
Map 5 C1. 21-354 44 44.
A restaurant and snack bar on two floors, Galeto is a good place to visit for a late night snack as it serves food into the early hours.

CAMPO PEQUENO: *Versailles*
Avenida da República 15a. **Map** 5 C1.
[21-354 63 40.
A well-known, turn-of-the-century restaurant café, the Versailles is ornately decorated in the Parisian style. Smartly attired waiters serve lunches, teas and dinners to a well-heeled clientele. **[H]**

CHIADO: *A Brasileira*
Rua Garrett 120. **Map** 7 A4.
[21-346 95 41.
This is one of Lisbon's oldest and best-known cafés. Founded in 1895, it became a haunt for artists and poets and continues to draw artists and media types. **[H] [ ]**

CHIADO: *Amo-te Chiado*
Rua Nova do Almada 105.
Map 7 B4. **[** 21-092 70 10.
This establishment is frequented by Lisbon's artistic community.

CHIADO: *Café Pastelaria Bénard*
Rua Garrett 104. **Map** 7 A4.
[21-347 31 33.
This café serves an excellent selection of cakes and pastries. It also has an outdoor terrace. **[ ]**

CHIADO: *Cervejaria Trindade*
Rua Nova da Trindade 20c.
Map 7 A4. **[** 21-342 35 06.
A huge beer hall-style restaurant with beautiful *azulejo* panels, it specializes in seafood. **[H]**

DOCAS: *Doca de Santo*
Doca de Santo Amaro. **Map** 3 A5.
[21-396 35 22.
This is one of several warehouses along the marina which have been converted into a bar. The terrace has a wonderful view of the marina and river. **[H] [ ]**

DOCAS: *Doca 6*
Doca de Santo Amaro, Arm. 6.
Map 3 A5. **[** 21-395 79 05.
A justifiably popular bar and restaurant, Doca 6 has a terrace with views over the marina. **[ ] [H]**

DOCAS: *Salsa Latina*
Gare Marítima de Alcântara 30.
Map 3 B4. **[** 21-395 05 55.
This smart bar and restaurant with a terrace overlooking the river, caters to an affluent crowd. Salsa and Latin music are played most evenings. **[H] [ ] [♫]**

GRAÇA: *Chapitô*
Costa do Castelo 1–7.
[21-886 73 34.
Chapitô is Lisbon's circus school, but its bar welcomes everybody. Great views from the terrace and an entertaining programme of creative events. **[H] [ ]**

PRAÇA DO CHILE: *Portugália*
Avenida Almirante Reis 117.
Map 6 E5. **[** 21-314 00 02.
Although there are now several Portugalias in Lisbon, this is the original. Popular with families, this is a classic beer-hall with a bar offering snacks and a restaurant with reasonably priced hearty meals in the back *(see p131).* **[H]**

PRÍNCIPE REAL: *Enoteca*
Rua da Mãe d'Água. **Map** 4 F1.
[21-342 20 79.
Lisbon's first and only wine bar is an excellent place to sample the country's best wines and ports. Imaginative snacks are also served.

RATO: *Real Fábrica*
Rua da Escola Politécnica 275.
Map 4 E1. **[** 21-385 20 90.
A tastefully renovated old ceramic factory on two floors. The bar on the ground floor serves beers and snacks. There is a smart restaurant on the upper floor. **[H] [ ]**

THE LISBON COAST

CASCAIS: *Bar 24*
Rua Marquês Leal Pancada 24.
[21-482 12 71.
One of the tiniest bars in town, with trendy decor, Bar 24 attracts a young crowd and can get quite packed. It offers a great range of alcoholic drinks.

CASCAIS: *Bar Trem Velho*
Alameda Duquesa de Palmela.
[21-486 73 55.
This relaxed bar is in a converted train carriage next to Cascais train station. Serves snacks and litre mugs of beer called *girafas.* **[H]**

CASCAIS: *Beefeaters*
Rua Visconde da Luz 1a.
[21-484 06 96.
This bar serves English ales, Dutch beer and Guinness among other beers. Also offers traditional British pub food. **[H] [ ]**

CASCAIS: *Casa do Largo*
Largo da Assunção 6.
[21-483 18 56.
The Casa do Largo is a favourite haunt of the fashionable Cascais population of all ages. Set in an old house and decorated with pictures of boats and other nautical themes. **[H] [ ]**

CASCAIS: *John Bull*
Largo Luís de Camões 4.
[21-483 33 19.
A British institution with wooden interiors on two floors, the John Bull serves a variety of local and foreign, especially British, beers on tap. **[H] [ ]**

ESTORIL: *Deck Bar*
Arcadas do Parque 21–22.
[21-468 03 66.
One of Estoril's most popular terraced cafés, the Deck Bar is situated under arches opposite elegant gardens. Serves meals till 1am. Closed Mondays. **[H] [ ]**

ESTORIL: *Rasputine Bar*
Rua Bartolomeu Gusmão 24.
[21-467 12 53.
A popular bar/disco with a relaxed, informal atmosphere and live music. Closed Mon & Wed. **[♫]**

ESTORIL: *Tamariz Bar*
Praia do Tamariz.
[21-468 10 10.
A lively, terraced bar overlooking Praia do Tamariz, the Tamariz Bar is a venue for live music every weekend. Serves salads, burgers and a variety of drinks including *caipirinhas* and jugs of *sangria.* Only open during summer months. **[ ] [♫]**

SINTRA: *Café da Natália*
Rua 1° de Dezembro 3–5, São Pedro de Sintra. **[** 21-923 56 79.
This old manor house, converted into an airy café, serves local food and wines. Dona Natália is known for her delicious quiches and crepes. Closed Sundays. **[H]**

SINTRA: *Café Paris*
Largo Rainha Dona Amélia 32.
[21-923 23 75.
An elegant, terraced café located on the main square opposite the Palácio Nacional, Café Paris is also open for lunches and dinners. **[H] [ ]**

SINTRA: *Casa da Sapa*
Volta do Duche 12.
[21-923 04 93.
A tiny cake shop, it has been baking its famous *queijadas* (cinnamon cheesecakes) since the mid-18th century. Lovely view of the Sintra valley. **[ ]**

SINTRA: *Pastelaria Piriquita*
Rua das Padarias 1–3.
[21-923 06 26.
One of Sintra's oldest cafés, it is situated on a narrow street opposite the Palácio Nacional. Serves good *queijadas* and *travesseiros* (almond pastries).

SINTRA: *Restaurante Café Cintia*
Avenida Miguel Bombarda 49.
[21-923 27 12.
A typical Portuguese café with a dark interior, it offers a glorious view of the Sintra valley and serves excellent *travesseiros.* **[H] [ ]**

For key to symbols see back flap

SHOPS AND MARKETS

LISBON offers a wide variety of shops to the visitor, with its combination of elegant high street shops, flea markets and modern shopping centres. The cobbled streets of the Baixa, and the chic Chiado district have traditionally been Lisbon's main shopping areas, but the numerous indoor shopping centres are becoming increasingly popular.

Portuguese ceramic cockerel

Markets in Lisbon, Sintra and Cascais provide more adventurous shopping. If you are after something typically Portuguese, the hand-woven tapestries and lacework are worth buying. Most of all, choose from a range of ceramics, such as *azulejos* or Vista Alegre porcelain. For lovers of wine, Lisbon's wine merchants offer the best from all over the country.

A delicatessen in the Bairro Alto

OPENING HOURS

TRADITIONAL SHOPPING hours are Monday to Friday 9am to 1pm and 3pm to 7pm, and Saturday 9am to 1pm.

However, in order to satisfy consumer demand, many shops, especially those in the Baixa, are now staying open during the lunch hour and on Saturday afternoons. Specialist shops such as hardware stores generally close for lunch at 12:30pm and reopen at 2:30pm. Shopping centres are open daily from 10am to midnight with most shops closing at 11pm. Generally, convenience stores, such as the **Select** chain, are open daily from 7am to 2am.

HOW TO PAY

MOST SHOPS in Lisbon accept Visa and, to a lesser extent, American Express and MasterCard. Many smaller shops outside the main shopping areas will not. An alternative is to obtain a cash advance with a credit card from one of the many Multibanco teller machines (ATMs). Note that these charge interest on the withdrawal from day one, in addition to a currency conversion fee.

VAT AND TAXES

NON-EUROPEAN UNION residents are exempt from IVA (Value Added Tax) in Portugal provided they remain in the country for no longer than 180 days. However, obtaining a rebate may be complicated in small shops or in areas less frequented by tourists. It is much simpler to buy in shops with a Tax Free sign outside.

To get your rebate, ask the shop assistant for an *Isenção na Exportação* form. This must then be presented to a customs officer on your departure from Portugal. The original of the document will be returned to the vendor who is responsible for the reimbursement.

SHOPPING CENTRES

LARGE SHOPPING CENTRES are now very much part of the shopping landscape in Lisbon. They combine vast supermarkets, international chain stores and small specialist shops. All have restaurants and underground car parks; most also have cinemas. The oldest and best-known is **Amoreiras**, which has 300 shops, 10 cinemas and 50 restaurants. **Galerias Monumental** is one of three smaller centers clustered near Praça Duque de Saldanha. **Armazéns do Chiado** in the Chiado area has an historic façade but a modern interior. The huge **Centro Columbo** in Benfica boasts a large children's leisure centre. The **Vasco da Gama** centre connects Oriente staton with Parque das Naçoes. The Spanish **El Corte Inglés** is at the top of Parque Eduardo VII. **Cascaishopping**, located between Estoril and Sintra, is one of many suburban centres.

The vast Amoreiras Shopping Centre, home to international chain stores

Shoppers browsing among the bric-a-brac in the popular Feira da Ladra

MARKETS

THERE ARE markets of every variety in Lisbon, from municipal markets selling fresh produce to the famous **Feira da Ladra** (Thieves' Market), a flea market on the slopes of the Alfama district. Although some stalls just sell junk, some bargains can be found among the array of bric-a-brac, second-hand clothes and general arts and crafts.

For more specialized markets, the **Feira Numismática** in Praça do Comércio has a fascinating selection of old Portuguese coins and notes. Located at Oriente rail station are the **Feira de Antiguidades E Velharias**, an antiques market, and the **Feira dos Alfarrabistas**, for old books. Set in picturesque surroundings outside Lisbon, the **Feira de São Pedro**, in Sintra, is a wonderful market selling everything from new clothes and old bric-a-brac, to maturing cheeses and cackling fowl.

Along the coast, the **Feira de Cascais** has some good clothes bargains, as does the **Feira de Carcavelos**. Arrive early to beat the crowds.

FOOD SHOPS

IT IS ALMOST IMPOSSIBLE to window shop in Lisbon's delicatessens (charcutarias) without buying. Lined with a vast array of mouth watering foods, from superb cheeses to tasty smoked meats and exquisite sweets, establishments such as **Charcutaria Brasil** are a must for all seasoned gourmets. Here you can buy almost all regional specialities, from cheeses such as serra and ilhas to wild game such as partridge. Smoked hams and spicy sausages are also popular. If you have a sweet tooth, try some delicious ovos moles (egg sweets) or an assortment of dried or crystallized fruits, including delicious Elvas plums.

Other good food shops include **Charcutaria Carvalho & Morais** and **Manuel Tavares**, which has a large selection of port and madeira. **Celeiro Dieta** is a good health food shop, and is well-known for stocking organic foods.

WINES AND SPIRITS

PORTUGAL HAS A large variety of wines, fortified wines and spirits, amply represented in Lisbon's specialist shops. From light vinhos verdes to powerful tintos (reds), from fruity young ruby ports to ancient tawny ports or madeira, from sweet amêndoa amarga (bitter almond liqueur) to fiery bagaceira (grapeskin distillate).

Napoleão, the best-known wine merchants in Lisbon, has outlets in many parts of the city, with its oldest shop in the Baixa. For port specifically, visit the **Solar do Vinho do Porto** (see p54), in Bairro Alto: this slightly fusty institution is actually a bar where you can sample a vast range of ports before deciding what to buy. **Garrafeira de Campo de Ourique** is one of Lisbon's best smaller wine merchants, and **Coisas do Arco do Vinho** has a good selection. Alternatively, large supermarkets are good for bargains, with frequent special offers on wines and spirits. You could visit the cellars of **J.M. da Fonseca** in Azeitão, where you can taste and buy many of the wines.

Fresh fish for sale at one of Lisbon's municipal markets

MUSIC AND MULTIMEDIA

THE MUSIC SCENE in Portugal is a lively mix of traditions and the very latest. Fado music remains hugely popular, while techno and trance dance music have a dedicated following. Lisbon is also an important centre for newer music from former African colonies such as Cape Verde.

FNAC operates two megastores in Lisbon, and these are widely regarded as the city's best music shops in terms of variety. FNAC also sells most kinds of electronic hardware and software, as well as books. **Valentim de Carvalho** is a chain of music shops with outlets all over the city. **Discoteca Amália** in the Baixa specialises in fado.

Frontage of Livraria Bertrand, one of Lisbon's oldest bookshops

BOOKSHOPS

PORTUGAL ENJOYS a great literary tradition with a range of authors, past and present, including Luís de Camões, Eça de Queiróz, Fernando Pessoa and José Saramago. Translations of their works, and those of other well-known Portuguese writers, are available in most large bookshops.

Livraria Bertrand and **Livraria Portugal**, both in the Chiado, are among Lisbon's oldest bookshops. **Livraria Buchholz** near the top of Avenida da Liberdade, was founded by a German and has a particularly large section of books in languages other than Portuguese, including travel guides, paperback fiction and history.

For an interesting selection of second-hand books, try visiting the **Feira dos Alfarrabistas** market, held at Oriente railway station on the first Sunday of every month.

Terracotta ware for sale in Setúbal

CLOTHES

MANY OF THE large chain stores, have outlets in Lisbon, particularly in the shopping centres (see p136). Perhaps most noticeable is the Spanish Zara chain, whose shops sell affordable clothes for everyone.

More exclusive shops, including designer outlets, can be found on and around Avenida da Liberdade. **Rosa & Teixeira**, sells classic mens-wear, **Loja das Meias** is a mid-range chain with several shops. **Ana Salazar** is one of an increasing number of known Portuguese designers.

CERAMICS

PORTUGAL'S CERAMICS are famous for their quality and variety. In Lisbon you can find everything, from delicate porcelain to rustic terracotta, and from tiles to tableware.

The very fine **Vista Alegre** porcelain tableware is inter-nationally known. Also famous are the hand-painted ceramics, including tiles from **Viúva Lamego**, **Santana** and **Cerâmica Artística de Carcavelos**. Known as *azu-lejos*, glazed tiles have long been used in Portugal to brighten up buildings. They may be plain, patterned or make up large figurative paint-ings. In Cascais, **Ceramicarte** is one of the largest ceramic centres. Perhaps the most ubi-quitous pottery originates from Barcelos, famous for its decoratively painted cockerel which has become the un-official national symbol.

REGIONAL CRAFTS

PORTUGAL HAS a rich history of fine regional craftwork (*artesanato*), in particular embroidery and fine lace, hand-knitted woolens, and delicate jewellery made from silver and gold thread. There are plenty of handicraft and gift shops in the Restauradores and Rossio areas of Lisbon, though these can be a little touristy. **Arte Rustica**, in the Baixa, is excellent for genuine crafts.

Regionália, in Estoril, and **Sintra Bazar** in central Sintra, are also both good for arts. Between July and August a wide variety of crafts can be seen at the **Estoril Craft Fair**, at which artisans from all over Portugal gather to exhibit their work. **Casa Quintão** specializes in fine hand-woven carpets and tapestries. Cork carvings and pottery can be found at **Santos Ofícios**.

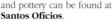
Lisbon offers regional crafts from all over Portugal

ANTIQUES

ANTIQUES OFTEN TEND to be overpriced in Portugal, especially in Lisbon where the shops are mostly geared to a fairly up-market clientele. You will generally find better value in towns outside the city. Look for shops that are members of APA (*Associação Portuguesa de Antiquários*), often indicated by a sign in the shop window.

The majority of Lisbon's antique shops, such as **Antiguidades Moncada**, are located either in Rua Dom Pedro V, at the top of the Bairro Alto, or in Rua de São Bento, by the Parliament building, and around the cathedral, in the Alfama. There are numerous religious artefacts to be found in the area and **Solar** specializes in 16th– 20th-century tiles (*azulejos*).

Beautiful prints (known as *gravuras*), sold at various second-hand bookshops in the Bairro Alto, are usually good value for money. **Livraria Olisipo** stocks books and also old prints of land-scapes, fauna and maps. For a good range of quality antiques, it is worth visiting the auc-tions held at **Cabral Moncada Leilões** (every Monday even-ing) and also the Antiques Fair, which is held in Lisbon annually during April.

SIZE CHART

Lisbon uses both British and American systems.

Women's dresses, coats and skirts

Portuguese	34	36	38	40	42	44	46
British	8	10	12	14	16	18	20
American	6	8	10	12	14	16	18

Women's shoes

Portuguese	36	37	38	39	40	41
British	3	4	5	6	7	8
American	5	6	7	8	9	10

Men's suits

Portuguese	44	46	48	50	52	54	56	58
British	34	36	38	40	42	44	46	48
American	34	36	38	40	42	44	46	48

Men's shirts

Portuguese	36	38	39	41	42	43	44	45
British	14	15	15½	16	16½	17	17½	18
American	14	15	15½	16	16½	17	17½	18

Men's shoes

Portuguese	39	40	41	42	43	44	45	46
British	6	7	7½	8	9	10	11	12
American	7	7½	8	8½	9½	10½	11	11½

DIRECTORY

SHOPPING CENTRES

Amoreiras
Avenida Eng. Duarte Pacheco, Amoreiras.
Map 5 A5.
21-381 02 00.
w www.amoreiras.com

Armazéns do Chiado
Rua do Carmo 2, Chiado. **Map** 7 B4.
21-321 06 00.

Cascaishopping
Estrada Nacional 9, Alcabideche - Estoril.
21-467 90 78.

Centro Colombo
Avenida Lusíada Benfica.
21-711 36 00/36.
w www.colombo.pt

El Corte Inglés
Avenida António Augusto Aguiar 31. **Map** 5 B5.
21-371.17 00.
w www.elcorteingles.pt

Galerias Monumental
Avenida Fontes Pereira de Melo 51, Saldanha.
Map 5 C4.
21-351 05 00.

Vasco da Gama
Avenida Dom João ll, Parque das Nações.
21-893 06 90.

MARKETS

Feira dos Alfarrabistas
Estação Oriente.

Feira de Antiguidades Velharas
Estação Oriente.

Feira de Carcavelos
Carcavelos.

Feira de Cascais
Cascais.

Feira da Ladra
Alfama. **Map** 8 E3.

Feira Numismática
Praça do Comércio.
Map 7 C5.

Feira de São Pedro
Sintra.

FOOD SHOPS

Celeiro Dieta
Rua 1º de Dezembro 65, Rossio. **Map** 7 B3.
21-342 24 63.

Charcutaria Brasil
Rua Alexandre Herculano 90–92, Rato. **Map** 5 C5.
21-388 56 44.

Charcutaria Carvalho and Morais
Avenida João XXI 54, Areeiro. **Map** 6 E1.
21-797 34 12.

Manuel Tavares
Rua da Betesga 1, Baixa. **Map** 7 B3.
21-342 42 09.

WINES AND SPIRITS

Coisas do Arco do Vinho
Centro Cultural de Belém.
Map 1 B5.
21-364 20 31.

Garrafeira de Campo de Ourique
Rua Tomás de Anunciação 29a, Campo de Ourique.
21-397 34 94.

J.M. da Fonseca
Vila Nogueira de Azeitão, Azeitão.
21-219 75 00.

Napoleão
Rua dos Fanqueiros 72–6, Baixa. **Map** 7 C4.
21-887 20 42.

Solar do Vinho do Porto
Rua São Pedro de Alcântara 45, Bairro Alto.
Map 7 A3.
21-347 57 07.
w www.ivp.pt

MUSIC AND MULTIMEDIA

Discoteca Amália
Rua do Ouro, 272.
Baixa. **Map** 7 B4.
21-342 09 39.

FNAC
Rua Nova do Almada 102, Chiado. **Map** 7 B4
21-322 18 00.

Velentim de Carvalho
Centro Cultural de Belém.
Map 1 B5.
21-362 63 65.

BOOKSHOPS

Livraria Bertrand
Rua Garrett 73, Chiado.
Map 7 A4.
21-346 86 46.

Livraria Buchholz
Rua Duque de Palmela 4, Marquês Pombal. **Map** 5 C5.
21-317 05 80.

Livraria Portugal
Rua do Carmo 70–74, Chiado. **Map** 7 B4.
21-347 49 82.

CLOTHES

Ana Salazar
Rua do Carmo 85–87, Chiado. **Map** 7 B3.
21-347 22 89.

Loja das Meias
Praça Dom Pedro IV 1, Rossio. **Map** 7 B3.
21-347 41 80.

Rosa & Teixeira
Avenida da Liberdade 204, Avenida. **Map** 5 C5.
21-311 03 50.

Zara
Rua Garrett 1, Chiado.
Map 7 B4.
21-324 37 10.

CERAMICS

Cerâmica Artística de Carcavelos
Avenida Loureiro 47b, Carcavelos.
21-456 32 67.

Ceramicarte
Largo da Assunção 3–4, Cascais. 21-484 01 70.

Santana
Rua do Alecrim 95, Chiado. **Map** 7 A5.
21-342 25 37.

Vista Alegre
Largo do Chiado 20–21, Chiado. **Map** 7 A4.
21-346 14 01.

Viúva Lamego
Calçada do Sacramento 29, Chiado. **Map** 7 B4.
21-346 96 92.

REGIONAL CRAFTS

Arte Rústica
Rua do Ouro 246–8, Baixa. **Map** 7 B4.
21-342 11 27.

Casa Quintão
Rua Serpa Pinto12, Chiado. **Map** 7 A4.
21-346 58 37.

Regionália
Arcadas do Parque 27, Estoril.
21-468 16 19.

Santos Ofícios
Rua da Madalena 87, Baixa. **Map** 7 C4
21-887 20 31.

Sintra Bazar
Praça da República 37, Sintra.
21-924 82 45.

ANTIQUES

Antiguidades Moncada
Rua Dom Pedro V 34, Bairro Alto. **Map** 4 F2.
21-346 82 95.

Cabral Moncada Leilões
Rua Miguel Lupi, 12, Estrela. **Map** 4 E2.
21-395 47 81.

Livraria Olisipo
Largo Trindade Coelho 7–8, Bairro Alto. **Map** 7 A3.
21-346 27 71.

Solar
Rua Dom Pedro V 68–70, Bairro Alto. **Map** 4 F2.
21-346 55 22.

ENTERTAINMENT IN LISBON

For a smallish European capital, Lisbon has a good and varied cultural calendar. Musical events range from classical and opera performances to intimate fado evenings, and large rock concerts. Dance, both classical and modern, is well represented in Lisbon. The Gulbenkian Foundation, long the only major arts patron, has been joined by other private funds as well as state institutions.

Football is a consuming passion of the Portuguese, and Lisbon's Sporting and Benfica teams play regularly at home. Lisbon outparties many larger capitals, with a nightlife known for its liveliness.

BOOKING TICKETS

Tickets can be reserved by phoning the Agência de Bilhetes para Espectáculos Públicos (**ABEP**). Pay in cash when you collect them from the kiosk. Some cinemas and theatres accept phone or credit card bookings – it is best to check first.

ABEP kiosk selling tickets on Praça dos Restauradores

LISTINGS MAGAZINES

Previews of forthcoming events and listings of bars and clubs appear weekly in major newspapers. English-language events publications include the monthly *Follow Me Lisboa* and the quarterly *Lisboa Step By Step*, which are available free from tourist offices. The monthly *Agenda Cultural* is in Portuguese.

CINEMA AND THEATRE

Movie-goers are very well served in Lisbon. Films are shown in their original language with Portuguese subtitles, and tickets are inexpensive. On Mondays most cinemas offer reductions. The city's traditional cinemas have now largely given way to modern multiplexes, usually in shopping centres such as Amoreiras or El Corte Inglés (*see p139*). While these screen mainstream Hollywood fare,

cinemas such as **King Triplex** show more European films. Classics and retrospectives can be seen at the **Cinemateca Portuguesa**, whose monthly programme is available at tourist offices.

Theatre performances are most often in Portuguese, but large institutions such as the **Teatro Nacional Dona Maria II** and the **Teatro da Trindade** occasionally stage guest performances by visiting companies. Less formally, **Chapitô** sometimes has open-air shows.

CLASSICAL MUSIC, OPERA AND DANCE

Lisbon's top cultural centres are the modern **Centro Cultural de Belém** (*see p68*) and the **Fundação Calouste Gulbenkian** (*see pp76–9*). They host a variety of national and international events including concerts and ballet. **The Teatro Nacional de São Carlos** is Portugal's national opera, with a season that mixes its own productions with guest performances. The **Coliseu dos Recreios** has no institution attached and so offers a variety of events.

Performance at the Chapitô circus school, Alfama

WORLD MUSIC, JAZZ, POP AND ROCK

Lisbon's musical soul may be *fado* (*see pp142–3*), but the city is no stranger to other forms of musical expression. African music, particularly that of former Portuguese colony Cape Verde, plays an big part in Lisbon's music scene. Venues include **B.Leza** and **Enclave**, both have frequent live performances.

The **Hot Clube** has been Lisbon's foremost jazz venue for as long as anyone can

The house orchestra playing at the Fundação Calouste Gulbenkian

Musician at Pé Sujo

remember, and has the right intimate atmosphere. **Speakeasy** is younger, slightly bigger, and varies live jazz with up-tempo blues, particularly at weekends.

Large rock and pop concerts are held at outdoor venues such as **Praça Sony** and football stadiums, or indoors at **Pavilhão Atlântico** or Coliseu dos Recreios.

NIGHTCLUBS

BAIRRO ALTO remains a lively area for Lisbon nightlife, although its mostly small bars don't usually have dance floors or keep very late hours. There are exceptions, including the doyen of Bairro Alto clubs, **Frágil**, and the recent DJ club **V Imperium**.

Among the larger and more mainstream dance venues are **Kremlin** and **Kapital**; the first a nearly historic house club, the second a very middle-of-the-road disco.

Farther westward by the Doca de Santo Amaro marina is the attractively housed **Salsa Latina**, one of Lisbon's few salsa places. Inland, in the Alcântara area, are **W** and **Alcântara Club**, while eastwards along the river near Santa Apolónia station, is **Lux**,

the cream of Lisbon's current club scene.

Details of recommended bars in Lisbon, Estoril, Cascais and Sintra can be found on pages 134–5.

SPECTATOR SPORTS

PORTUGAL IS HOSTING the 2004 European Football Championship, and Lisbon's two main teams, Sporting and Benfica, are both building new stadiums for the event. The Portuguese football cup finals, as well as other events such as the Estoril Open tennis tournament, are held at the **Estádio Nacional-Jamor**. The Pavilhão Atlântico is also used for indoor events such as tennis, volleyball and basketball. Estoril's **Autódromo** Fernanda Pires da Silva is a motor racing venue.

DIRECTORY

BOOKING TICKETS

ABEP
Praça dos Restauradores.
Map 7 A2.
☎ 21-347 58 24.

FNAC
Centro Colombo.
☎ 21-711 42 37.

CINEMA AND THEATRE

Cinemateca Portuguesa
Rua Barata Salgueiro 39.
Map 5 C5.
☎ 21-359 62 62.

Chapitô
Costa do Castelo 7. **Map** 7 C3. ☎ 21-886 73 34.

King Triplex
Avenida Frei Miguel Contreiras 52a. **Map** 6 E1.
☎ 21-848 08 08.

Teatro da Trindade
Rua Nova da Trindade 9.
Map 7 A3.
☎ 21-342 32 00.

Teatro Nacional Dona Maria II
Praça Dom Pedro IV. **Map** 7 B3. ☎ 21-325 08 00.

CLASSICAL MUSIC, OPERA AND DANCE

Centro Cultural de Belém
Praça do Império. **Map** 1 C5. ☎ 21-361 24 00.

Coliseu dos Recreios
Rua das Portas de Santo Antão 92. **Map** 7 A2.
☎ 21-324 05 80.

Fundação Calouste Gulbenkian
Avenida de Berna 45.
Map 5 B2.
☎ 21-782 30 00.

Teatro Camões
Parque das Nações.
☎ 21-892 34 70.

Teatro Nacional de São Carlos
Rua Serpa Pinto 9. **Map** 7 A4. ☎ 21-325 30 00.

WORLD MUSIC, JAZZ, POP AND ROCK

B. Leza
Largo do Conde Barão 50.
Map 4 E3.
☎ 21-396 37 35.

Enclave
Rua do Sol ao Rato 71A.
Map 4 D1.
☎ 21-388 87 38.

Hot Clube
Praça da Alegria 38–9. **Map** 4 F1. ☎ 21-346 73 69.

Pavilhão Atlântico
Parque das Nações.
☎ 21-891 84 09.

Praça Sony
Parque das Nações.
☎ 21-891 90 00.

Speakeasy
Cais das Oficinas, Armazém 115, Rocha Conde d'Óbidos. **Map** 4 D4.
☎ 21-395 73 08

NIGHTCLUBS

Alcântara Club
Rua da Cozinha Económica 11. ☎ 21-346 52 50.

Frágil
Rua da Atalaia 128. **Map** 4 F2. ☎ 21-346 95 78.

Kapital
Avenida 24 de Julho 68.
Map 4 E3.
☎ 21-395 71 01.

Kremlin
Escadinhas da Praia 5. **Map** 4 D3. ☎ 21-395 71 01.

Lux
Avenida Infante Dom Henrique. **Map** 8 D5.
☎ 21-882 08 90.

Salsa Latina
Gare Marítima de Alcântara. **Map** 3 A5/B5.
☎ 21-395 05 55.

V Imperium
Calçada do Tijolo 8. **Map** 4 F2. ☎ 96-743 03 03.

W
Rua Maria Luísa Holstein 13. **Map** 3 A4.
☎ 21-363 68 30.

SPORTS

Autódromo Estoril
Alcabideche.
☎ 21-469 14 62.

Estádio José Alvalade
(Sporting) Rua Francisco Stromp 2.
☎ 21-756 79 30.

Estádio da Luz
(Benfica) Avenida General Norton Matos 1500.
☎ 21-862 70 00.

Estádio Nacional-Jamor
Cruz Quebrada
☎ 21-419 72 12.

Fado: the Music of Lisbon

L IKE THE BLUES, *fado* is an expression of longing and sorrow. Literally meaning "fate", the term may be applied to an individual song as well as the genre itself. The music owes much to the concept known as *saudade*, meaning a longing both for what has been lost, and for what has never been attained, which perhaps accounts for its emotional power. The people of Lisbon have nurtured this poignant music in back-street cafés and restaurants for over 150 years, and it has altered little in that time. It is sung as often by women as men, always accompanied by the *guitarra* and *viola* (acoustic Spanish guitar). *Fado* from Coimbra has developed its own lighter-hearted style.

A guitarra accompanist

A graphic depiction of the music's low-life associations from the 1920s

Maria Severa (1810–36) was the first great fadista and the subject of the first Portuguese sound film in 1931. Her scandalous life and early death are pivotal to fado history, and her spiritual influence has been enormous, inspiring fados, poems, novels and plays.

All female *fadistas* wear a black shawl in memory of Maria Severa.

The *guitarrista* plays the melody and will occasionally perform a solo instrumental piece.

THE GUITARRA

Peculiar to Portuguese culture, the *guitarra* is a flat-backed instrument shaped like a mandolin, with eight, ten or twelve strings, arranged in pairs. It has evolved from a simple 19th-century design into a finely decorated piece, sometimes inlaid with mother-of-pearl. The sound of the *guitarra* is an essential ingredient of a good *fado*, echoing and enhancing the singer's melody line.

Most instruments have 12 paired strings, like this one. The double strings produce a resonant, silvery-sweet tone.

Delicate mother-of-pearl inlaid flower motifs

Mother-of-pearl finger plate

All kinds of themes may occur in fado. *This song of 1910, for example, celebrates the dawning of the liberal republic. Such songsheets remained a favoured means of dissemination, even after the first records were made in 1904.*

Alfredo Duarte (1891–1982) was a renowned writer of fado lyrics dealing with love, death, longing, tragedy and triumph. Affectionately known as O Marceneiro (the master carpenter) because of his skill as a joiner, he is still revered and his work widely performed.

A cultural icon for the Portuguese, Amália Rodrigues (1921–99) was the leading exponent of fado for over 50 years. She crystallized the music's style in the postwar years, and made it known around the world.

The viola provides rhythm accompaniment, but the player will never take a solo.

The music has long inspired great writers and painters. O Fado (1910) by José Malhôa (1855–1933) shows it in an intimate setting with the fadista captivating his listener. The air of abandonment underlines the earthiness of many of the songs.

THE FADO HOUSE

Lisbon's best *fado* houses are those run by *fadistas* themselves. Based on a love of the music and on relationships with other performers, such houses usually offer a truer fado experience than the larger, tourist-oriented houses. A good example is the Parreirinha de Alfama, owned by Argentina Santos (shown above). Less slick, but more emotionally charged, are performances of *fado vadio*, "itinerant" fado, in humbler restaurants and bars such as Tasca do Chico in Bairro Alto.

WHERE TO ENJOY FADO IN LISBON

Any of these fado houses will offer you good food, wine and music. Or visit the Casa do Fado for a fascinating exhibition of the history of Fado.

Arcadas do Faia
Rua da Barroca 54–6.
Map 4 F2. 〖 21-342 67 42.

Casa do Fado
Largo do Chafariz de Dentro 1. 〖 21-882 34 70. ☐ 10am–1pm, 2–6pm daily (to 2pm Fri–Sun).

Parreirinha de Alfama
Beco do Espírito Santo 1.
Map 7 E4. 〖 21-886 82 09.

Senhor Vinho
Rua do Meio à Lapa 18.
Map 4 D3.
〖 21-397 74 56

Tasca do Chico
Rua Diário de Notícias 39.
Map 7 A4. 〖 21-343 10 40.

Taverna do Embuçado
Beco dos Cortumes.
Map 8 E4. 〖 21-886 50 88.

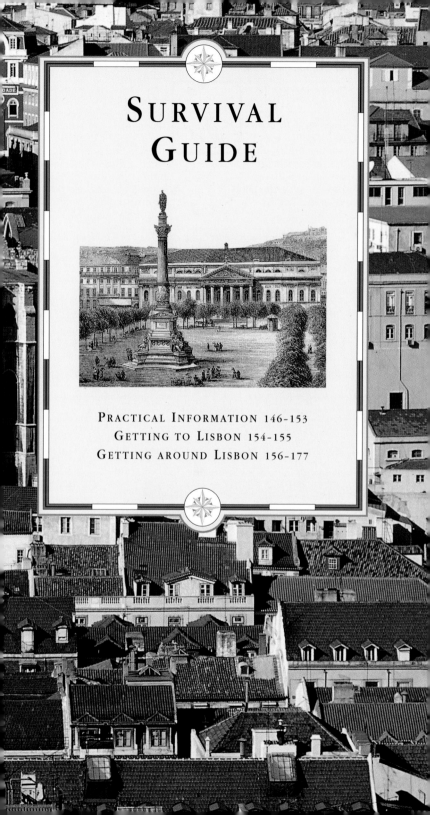

SURVIVAL
GUIDE

PRACTICAL INFORMATION

LISBON has grown up over the past decade. It has become increasingly modern and cosmopolitan, with the advantages and a few disadvantages that that brings. The city is better-equipped to receive visitors than it was, with professional tourist services particularly at the Lisboa Welcome Centre in the Baixa

Tourist information sign

area. But Lisbon has also become more expensive and traffic-ridden, and perhaps slightly less eccentric than it was. Still, visitors seeking the older Lisbon need only explore the Alfama, or any of the city's smaller areas. The best way to appreciate the city is on foot, using trams only for the steeper hills, and pausing to enjoy the varied views.

CUSTOMS

ON 30 JUNE 1999, the intra-EU Duty and Tax Free Allowances, better known as Duty-free, were abolished. Consulates will be able to provide up-to-date details on particular customs regulations. For more information on customs and other tax-related matters, see page 136.

VISAS

NATIONALS of the EU need only a valid passport to enter Portugal; for stays longer than six months a residence permit is required. Americans, Canadians, Australians and New Zealanders may stay for 90 days without a visa. Travellers from outside the EU should check with the nearest Portuguese embassy or consulate as regulations change.

TOURIST INFORMATION

THE TOURIST OFFICES' opening hours are generally the same as those of local shops. Offices in the centre of Lisbon

have been marked on the Street Finder *(see pp170–77)*. Offices may also be found at Portela airport and at Santa Apolónia station. Addresses of offices in the Lisbon Coast area are given in the information at the top of each light entry. Portuguese tourist offices abroad can provide you with helpful information before you travel that will help you plan your holiday.

ADMISSION CHARGES

MOST MUSEUMS and monuments, except churches, charge an entrance fee, which often increases in the summer. Entry is often free on Sunday mornings and public holidays. Pensioners and children under 14 are entitled to a 40 per cent discount. Visitors under 26 with a *Cartão Jóvem* (youth card) or an ISIC card (international student identity card) are entitled to half-price entrance. Visitors to Lisbon can buy a LISBOA card, which

Museum tickets

permits free entry to Lisbon's state museums and also free travel on all the city's public transport *(see p158)*.

OPENING TIMES

MOST MUSEUMS open from 10am–5pm daily with many closing for lunch from 12–2pm or from 12:30–2:30pm. Smaller museums, or privately-owned ones, may have different opening times. Note that state-run museums and some sights close on Mondays and public holidays. Major churches are open all day although some may close from 12–4pm. Smaller ones may only open for services.

FACILITIES FOR THE DISABLED

DISABLED FACILITIES in Lisbon are slowly improving. Adapted toilets are available at airports and the main stations and reserved car-parking is now more evident. Ramps and lifts are gradually being installed in public places.

LANGUAGE

WRITTEN Portuguese is fairly similar to Spanish, so if you know Spanish you should have little difficulty reading Portuguese text. Spoken Portuguese, however sounds very different from Spanish. The Portuguese are proud of their language, and may take offence at being addressed in Spanish. A phrasebook with some useful words and phrases is on pages 191–2.

Façade of the Museu Nacional de Arqueologia in Lisbon

◁ **View across Lisbon's skyline, with the Elevador de Santa Justa in the foreground**

Informally-dressed Portuguese families leaving church

ETIQUETTE

Although English is more widely spoken in Portugal than in neighbouring Spain, the Portuguese appreciate visitors' efforts, however small, to communicate in their language. A simple *bom dia* (good day) or *boa tarde* (good afternoon) can work wonders. Portuguese retains some old-fashioned modes of address which are seen as polite rather than formal, including *o senhor* and *a senhora* where English uses "you". This contrasts with the informality of cheek-kisses, used between men

and women as well as between women in most situations. Men generally shake hands.

PORTUGUESE TIME

Portugal follows Britain in adopting Greenwich Mean Time (GMT) in winter and moving the clocks forward one hour in summer. The 24-hour clock is commonly used.

ELECTRICITY

Voltage in portugal is 220 volts. Plugs have two round pins and most hotel bathrooms offer built-in adaptors for shavers only.

NEWSPAPERS, RADIO AND TELEVISION

Portuguese newspapers

English-language newspapers printed in Europe are widely available on the day of publication. Various other European newspapers and periodicals are on sale the day after home publication. Pórtuguese daily newspapers include *Diário de Notícias* and *Público*. The *Anglo-Portuguese News* (APN) is Lisbon's main English-language publication. Catering largely to the British expatriate community along the Estoril coast, it is published weekly. Portugal has two state-owned television channels, RTP1 and RTP2, and two privately-owned channels, SIC and TVI. Most foreign-language programmes are broadcast in the original language, with Portuguese subtitles. Other international broadcasts are available via satellite and cable. Comprehensive listings of programmes can be found in the weekly TV guide, *TV Guia*, as well as in most newspapers.

Newspaper stall in the Café Brasiliera (p53)

CONVERSION CHART

Imperial to Metric
1 inch = 2.54 centimetres
1 foot = 30 centimetres
1 mile = 1.6 kilometres
1 ounce = 28 grams
1 pound = 454 grams
1 pint = 0.6 litres
1 gallon = 4.6 litres

Metric to Imperial
1 millimetre = 0.04 inches
1 centimetre = 0.4 inches
1 metre = 3 feet 3 inches
1 kilometre = 0.6 miles
1 gram = 0.04 ounces
1 kilogram = 2.2 pounds
1 litre = 1.8 pints

DIRECTORY

EMBASSIES AND CONSULATES

Australia
Avenida da Liberdade 198, 2°, E
Edifício Victoria, 1269-121, Lisbon.
Map 5 C5.
21-310 15 00.

Canada
Avenida da Liberdade 196–200, 3°,
Edifício Victoria, 1269-121, Lisbon.
Map 5 C5.
21-316 46 00.

United Kingdom
Rua de São Bernardo 33,
1249-082, Lisbon. **Map** 4 D2.
21-392 40 00 (embassy).

United States
Avenida das Forças Armadas,
1600-081, Lisbon.
21-727 33 00.

GOVERNMENT TOURIST OFFICES

In Lisbon:
Lisboa Welcome Center, Rua do
Arsenal 15, 1100-038, Lisbon.
Map 7 B5. 21-031 27 00;
toll free: 800-296 296.
www.atl-turismolisboa.pt

At Lisbon airport:
21-845 06 60 (municipal).
21-849 43 23 (ICEP – Portugal).

Canada
416-921 7376.

United Kingdom
09063-640 610.

United States
212-220 5772.

Personal Health and Security

L ISBON does not have a serious crime problem, but simple precautions can and should be taken. Watch out for pickpockets in busy areas and on public transport, avoid carrying large amounts of cash and don't leave valuables in parked cars. The police are generally helpful, but bureaucratic; reporting a crime can take time. In case of a medical emergency, dial 112 and ask for an ambulance. For minor complaints consult a pharmacist at first.

WHAT TO DO IN AN EMERGENCY

T HE NUMBER to contact in the event of an emergency is 112. Dial the number and then indicate which service you require – the police *(polícia)*, an ambulance *(ambulância)* or the fire brigade *(bombeiros)*. If you need medical treatment, the casualty department *(serviço de urgência)* of the closest main hospital will treat you. On motorways and main roads, use the orange SOS telephone to call for help should you have a car accident. The service is in Portuguese; press the button and then wait for an answer. The operator will put you through.

HEALTH PRECAUTIONS

N O VACCINATIONS are needed for visitors, although doctors recommend being up-to-date with tetanus, diptheria and measles jabs. Tap water is safe to drink throughout the country. If you are visiting during the summer, it is advisable to bring insect repellent, as mosquitoes, while they do not present any serious health problems, can be a nuisance.

PHARMACIES

P HARMACIES *(farmácias)* in Lisbon can diagnose simple health problems and suggest appropriate treatment. Pharmacists can dispense a range of drugs that would normally only be available on prescription in many other countries. The sign for a *farmácia* is a green cross. They are open from 9am to 1pm and 3pm to 7pm. Each pharmacy displays a card in the window showing the address of the nearest all-night pharmacy and a list of those that are open until late (10pm).

MEDICAL TREATMENT

S OCIAL SECURITY coverage is available for all EU nationals, but you may have to pay first and reclaim later. You must have an E111 form before travelling which is available at post offices or from the Department of Health. The E111 covers emergencies only, so visitors need insurance for all other medical treatments.

Pharmacy sign

US visitors should check with their insurance carriers before leaving home to ensure that they are covered. Many medical facilities will require that treatment is paid in full at the time of service. Bear in mind that private health care is expensive in Portugal and get an itemized bill for your carrier.

The **British Hospital** in Lisbon has English-speaking doctors, as do international health centres on the Lisbon Coast.

Motorway SOS telephone

PORTUGUESE POLICE

I N LISBON and other main towns, the police force is the *Polícia de Segurança Pública* (PSP). In rural areas, law and order is kept by the *Guarda Nacional Republicana* (GNR). The *Brigada de Trânsito* (traffic police) are a division of the GNR, and are recognizable by their red armbands. They are responsible for patrolling roads.

PERSONAL SECURITY

V IOLENT CRIME is fairly rare in Lisbon and in Portugal generally, and the majority of visitors will experience no problems whatsoever. Nonetheless, a few sensible precautions are worth taking: avoid quiet areas such as the Baixa after dark, and don't stroll alone through Bairro

Traffic policeman   **Male PSP officer**   **Female PSP officer**

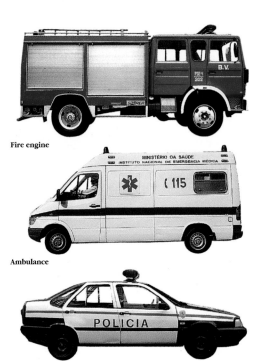

Fire engine

Ambulance

Police car

DIRECTORY

EMERGENCY NUMBERS

**General Emergency
(Fire, Police, Ambulance)**
112.

**Assistentes Intérpretes
de Portugal**
Avenida da República 41, 3°,
1050-187 Lisbon.
21-799 43 60.

British Hospital
Rua Saraiva de Carvalho 49,
1269-098 Lisbon.
21-394 31 00.

Ordem dos Advogados
Largo de São Domingos 14, 1°,
1169-060 Lisbon.
21-887 56 21.

Alto, Alfama or around Cais do Sodré after bars' closing time. In the daytime, be alert to the possibility of pickpockets or, more rarely, bagsnatchers. Some poorer neighbourhoods and outlying slums see more serious daytime crime, but they are not on the typical visitor's itinerary.

It is generally a good idea to ignore any jeering, heckling or other provocations – they are usually not as serious as they can sound. Other general precautions include not carrying or showing large amounts of cash, not leaving possessions visible in parked cars, and holding on to equipment such as mobile phones and cameras. If you are robbed, you are advised not to try to resist.

REPORTING A CRIME

IF YOU HAVE any property stolen, you should immediately contact the nearest police station. Theft of documents, such as a passport, should also be reported to your

consulate. Many insurance companies insist that policy holders report any theft within 24 hours. The police will file a report which you will need in order to claim from your insurance company on your return home. Contact the PSP in towns or cities, or the GNR in rural areas. In all situations, keep calm and be polite to the authorities to avoid delays. The same applies should you be involved in a car accident. In rural areas you may be asked to accompany the other driver to the nearest police station to complete the necessary paperwork. Ask for an interpreter if no one there speaks English.

LEGAL ASSISTANCE

AN INSURANCE POLICY that covers the costs of legal advice, issued by companies such as Europ Assistance or Mondial Assistance, will help with the legal aspects of your insurance claim should you have an accident. If you have not arranged this cover, call your nearest consulate or the **Ordem dos Advogados** (lawyers' association) who can give you names of English-speaking lawyers and help you with obtaining representation. Lists of interpreters, if you require one, are given in the local Yellow Pages (Páginas Amarelas) under *Tradutores e Intérpretes*, or can be contacted through the **Assistentes Intérpretes de Portugal**, which is based in Lisbon.

PUBLIC CONVENIENCES

THE PORTUGUESE for toilets is *casa de banho*. If the usual figures of a man or woman are not shown, look for *homens* (men) and *senhoras* (ladies). Toilet facilities are provided at service areas every 40 km (25 miles) and at drive-in rest areas on the motorways. In some cases you may have to pay to use ladies' toilets, but men's facilities are always free.

Ladies' toilet sign

Men's toilet sign

Banking and Local Currency

BPI Bank Logo

Portugal is one of the founding members of the European Monetary Union and one of the countries that launched the euro in 2002. Conversion to the new currency went more smoothly than anyone had dared hope, but in some cases prices may still be quoted in both currencies. Traveller's cheques are the safest way to carry money, but cashing them can be quite expensive in Lisbon, and they are rarely accepted as payment. Credit and debit cards are often a more convenient option. Still, it is always a good idea to arrive with enough euros in cash to cover one or two days' expenditure.

Bank façade on Rua do Ouro

BANKING HOURS

Banks are open between 8:30am and 3pm, Monday to Friday. Some branches stay open for longer, usually until 6pm – enquire at individual banks to find out which these are, as they sometimes change. Banks are closed at weekends and on public holidays.

CHANGING MONEY

Money can be changed at banks, bureaux de change *(agências de câmbios)* and at many hotels. Bank branches are everywhere, but their rates of exchange and commissions vary. Waiting times and bureaucratic practices at banks may also make them a worse option. Bureaux de change charge higher commissions than many banks but offer a more expedient service, as well as longer opening hours (including weekends). As a rule, hotels have the worst rates of exchange. At banks

and bureaux de change you may be asked to show your passport or some other form of identification for exchange transactions.

An alternative is to use a currency exchange machine, of which there are a few in central Lisbon.

CHEQUES AND CARDS

Traveller's cheques are a safe but not very convenient way of carrying money in Lisbon. It is rare for shops or hotels to accept them as payment, and cashing them may be quite expensive. In general, bureaux de change are better for this than banks, whose commissions may be high.

The best place to cash traveller's cheques is at the **Top Tours** travel agency, the local American Express representative. They will cash US dollar- or pounds-denominated traveller's cheques without charging a commission.

Most visitors, however, find it most practical and convenient

to withdraw cash from an automatic teller machine (Multibanco or MB) using their credit/debit card. Multibanco machines are typically found outside bank branches or in shopping centres. Most accept Visa, MasterCard, American Express, Maestro and Cirrus.

DIRECTORY

MAJOR BANKS

Banco Bilbao Vizcaya Argentária
Avenida da Liberdade 222.
(21-311 72 00.

Banco Espírito Santo
Avenida da Liberdade 195.
(21-359 70 00.

Barclays Bank
Avenida da República 50.
(21-351 00 00.

Caixa Geral de Depósitos
Rua do Ouro 49.
(21-340 50 00.

TRAVELLER'S CHEQUES

Top Tours
Avenida Duque de Loulé 108.
(21-310 88 00.

LOST CARDS OR TRAVELLER'S CHEQUES

American Express
(800 204 050.

MasterCard
(800 811 272.

Travelex
(01 733 294 451 or 452 (UK).

Visa
(800 811 824.

Fortress-like head office of Caixa Geral de Depósitos in Arco do Cego

The Euro

TWELVE COUNTRIES have replaced their traditional currencies with a single European currency called the euro. Austria, Belgium, Finland, France, Germany, Greece, Ireland, Italy, Luxembourg, Netherlands, Portugal and Spain chose to join the new currency; the UK, Denmark and Sweden stayed out, with an option to review their situation. The euro was introduced on 1 January, 1999, but only for banking purposes. Notes and coins came into circulation on 1 January 2002. A transition period allowed euros and escudos to be used simultaneously, with national notes and coins phased out in March 2002. Euros can be used anywhere within the participating member states.

Bank Notes

Euro bank notes have seven denominations. The 5-euro note (grey in colour) is the smallest, followed by the 10-euro note (pink), 20-euro note (blue), 50-euro note (orange), 100-euro note (green), 200-euro note (yellow) and 500-euro note (purple). All notes show the stars of the European Union.

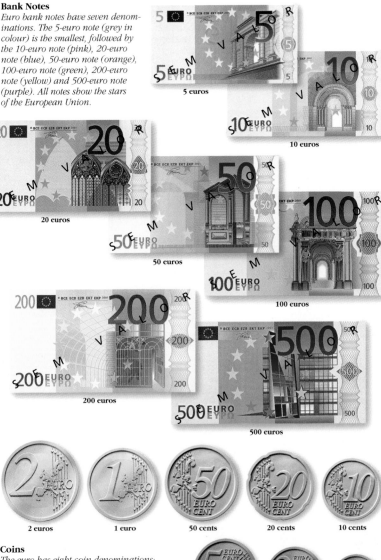

5 euros

10 euros

20 euros

50 euros

100 euros

200 euros

500 euros

2 euros

1 euro

50 cents

20 cents

10 cents

Coins

The euro has eight coin denominations: 2 euros and 1 euro; 50 cents, 20 cents, 10 cents, 5 cents, 2 cents and 1 cent. The 2- and 1-euro coins are both silver and gold in colour. The 50-, 20- and 10-cent coins are gold. The 5-, 2- and 1-cent coins are bronze.

5 cents

2 cents

1 cent

Using the Telephone

ONCE NOTORIOUS for its unreliability, Portugal's telecommunications system is now fully modern. In Lisbon, the visitor should have few problems using the telephone, with the possible exception of a few remaining old-fashioned telephone booths. The previous monopoly of the state operator, Portugal Telecom, has been broken, and a price war is in full swing. Look out for special offers on phone cards, which are much the best option when using a public telephone.

English-style phone box There are three mobile phone operators in Portugal: Telece/Vodafone, TMN and Optimus.

Post office *cabine* phone

USING A COIN PHONE

1 Lift receiver and wait for the dialling tone.

2 Insert coins in this slot one at a time.

3 The display shows amount of credit. If more money is required the message "*Inserir mais moedas por favor*" appears.

4 Key in telephone number and wait to be connected.

5 To make another call, press the follow-on call button.

6 Replace receiver after call. Unused coins will be refunded.

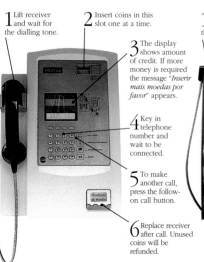

USING A CARD PHONE

1 Lift receiver and wait for the dialling tone.

2 Insert phonecard arrow side up, or credit card magnetic strip down.

3 The screen will display number of units available, then tell you to key in telephone number.

4 Key in number and wait to be connected.

5 If phonecard runs out in the middle of a call, it will re-emerge. Remove it and in-sert another one.

6 Replace receiver after call. When card re-emerges, remove it.

10 cents **20 cents** **50 cents** **1 euro**

Phonecards are available in varying amounts

TELEPHONING IN LISBON

PUBLIC PAY PHONES come in both the coin and the card variety, as well as in combinations of the two. They are found in booths in the street as well as in bars, cafés and shopping centres. Coin-operated phones now accept all denominations of euro and cent coins except the one-cent coin. Card operated phones are more common and more convenient, accepting a variety of phone cards available from post offices, newsagents, tobacconists and Telecom company outlets. Some also accept credit cards, although that incurs a small extra charge.

The cheapest way to use a payphone is with a phone card. The main operator, PT Comunicações (previously the monopoly holder and still the owner of the network), charges about 3 European cents per minute for a local call. International calls and calls to mobile phones are more expensive again, but there are special cards and deals to be had. An alternative is to phone from a post office, without having either change or card. You simply step into a free booth, make your call, and pay the cashier after-wards. The cost per unit is relatively low. Some cafés, restaurants and bars also have a units meter connected to their phone and calculate the cost of your call. They charge more than the post office but less than hotels.

For international calls and calls to mobile phones in particular, bear in mind that rates are lower between 9pm and 9am and at weekends.

REVERSE CHARGE CALLS

REVERSE CHARGE calls can be made from any telephone. Dial the *directo* number listed at the front of the telephone directory after the country and city dialling codes, or dial 179 and ask for the *directo* number of the country you wish to call. This number will put you in touch with an operator in that country. For some countries, including the USA, there is a choice of carriers (e.g., AT&T or MCI).

A beige coin telephone outside a café, covered by a shelter

DIALLING CODES

- All numbers in Portugal now have nine digits, including the area code, regardless of where you are calling from.
- To call Portugal use the country code 351.
- To phone Lisbon, and most places in the Lisbon Coast area from abroad, first dial 00 351 21 and then the local number.
- To call abroad from Lisbon, dial 00 and then the country code. The code for Australia is 61; Ireland: 353; New Zealand: 64; UK: 44 and US and Canada: 1.
- Lisbon's directory enquiries number is 118. For international directory enquiries dial 177.
- The Algarve is covered by Portimão (282), Faro (289), and Tavira (281). Madeira's code is 291.

Postal Services

Correios (postal service) logo

THE POSTAL SERVICE is known as the *Correios*. It is reasonably efficent: a letter sent to a country within the EU should take five to seven days, and a letter sent to the USA or further afield should take about seven to ten days. The *Correios* sign features a horse and rider in white on a red background.

SENDING A LETTER

FIRST-CLASS MAIL, known as *correio azul*, promises delivery within Portugal by the following day, while second-class mail, or *normal*, usually takes longer. First-class postboxes are blue; second-class ones are red. At post offices there may be a separate slot for international mail. There is also an express mail service called EMS and, for valuable letters, recorded delivery *(correio registado)* is available. Stamps *(selos)* can be bought from post offices or from any shop displaying the *Correios* sign. You can also buy stamps from vending machines in airport terminals, railway stations and on the streets of large towns.

Portuguese stamps

POSTE RESTANTE

A MAIL-HOLDING service *(posta restante)* is also available at most major post offices. The envelope should carry the name of the recipient in block capitals, underlined, followed by *posta restante* together with the postcode and the name of the destination town. To collect the mail, take your passport and look for the counter that is marked *encomendas*. A small fee is charged for this service.

POST OFFICES

POST OFFICES are usually open from 9am until 6pm from Monday to Friday. The main post office in Praça dos Restuaradores is open between 8:30am and 10pm, Monday to Friday and 9am–6pm on Saturdays and Sundays.

LISBON'S ADDRESSES

LISBON'S ADDRESSES often include both the storey of a building and the location within that floor. The ground floor is the *rés-do-chão* (r/c), first floor *primeiro andar* (1°), the second floor is expressed as 2°, and so on. Each floor is divided into left, *esquerdo* (E or Esq^{do}), right, *direito* (D or D^{to}).

Information on collection times   **First-class postbox**

Lisbon's Postboxes
First-class letters should be posted in blue (Correio Azul) boxes and second-class letters in red boxes.

Second-class postbox

TRAVEL INFORMATION

L ISBON IS SERVED by an international airport and has good rail and road links. It is also a popular port with cruise liners. The road network surrounding the city has improved significantly over the last decade, with new ring roads and motorways. A second bridge across the Tagus opened in 1998, lightening the load on the older 25 de Abril bridge. Trams provide fascinating trips through some of Lisbon's oldest neighbourhoods, whose steep hills and narrow streets no other form of public transport can negotiate. For the rest of the city, the Metro is the best way to get around. The bus network is huge, but despite separate lanes buses get held up in Lisbon's daily traffic jams. The Lisbon Coast is easily accessible by train, as is Sintra. Both of these are now suburbs of Lisbon, and motorway access can be slow during rush hours. Ferries are a pleasant way of crossing the Tagus, to Caparica's beaches.

TAP, the Air Portugal logo

AIR TRAVEL

L ISBON HAS regular scheduled flights from European capitals and major cities, including London, Paris, Madrid, Rome, Frankfurt, Munich, Zurich and Milan. Most of these are daily, and in many cases there are several daily connections. **TAP**, Portugal's national carrier, currently operates five daily flights from London (three from Heathrow and two from Gatwick) to Lisbon.

Travellers from North America will usually have to change at some European hub. **Delta** flies to Lisbon via Paris (using a partner airline) daily or twice daily. TAP's only direct flights from the US are out of Newark, New Jersey. South America is better served thanks to Portugal's ties with Brazil: TAP has direct flights to and from several Brazilian destinations, as does the Brazilian national carrier, **VARIG**.

There are no direct flights to Lisbon from Canada, Australia or New Zealand. London is the usual hub for flights from these countries.

TAP also flies to domestic destinations, including Oporto, Faro and Funchal. **Portugália**, Portugal's privately owned airline, has a wide domestic network and a growing European one. SATA, in partnership with TAP, serves the Azores.

Signs at Lisbon's Portela airport

Carros de "Aluguer Rent a Car	←
Autocarros Bus	←
Depósito de Bagagem Left Luggage	↘
Parque Acesso de peões	↘

Charter flights are available to Lisbon, particularly during the summer months. Tickets always have fixed outward and return dates, but as they are often cheaper than a regular one-way ticket, many passengers only use the outward flight. Some charter companies now re-sell empty return seats at lower prices. Student travellers can get reduced rates through specialist travel agencies, and it is worth checking the Internet for bargains. Many of the budget options will be via London. Tickets are pricier in summer.

LISBON AIRPORT

P ORTELA AIRPORT is located only 7 km (4 miles) north of Lisbon's city centre. It is a one-terminal airport, with around one hundred arrivals and departures daily. There are no huge distances to cover within the airport, but not all gates have direct boarding facilities, which means passengers are taken to the aircraft by bus.

CONNECTIONS WITH THE AIRPORT

T HE AIRPORT'S proximity to the city centre means that it is reasonably cheap to get to the heart of Lisbon. Taxis are available from the taxi rank just outside the arrivals hall *(see p157)*. Fares to the city centre are metred and cost between seven and ten euros with a small extra charge for luggage.

The Aero-Bus shuttle service departs every 20 minutes (7:45am–8:45pm) from the airport bus stop immediately beyond the taxi rank. It stops at Entrecampos, Saldanha, Marquês Pombal, Restauradores, Rossio, Praça do Comércio and Cais do Sodré station. Tickets cost 2.35 euros and are then valid for the rest of the day on buses, trams and funiculars.

Cheaper normal buses stop a little further to the right as you exit the arrivals hall. Nos. 44, 45, 22, 83 and 5 stop at various central Lisbon locations.

Shuttle bus waiting to depart from the airport to the city centre

Entrance to the Ponte 25 de Abril, one of the main routes into Lisbon

ARRIVING BY TRAIN

To the east of the Alfama district, on Avenida Infante Dom Henrique, is **Santa Apolónia**, the main station for long distance trains from Coimbra, Porto and the north, as well as from Madrid and Paris. It is 15 minutes' walk east of Praça do Comércio.

There is a tourist information office (open 8am–1pm and 2pm–4pm daily) and a bureau de change inside the station. Outside the main entrance there is a taxi rank.

Since 1998, the impressive, ultra-modern **Gare do Oriente** has provided an alternative international terminus to Santa Apolónia. Although located much farther north at the old Expo site Parque das Nações, it has excellent links into the city by both bus and metro.

Trains from the south and east of the city arrive at **Barreiro** station on the south bank of the Tagus and connect with the ferry which docks at Terreiro do Paço.

Nearby, **Cais do Sodré** station serves the resort towns of Cascais and Estoril. **Rossio** station, off Praça dos Restauradores, some 20 minutes away, and Sintra, about 45 minutes from Lisbon. For more details on travelling by train, see page 161.

The Fertagus rail link is a useful commuter service to the south bank of the Tagus.

ARRIVING BY ROAD

There are at present seven major entry routes into Lisbon: two from the south and east, two from the north, and three from the west.

Those arriving from the Algarve and the south, the A2 (E1) motorway, as well as Madrid and the east (A6) can either cross to central Lisbon via the busy Ponte 25 de Abril, Lisbon's landmark bridge, or to the northeastern part of the city via the newer and longer Ponte Vasco da Gama. Both of these are toll bridges; Vasco da Gama costs considerably more.

From Oporto and the north, the A1 (E1) motorway brings you to Lisbon's northeastern outskirts. To reach central Lisbon, follow signs indicating Campo Grande and then Centro. If you wish to head straight to the coastal resorts of Estoril and Cascais, without passing through central Lisbon, you should turn off the A1 (E1) on to the A9 at Alverca, 20 km (12 miles) north of Lisbon, immediately after the toll. The A9 is also known as the C.R.E.L. (the exterior ring road) and will be signposted to Cascais. It is toll-free.

Those arriving from Cascais and the Lisbon coast enter via the A5 motorway or the coastal N6 road, known as the Avenida Marginal. From Sintra, you enter via the IC19 which links up with Avenida

General Norton de Matos in the north of Lisbon. The A8 from northern Estremadura enters the city from the north.

LISBON'S BRIDGES

One of Lisbon's most famous landmarks, the Ponte 25 de Abril, provides the main link between Lisbon and Almada on the southern bank of the Tagus. Built in the 1960s, when cars were still a rarity in Portugal, it became a bottleneck in the late 1980s. In the 1990s more lanes were added and a rail line ingeniously slung underneath, in the hope of alleviating the congestion. The toll, which is charged only on the way into Lisbon to lessen queuing, was also raised significantly to help pay for a second bridge.

This second bridge, the Ponte Vasco da Gama *(see p81)*, links Lisbon's northeastern outskirts – the Expo area, now Parque das Nações, is immediately next to it – with Montijo on the other side of the wide Tagus estuary.

Getting Around Lisbon

A N ATTRACTIVE CITY, Lisbon is a pleasure to explore and walking can be one of the best ways to see it. However, it is also hilly and even the fittest of sightseers will soon tire. The trams and funiculars (*elevadores*) offer a welcome rest for the foot-weary as well as some great views. They are an essential Lisbon experience, but may not always be the most efficient means of transportation. For that, buses and the metro are better choices. Driving around Lisbon is not generally recommended: the city suffers from near-chronic congestion and its street plan is full of unexpected surprises. As a result, patience is in short supply among Lisbon drivers. Taxis offer the convenience of car travel and are relatively cheap too.

A typical alleyway in the Alfama district, Lisbon

WALKING AROUND LISBON

L ISBON IS a delightful city to wander around taking in the sights, especially in the old neighbourhoods such as the Alfama and Bairro Alto. Narrow cobbled streets, picturesque buildings and alleyways provide a charming setting to experience traditional Lisbon life.

However, it is important to remember that Lisbon is built on a number of hills, and unless you are fairly fit, it is wise to take advantage of public transport as much as possible for the uphill climbs. The 28 tram (*eléctrico*) goes almost all the way up to the Castelo de São Jorge; you can then walk down through the Alfama, and enjoy the views. Similarly, the Glória funicular will take you from Praça dos Restauradores up to Bairro Alto.

Lisbon's most central shopping area is made up of the Baixa and Chiado, where pedestrianized streets are filled with bustling shoppers,

street performers and vendors. A wide variety of shops, shopping centres, banks, outdoor cafés and restaurants offer plenty of opportunity to buy souvenirs, change money or enjoy a coffee or a meal, or simply to enjoy soaking up the atmosphere.

DRIVING AROUND LISBON

U SING A CAR to get around the busy city centre of Lisbon is not advisable. Finding your way around the complex street plan isn't easy, and traffic jams don't make it any easier. Portuguese drivers do not suffer what they perceive as fools gladly, and parking can be very difficult to find. Policemen in the wrong mood may issue on-the-spot fines to foreign drivers, although they are usually quite understanding of, and tolerant towards, confused car tourists.

Lisbon's larger roundabouts have traffic lights; on those that don't, cars travelling around the roundabout have priority over cars waiting to enter it. At all other intersections, unless there are signs or lights to the contrary, traffic from the right has priority. That, at least, is the rule; the common practice has more to do with seizing priority before the other driver does.

If it is absolutely necessary for you to drive in Lisbon, try to avoid the rush hours (roughly 8–10am and 5:30–8pm). Also, driving at weekends is much easier than during the week. Above all, try to keep calm even if other drivers are aggressive. You should also look out for pedestrians; crossings are badly marked, and Lisboetas seem to prefer dashing across the road at any point that is convenient to themselves.

PARKING

P ARKING IN Lisbon has become a little easier and a lot more expensive over the last few years. Most central Lisbon streets are now lined with pay and display spaces, marked at regular intervals by a P sign with a hand and a coin. Tickets are bought from machines along the pavement; the charge is quite low and only applies between 8am and 8pm on weekdays (and on Saturday mornings in some areas). However, there is a limit to the number of hours you can buy, and the machines don't give change, so come equipped with small coins. Illegally parked cars may be clamped or towed away, and will only be released upon payment of a fine.

Safer and longer-term parking is available in Lisbon's numerous underground car parks. These are marked by signs with a white P on a blue background and usually display whether there are spaces or not by means of a red full (*completo*) or green free (*livre*) light. Tickets are taken from a machine on

RETIRE AQUI O SEU BILHETE

Pay and display sign

The Marquês de Pombal roundabout in central Lisbon

entering and paid before leaving. More expensive than parking in the street, some of the larger ones in the centre of Lisbon are beneath Marquês de Pombal, Praça dos Restauradores and Praça da Figueira.

CAR HIRE

MOST OF THE major hire companies such as Hertz and Avis have offices at the airport inside the arrivals hall. To rent a car in Portugal you must have an international driving licence (unless you hold a licence from an EU member state). Drivers must be over the age of 21 and have held their licence for at least one year.

It is usually more expensive to hire a car at an airport, as is renting in summer; most companies offer special off-peak and weekend deals. The price depends on whether unlimited mileage is included and if you want comprehensive insurance *(todos-os-riscos)*. Normally, the car is provided with a full tank of petrol; it is best to return it with the tank full, as the agency will charge to fill it themselves.

A typical Lisbon taxi

PETROL

PETROL, CALLED *gasolina*, is relatively expensive in Portugal. Prices may vary slightly between stations, but the current level is just under one euro per litre. Diesel *(gasóleo)* costs considerably less and is the cheapest vehicle fuel. Unleaded fuel *(gasolina sem chumbo)* comes in two types: 95-octane normal and 98-octane super. The latter is more expensive. Leaded fuel is also widely available.

Filling stations use a colour coding system on the pumps to help clients distinguish between the different types of fuel: normal is marked green, super is white, diesel is black and leaded petrol is red.

There are plenty of small petrol stations in central Lisbon, some of which are open 24 hours a day. They are usually manned by attendants and it is customary but not obligatory to give them a tip.

TAXIS

COMPARED TO THE rest of Europe, taxis in Portugal remain relatively inexpensive and if costs are shared between two or more people they can work out cheaper than travelling by bus or tram. Most taxis are beige but a few of the older black and green cabs still exist. All are metered although costs depend on the time of day.

Vacant taxis have their rooftop "taxi" signs switched on, but it is sometimes difficult to see if they are lit. (Taxis can also be ordered by phone from companies such as **Autocoope**.) The green lights indicate that the taxi is taken; two green lights mean that the higher rate is being charged (10pm–6am, weekends and public holidays), one that the normal rate applies.

The starting rate for a taxi hailed in the street or taken at a taxi rank is 1.80 euros. The meter should always be used, although the driver might suggest agreeing on a price for long trips. A fee will be added for the taxi's returning empty.

Getting Around by Public Transport

Metro logo

Lisbon's public transport system provides access to all parts of the city by a variety of means: trams old and new, lifts and funiculars, buses and the underground Metropolitano. The technological spectrum is vast, from early 20th-century trams and funiculars to modern Metro trains, sleek new trams and articulated buses. Buses have the most extensive network, while trams cover a smaller area but offer good sightseeing opportunities. Both are prone to delays due to traffic jams and are run, as are lifts and funiculars, by the state-owned Carris company. The Metro, run separately but also state-owned, is the most efficient form of public transport.

Tickets

Tickets for buses, trams and funiculars can be bought on boarding, but it is cheaper to buy one of various multiple-trip tickets beforehand. These are available from Carris kiosks in many parts of the city, such as at the bottom of the Elevador de Santa Justa, at railway stations, by the Basílica da Estrela, in Praça da Figueira and by Marquês de Pombal. Some post offices and newsagents also sell Carris tickets.

The basic multiple-trip Carris ticket is for two trips and costs about the same as a single ticket. They are valid for an unlimited number of days, so several can be bought at the same time. Other options are 1-day and 3-day tickets, if you plan to use buses and trams a lot over a short period. Upon boarding, always validate your ticket in the *obliterador* machine next to the driver. Day passes only need to be validated on the first journey.

Metro tickets are bought in machines or from ticket offices at the stations. The choice is

between a single-trip (€0.65) or a two-trip ticket, or a ten-trip ticket (€5.70) valid for an unlimited number of days. There are also 1 (€1.40), 7 (€4.80) or 30-day passes. Tickets must be validated on entering the platform area and on leaving the station. In most stations, there are now gates that open on insertion of a valid ticket, or there is a small stamping machine to use.

There is also a combined Carris/Metro 1-day ticket (€2.75), as well as Tourist Passes valid for 4 (€9.95) or 7 (€14.10) days on both Carris and the Metro. Buying Tourist Passes may involve showing some form of identification.

Children between the ages of four and twelve, adults over 65 and students all pay half price on public transport. Children under the age of four travel free of charge. Visit www.metrolisboa.pt for further information.

Metro *obliterador* machine

Tourist Routes

One of the quickest and easiest ways of getting between museums and other popular sights is to hop on an ArtShuttle mini-bus, which stops every 15 minutes at most museums on a continuously repeated circuit. You buy your ticket on the bus and may then use the shuttle service as you need it for the rest of the day.

Travelling by Metro

The fastest and cheapest way by far to get around town is by the *Metropolitano*. Metro stations are signposted with a red M and the service operates from 6:30 to 1am each day. Although the Metro becomes quite packed during the morning and evening rush hours, there are frequent trains. The system is safe to travel on, even at night, since the stations and trains are regularly patrolled by the police. Most stations now have automatic gates at the entrance to the platform areas; a valid ticket must be inserted both on entering and leaving. Bear in mind that Metro ticket inspectors can fine you up to 100 times the value of a single-trip ticket if you are caught without a valid ticket.

The Metro first opened in December 1959 and consisted of one Y-shaped line running between Jardim Zoolológico,

The Lisboa Card

This comprehensive tourist pass allows free access to most forms of public transport (not ferries) and reduced rates on some tourist tours (including the Carris open-top bus tour, the Colinas tour in the red trams, and Transtejo river tours). Additionally, admission charges are waived at 25 national museums and other sights, and reduced at a number of other ones (20 per cent off at the Gulbenkian Museum, for instance). It is an impressive offer, and competitively priced, but with only 24, 48 or 72 hours in which to make use of it, you might be rushed off your feet. The Lisboa Card is on sale at the airport's arrival hall, tourist offices, selected hotels, travel agents and sights, as well as in Carris kiosks.

Lisboa card tourist pass

THE LISBON METRO SYSTEM

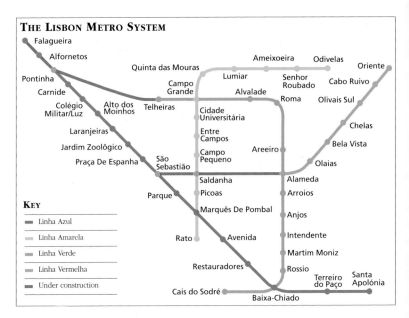

Falagueira
Alfornetos
Pontinha
Carnide
Colégio Militar/Luz
Alto dos Moinhos
Laranjeiras
Jardim Zoológico
Praça De Espanha
Quinta das Mouras
Campo Grande
Telheiras
Cidade Universitária
Entre Campos
Campo Pequeno
São Sebastião
Saldanha
Picoas
Parque
Marquês De Pombal
Rato
Avenida
Restauradores
Cais do Sodré
Baixa-Chiado
Ameixoeira
Odivelas
Oriente
Lumiar
Senhor Roubado
Cabo Ruivo
Alvalade
Roma
Olivais Sul
Areeiro
Chelas
Bela Vista
Olaias
Alameda
Arroios
Anjos
Intendente
Martim Moniz
Rossio
Terreiro do Paço
Santa Apolónia

KEY

- ▬ Linha Azul
- ▬ Linha Amarela
- ▬ Linha Verde
- ▬ Linha Vermelha
- ▬ Under construction

Entrecampos and Restauradores. Today, there are some 37 stations operating on four lines: the Linha Azul (Blue line), the Linha Amarela (Yellow line), the Linha Verde (Green line) and the Linha Vermelha (Red line). These lines link the Metro to major bus, train and ferry services, and provide transport from Lisbon's suburbs to the commercial heart of the city, along the north bank of the river. Plans are underway to greatly extend the city's Metro system and a number of stations are currently under construction.

TRAVELLING BY TRAM

TRAMS (eléctricos) are one of the most pleasant ways of sightseeing in Lisbon. However, they only operate in a very limited area of the city, along the river to Belém and around the hilly parts of Lisbon. There are presently two types of tram operating in Lisbon: the charming, old, pre-World War I models, and the much longer new trams with sleek interiors.

Single tickets for all rides are very cheap except for those on the red Colinas or Tejo trams, which provide special sightseeing rides for tourists and are much more

expensive than the ordinary routes. These sightseeing services operate throughout the year and take you through the hilly parts of Lisbon and along the Tagus. However, it is better value to catch one of the following trams:

No.25 runs from the Cemitério des Prazeres in Campo de Ourique, past the Basílica da Estrela to the attractive residential district of Lapa, on a steep hill facing the river. It descends to the river

and then runs past Praça do Comércio to where Alfama begins, ending its route in Rua da Alfândega.

No.28 shares some of its route with No.25, running via Estrela down past the Palácio de São Bento and up again to Bairro Alto and Chiado. It descends to the Baixa, passes Lisbon's cathedral, then climbs to Castelo São Jorge. It offers an excellent sightseeing tour of old Lisbon – often most of its passengers are tourists.

New-style tram

Sightseeing tram

Lisbon's Elevador da Glória ascending to the Bairro Alto

FUNICULARS AND LIFTS

DUE TO LISBON's hilly terrain, funiculars and lifts are a convenient and popular means of getting from river level to the upper parts of the city, particularly Bairro Alto. Although expensive in relation to the distance covered, this form of transport certainly helps take the effort out of negotiating Lisbon's hills, and in addition offers some superb views over the city.

Elevador da Bica climbs from the São Paulo area up to the lower end of Bairro Alto. **Elevador da Glória** goes from Praça dos Restauradores to the upper end of Bairro Alto. Currently closed for renovation, but due to re-open soon, the walkway at **Elevador de Santa Justa** links the Baxia with the Bairro Alto (see p52). **Elevador da Lavra,** climbs from Praça dos Restauradores up to the Hospital São José.

TRAVELLING BY BUS

LISBON BUSES (autocarros) are yellow or orange. Most inner-city services run about from 5:30am to 1am. A smaller number of night buses operate between 1am and 5:30am.

The bus network is Lisbon's most extensive public transport system, and buses go just about everywhere. Their timetable suffers from Lisbon's traffic problems, which means you sometimes have to wait a long time to get on a very crowded bus. Most public vehicles are smooth-riding, air-conditioned buses that bend at the middle.

Stops are indicated by a sign marked *paragem* where details of the specific route are shown. The final destination is always displayed on the front of the bus, along with its number. Tickets can be bought on boarding, and must be clipped in the *obliterador* machine by the driver. Buses, trams and funiculars use the same tickets.

Orange and white Lisbon bus heading for Praça do Comércio

USEFUL BUS AND TRAM ROUTES IN LISBON

It is easy to get around Lisbon thanks to the large number of bus and tram services supplied by Carris. Services are fairly frequent and often provide wonderful views of the city. This map indicates some of the best bus and tram routes which link up the major sights.

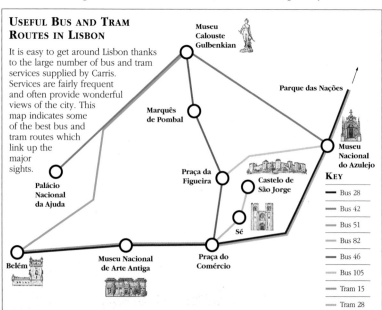

Museu Calouste Gulbenkian

Parque das Nações

Marquês de Pombal

Museu Nacional do Azulejo

Palácio Nacional da Ajuda

Praça da Figueira

Castelo de São Jorge

KEY

──	Bus 28
──	Bus 42
──	Bus 51
──	Bus 82
──	Bus 46
──	Bus 105
──	Tram 15
──	Tram 28

Sé

Belém

Museu Nacional de Arte Antiga

Praça do Comércio

Travelling Around the Lisbon Coast

Logo for Caminhos de Ferro Portugueses

LISBON AND ITS surroundings offer numerous sightseeing opportunities and the good road network means that most sights are only 30 minutes or so from the city centre. Buses, coaches and local trains are available for visiting Cascais and Estoril. Although no public buses go to Sintra, there are organized coach tours to the palaces and the glorious countryside around the town. A frequent rail service operates from Rossio station to Sintra. To visit Sesimbra and other areas to the south of the Tagus, ferries depart from Praça do Comércio, in Lisbon, and offer a more leisurely way to cross the river than the busy Ponte 25 de Abril. Alternatively, the Fertagus train also crosses the bridge on the lower level. Trains and buses can then be picked up on the south bank of the river.

High-speed Alfa train at Santa Apolónia station in Lisbon

TRAVELLING BY TRAIN

THE STATE-OWNED railway company, Caminhos de Ferro Portugueses (CP), operates all trains in Portugal.

There are four main rail lines out of Lisbon. Most popular with tourists is the line which runs from Cais do Sodré to Cascais on the coast, and the line linking Rossio station to the town of Sintra. Rossio station (metro Restauradores) is currently closed for renovation. Trains to Sintra now leave from Entre Campos (Tel: 800 200 904) and Sete Rios Metro stations, and the journey takes about 45 minutes. Santa Apolónia is the main station for trains travelling north as well as for most international arrivals. For those travelling east or south of Lisbon, a ferry departs from Terreiro do Paço station, on the north bank of the Tagus, to Barreiro station on the south side, from where train services depart. The Gare do

Façade of Rossio station

Oriente near the Parque das Nações, opened in 1998. It serves as an alternative international terminus as well as an interchange for local destinations.

To reach Estoril and Cascais take the train from Cais do Sodré station. The journey follows the coastline and takes about 45 minutes. Check destinations on the screens at the station before you travel as some trains terminate at Oeiras. You can also catch the train to Alcântara from Cais do Sodré, only five minutes away, or to Belém, ten minutes away.

TICKETING SYSTEM

DISCOUNTS of 50 per cent are available on all CP tickets for children aged from four to twelve years, students (you will need to show your student ID), and adults over 65. Children under the age of four travel free. However, there are no special discounts available for groups travelling together.

Return tickets can be bought on the Cais do Sodré-Cascais and Rossio-Sintra lines; however this will only save time rather than money, as returns are simply double the cost of single tickets.

If you wish to take a bicycle on these trains you will only be permitted to do outside rush hours and a fee will be charged (except on weekends and holidays). Passengers without a ticket will be fined.

Departures board in Santa Apolónia station giving times and destinations

HORA	DESTINO	LINHA	COMBOIO	OBSERVAÇÕES
13H34	ALVERCA	7	SUBURB	TODAS EST E APEAD
14H00	PORTO CAMP	1	RAPIDO	SERVICO ALFA
14H14	TOMAR	6	REGIONAL	
14H34	ALVERCA		SUBURB	SO 3 CARRUAG.FRENT
15H05	PORTO CAMP		INTERREG	
15H14	TOMAR		REGIONAL	
15H34	ALVERCA		SUBURB	TODAS EST E APEAD
16H00	HENDAYE		INTERNAC	SUD EXPRESS
16H03	COVILHA		REGIONAL	

TRAVELLING BY CAR

WHEN DRIVING, always carry your passport, licence, car insurance and rental contract. Failure to produce these *documentos* if the police stop you will incur a fine.

The road network in and around Lisbon has seen significant improvements in the last decade, with the construction of new ring roads as well as motorways. If you are heading west out of Lisbon towards the coast and Estoril and Cascais, the quickest route is to take the A5 motorway.

Local signs giving directions to Estoril, the south via the bridge and Sete Rios

However, try to avoid rush hour traffic (8–10am and 5:30–8pm). To get on to the A5, follow the road out from Praça de Espanha or from Marques Pombal past Amoreiras.

Alternatively, if you prefer to take the scenic coastal route (N6), follow the A5 out of Lisbon for 8 km (5 miles), and turn off at the sign to Avenida Marginal.

To get to Sintra, the best route to take is either the A5 motorway, or to follow the IC19 past Queluz. The A5 motorway passes through small areas of countryside.

To reach Caparica, Tróia and Setúbal, south of the Tagus, you can either cross the Ponte 25 de Abril at Alcântara or take the car ferry which departs regularly from Cais do Sodré port to Cacilhas. Once across the river, follow the A2 south.

MOTORWAYS

MOTORWAYS AROUND Lisbon have toll charges and most are privately owned by a company called **Brisa**.

In general, they are the quickest way to travel around Portugal, as they have better surfaces than minor roads. There are also motorway rest areas where you can have something to eat and fill the car up with petrol.

There are two systems for paying tolls on motorways. Most drivers take a ticket (*título*) at the entrance and pay at the exit where the fee is displayed at the toll booth.

The other system, known as the Via Verde, is primarily for residents in the area and is not intended for general use. Drivers subscribing to the system drive through the Via Verde channel without stopping. Their passage is registered automatically and billed later. It is strictly forbidden for anyone who does not subscribe to drive through the *Via Verde*, so make sure that you are in the correct lane as you approach the toll booths.

BREAKING DOWN

THE LOCAL motoring association, **ACP** (Automóvel Club de Portugal), has a reciprocal breakdown service with most other international motoring organizations. To qualify, drivers should take out European cover with their own organization.

Should you suffer a road accident, the emergency services number is 112. If you have simply broken down, call the ACP. There are SOS phones at regular intervals along motorways. Unless you state that you are a member of an ACP-affiliated organization, a private tow truck will be sent to help you.

Breakdown assistance will try to repair your car on the spot, but if it is a more serious problem they will tow your car to a garage. Depending on your insurance, the ACP can make arrangements for you to have a hire car until yours is repaired.

In Portugal, international rules apply to breakdowns, including placing a red warning triangle behind the car to alert other drivers. Be sure to check that you have one in your car before you travel.

A sightseeing coach from one of the many tour operators

TRAVELLING BY COACH

FOLLOWING the privatization of the Rodoviária Nacional (RN), concessions have been made available to private enterprise. Competitive pricing has developed between rival coach companies, but the absence of a central coach service can make it difficult to know which company serves which destination.

Each of the companies operates its own ticketing system. As a general rule, however, you buy your ticket from the driver when you board the coach, although it is possible to get cheaper tickets, known as *modulos*, beforehand from the relevant coach company's kiosk. As on the trains, there are no group discounts though children between the ages of four and twelve travel half price.

At present, the only direct coach service operating between Lisbon and Cascais is run by the Scottish bus company **Scotturb** and **Rodoviária de Lisboa**. This hourly service departs from Lisbon airport via Campo Grande to Cascais, returning on an hourly basis as well. The two companies run one bus each, on alternate hours. **TST** (Transportes Sul do Tejo) serves destinations south of the Tagus. Buses leave from Praça de Espanha (Metro Praça de Espanha) for destinations such as Costa da Caparica (1hr) and Sesimbra (1hr 45 mins).

For destinations northwest of Lisbon, contact Rodoviária de Lisboa. **Rede Expressos** and **EVA** are two coach companies that operate direct services to destinations all over the country. EVA covers the Algarve particularly well. Both are based at the Sete Rios bus terminal in Praça Marechal Humberto Delgado, while Rodoviária de Lisboa operates from Campo Grande among other places.

To date there is no coach link between Lisbon and Sintra. However, Scotturb operates three routes to Sintra from Cascais and Estoril. The No. 403 departs from near Cascais railway station every 90 minutes, via Cabo da Roca. The No. 417 runs from Cascais via Alcabideche and the No. 418 departs hourly from outside Estoril train station. All three buses stop at Sintra station and in the town centre. In Sintra, Scotturb also runs a service from the train station to Palácio da Pena and Castelo dos Mouros from Tuesday to Sunday.

COACH TOURS

THERE ARE MANY coach tours operating in the Lisbon area, offering a wide choice of destinations, from a short local trip around the city's sights to longer trips to other cities in Portugal such as Oporto. For those who just wish to tour Lisbon itself, short half-day tours are available. Sintra, Cabo da Roca, Estoril and Cascais are all easily reached in a day trip. Alternatively, you can head

southwards to Sesimbra and Arrábida, or north to Mafra. Prices depend on whether meals or special events, such as *fado* or bullfighting, are included. Most tours offer reductions to children under the age of ten.

Tours can be booked directly with the tour operator, through a travel agent or at some hotels. If you are staying at one of Lisbon's major hotels, some tours will provide a pick-up service.

FERRIES ACROSS THE TAGUS

MOST FERRY SERVICES are operated by **Transtejo**. There are several different points at which you can cross the Tagus by ferry. The trips are worth making purely for the fabulous views of Lisbon.

From Terreiro do Paço (Estação Fluvial) there are crossings to Cacilhas (6am–10:30pm daily) which take 15 minutes. Ferries also cross from Terreiro do Paço to Seixal and Montijo (6am–10:30pm daily) and take 20 and 30 minutes respectively. Ferries owned by Soflusa operate a 15-minute service from Terreiro do Paço to Barreiro (5:45–2:45am daily). There are also ferries between Parque das Nações and Seixal via Barreiro and from Cacilhas to Parque das Nações (7am–8pm daily), taking 45 and 30 minutes respectively. From Belém, ferries go to Porto Brandão and Trafaria (6:30am–11:30pm daily), where you can get a bus to the beaches at Caparica.

Ferry docking at Terreiro do Paço

LISBON STREET FINDER

AP REFERENCES given in this guide for sights and entertainment venues in Lisbon refer to the Street Finder maps on the following pages. Map references are also given for Lisbon's hotels *(see pp114–119)* and restaurants *(see pp128–33)*. The first figure in the map reference indicates which Street Finder map to turn to, and the letter and number which follow refer to the grid reference on that map. The map below shows the area of Lisbon covered by the eight Street Finder maps. Symbols used for sights and useful information are displayed in the key below. An index of street names and all the place of interest marked on the maps can be found on the following pages.

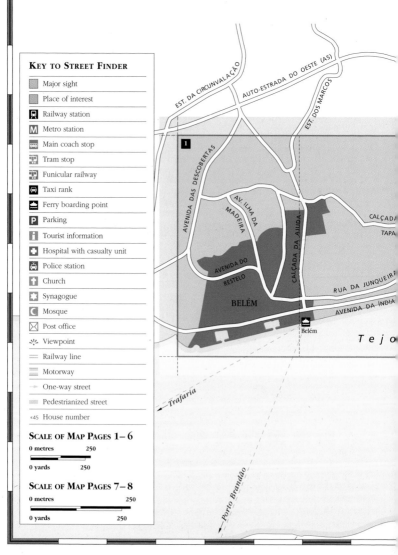

KEY TO STREET FINDER

	Major sight
	Place of interest
🚉	Railway station
M	Metro station
🚌	Main coach stop
🚊	Tram stop
🚟	Funicular railway
🚕	Taxi rank
⛴	Ferry boarding point
P	Parking
i	Tourist information
✚	Hospital with casualty unit
🚔	Police station
✝	Church
✡	Synagogue
☾	Mosque
⊠	Post office
⁂	Viewpoint
=	Railway line
=	Motorway
→	One-way street
▬	Pedestrianized street
◄45	House number

SCALE OF MAP PAGES 1–6

0 metres	250
0 yards	250

SCALE OF MAP PAGES 7–8

0 metres	250
0 yards	250

Street Finder Index

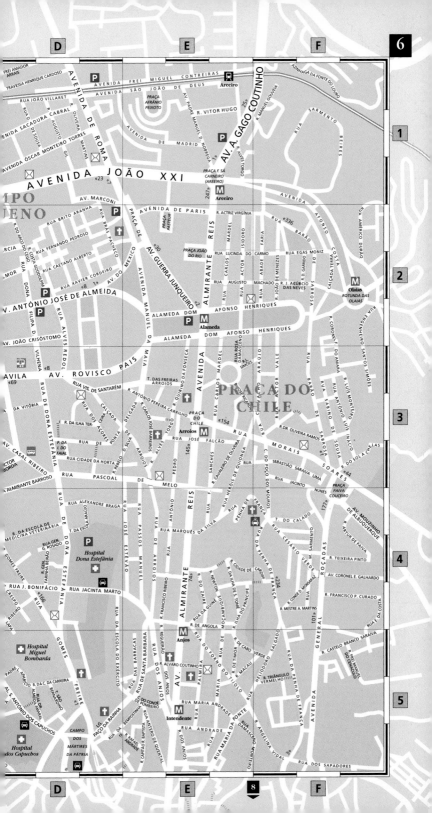

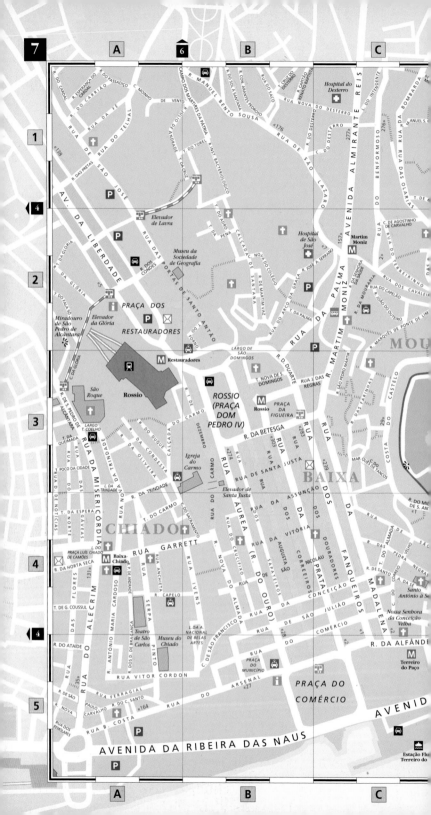

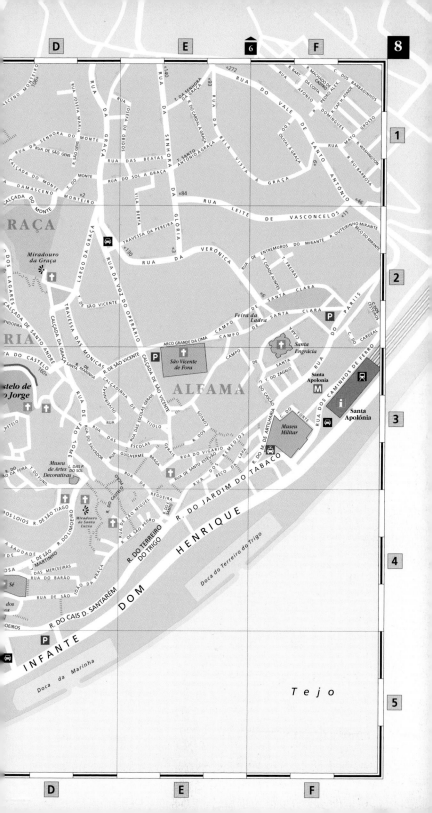

General Index

Acknowledgments

DORLING KINDERSLEY would like to thank the following people whose contributions and assistance have made the preparation of this book possible.

CONTRIBUTORS

SUSIE BOULTON studied History of Art at Cambridge University. A freelance travel writer, she is the author of *Eyewitness Venice and the Veneto*. SARAH MCALISTER is a freelance writer and editor for the *Time Out* guides. Her knowledge of Lisbon and the surrounding area is a result of extensive visits to the country.

CONSULTANT

MARTIN SYMINGTON was born in Portugal and is a freelance travel writer. He contributes to numerous British newspapers including the *Daily Telegraph* and the *Sunday Telegraph*. He is the author of guides to *The Loire Valley* (Hodder and Stoughton), *Portugal* (AA) and *Denmark* (AA/Thomas Cook). He has also contributed to *The Algarve and Southern Portugal* (AA/Thomas Cook), *Portugal* (Insight), *Eyewitness Great Britain* and *Eyewitness Seville and Andalusia*.

ADDITIONAL CONTRIBUTORS

Paul Vernon, Edite Vieira.

FACT CHECKER

Mihaela Rogalski.

DESIGN AND EDITORIAL ASSISTANCE

Gillian Allan, Douglas Amrine, Gillian Andrews, Andrew Costello, Angela Marie Graham, Paul Hines, Esther Labi, Kathryn Lane, Michelle de Larrabeiti, Adam Moore, Naomi Peck, Andrea Powell, Tom Prentice, Jake Reimann, Sands Publishing Solutions, Sadie Smith, Rachel Symons, Amanda Tomeh, Tomas Tranaeus, Ingrid Vienings, Fiona Wild.

INDEXER

Hilary Bird.

ADDITIONAL PHOTOGRAPHY

Steve Gorton, John Heseltine, Dave King, Martin Norris, Roger Philips, Clive Streeter.

PHOTOGRAPHIC AND ARTWORK REFERENCE

Joy FitzSimmons, Veronica Wood.

PHOTOGRAPHY PERMISSIONS

DORLING KINDERSLEY would like to thank the following for their assistance and kind permission to photograph at their establishments: Instituto Português do Património Arquitectónico e Arqueológico (IPPAR), Lisboa; Instituto Português de Museus (IPM), Lisboa; Museu do Mar, Cascais; Museu da Marinha, Lisboa; Fundação da Casa de Alorna, Lisboa, and all other churches, museums, parks, hotels, restaurants and sights too numerous to thank individually.

SPECIAL ASSISTANCE

Emília Tavares, Arquivo Nacional de Fotografia, Lisboa; Luísa Cardia, Biblioteca Nacional e do Livro, Lisboa; Marina Gonçalves and Aida Pereira, Câmara Municipal de Lisboa; Caminhos de Ferro Portugueses; Carris; Enatur, Lisboa; Karen Ollier-Spry, John E. Fells and Sons Ltd; Maria Helena Soares da Costa, Fundação Calouste Gulbenkian, Lisboa; Pilar Serras and José Aragão, ICEP, London; Instituto do Vinho de Porto, Porto; Simoneta Afonso, IPM, Lisboa; Mário Abreu, Dulce Ferraz, IPPAR, Lisboa; Pedro Moura Bessa and Eduardo Corte-Real, Livraria Civilização Editora, Porto; Metropolitano de Lisboa; Raquel Florentino and Cristina Leite, Museu da Cidade, Lisboa; Joao Castel Branco G. Pereira, Museu Nacional do Azulejo; and the staff at all the other tourist offices and town halls in Portugal.

PICTURE CREDITS

t = top; tl = top left; tlc = top left centre; tc = top centre; tr = top right; cla = centre left above; ca = centre above; cra = centre right above; cl = centre left; c = centre; cr = centre right; clb = centre left below; cb = centre below; crb = centre right below; bl = bottom left; b = bottom; bc = bottom centre; bcl = bottom centre left; br = bottom right; d = detail.

Works of art have been reproduced with the permission of the following copyright holders: *Terreiro do Paço* by Dirk Stoop 81b is reproduced by kind permission of the Museu da Cidade, Lisboa.

DORLING KINDERSLEY would like to thank the following individuals, companies and picture libraries for permission to reproduce their photographs:

AISA: 16tr, 17tc/br, 66b; ARQUIVO NACIONAL DE FOTOGRAFIA-INSTITUTO PORTUGUÊS DE MUSEUS: Museu Conde de Castro Guimarães/Manuel Palma 12; Biblioteca da Ajuda/José Pessoa 14c; Museu Grao Vasco/José Pessoa 18bl; Museu Nacional dos Coches/José Pessoa 17bc, 63bl; Henrique

Ruas 64b; Igreja São Vicente de Fora/Carlos Monteiro 17bl; Museu Nacional de Arte Antiga/Luís Pavão 28t, 56bl/br, 57t/c/b, 59c; Francisco Matias 19tl, José Pessoa 19tr, 56tl/tr, 58b, 59b; Pedro Ferreira 58t, 59t; Museu Nacional de Arqueologia/ José Pessoa 65c; Arnaldo Soares 142tr, 143tl; Museu Nacional do Teatro/Arnaldo Soares 142cl; Luisa Oliveira 143tr; José Pessoa 142b, 20–21t; San Payo 17tr; Tony Arruza: 16c, 20–21lc.

© Trustees of the British Museum, London: 18br; Boutinot Prince Wine Shippers, Stockport: 126br.

Câmara Municipal de Oeiras: 15c; Câmara Municipal de Lisboa: Antonio Rafael 20cl; Centro do Arte Moderna: José Manuel Costa Alves 80tl; Cephas: Peter Stowell 24b; Mick Rock 124cb, 125c, Peter Stowell 24b; Chapitô: 140tr; Cockburn Smithes & cia, S. A. – an Allied Domecq Company: 126crb; CTT Correios: 152br, 153cr.

Dow's Port 229cra.

European Commission: 152bl.

Fototeca Internacional, Lisboa: César Soares 16bl; Luís Elvas 25b/t; Fundação Ricardo do Espírito Santo Silva: Museu-Escola de Artes Decorativas Portuguesas 34c.

Giraudon: 18cl; Calouste Gulbenkian Foundation, Lisboa: 140b.

Ideal Photo: N. Adams 116cl; The Image Bank: José Manuel 4b, 23b; Moura Machado 24c; Instituto da Biblioteca Nacional e do Livro, Lisboa: 13b, 14b, 105bl.

Lusa: Luís Vasconcelos 52b; André Kosters 53t; António Cotrim 143c.

José Manuel: 21br; Mary Evans Picture Library: 21tr, 101b; Museu Calouste Gulbenkian, Lisboa: Enamelled Silver Gilt Corsage Ornament, Rene Lalique, © ADAGP, Paris and DACS, London 1997, 76t/ca/cb/b, 77t/ca/cb/b, 78c/b/t,79b/t/c; Museu da Cidade, Lisboa: Antonio Rafael 20tl/cl/bl/br, 21c/bl; Museu da Marinha, Lisboa: 16br, 68b.

Nationalmuseet, Copenhagen: 18tr; Naturpress: Juan Hidalgo-Candy Lopesino 22t.

Oronoz, Madrid: 16bc.

Palacio de Pena: 100cl.

RCL, Parede: Rui Cunha 141t; Dias dos Reis: 81tl, 150tr; Rex Features: Sipa Press, Michel Ginies 15b.

Science Photo Library/CNES 1993, Distribution Spot Image: 10.

Symington Port & Madeira Shippers: Claudio Capone 125cl, 127t, cla, bc.

Tomas Tranæus: 150b.

Peter Wilson: 30 (front endpaper tr), 44tl, 53b, 136b, 137c, 138c, 47br; Woodfall Wild Images: Mike Lane 109b; World Pictures: 23t.

Jacket
Front – DK Picture Library: Clive Streeter cb; Peter Wilson bca, bl; Getty Images: Simeone Huber main image. Back – DK Picture Library: Linda Whitwam b; Peter Wilson t.
Spine – Getty Images: Simeone Huber.

All other images © Dorling Kindersley. For further information see www.DKimages.com

facebook. Christina andersson (.dg)
blue bird pic

DORLING KINDERSLEY SPECIAL EDITIONS

Dorling Kindersley books can be purchased in bulk quantities at discounted prices for use in promotions or as premiums. We are also able to offer special editions and personalized jackets, corporate imprints, and excerpts from all of our books, tailored specifically to meet your own needs.

To find out more, please contact: (in the United Kingdom) Sarah.Burgess@dk.com or Special Sales, Dorling Kindersley Limited, 80 Strand, London WC2R 0RL; (in the United States) Special Markets Dept, DK Publishing, Inc., 375 Hudson Street, New York, NY 10014.

Phrase Book

In Emergency

Help!	Socorro!	soo-**koh**-roo
Stop!	Páre!	**pahr'**
Call a doctor!	Chame um médico!	**shahm'** ooñ **meh**-dee-koo
Call an ambulance!	Chame uma ambulância!	**shahm'** oo-muh añ-boo-**lañ**-see-uh
Call the police!	Chame a polícia!	**shahm'** uh poo-**lee**-see-uh
Call the fire brigade!	Chame os bombeiros!	**shahm'** oosh bom-**bay**-roosh
Where is the nearest telephone?	Há um telefone aqui perto?	ah ooñ te-le-**fon'** uh-**kee pehr**-too
Where is the nearest hospital?	Onde é o hospital mais próximo?	ond' **eh** oo ohsh-pee-**tahl' mysh pro**-see-moo

Communication Essentials

Yes	Sim	seeñ
No	Não	nowñ
Please	Por favor, Faz favor	poor fuh-**vor** fash fuh-**vor**
Thank you	Obrigado/da	o-bree-**gah**-doo/duh
Excuse me	Desculpe	dish-**koolp'**
Hello	Olá	oh-**lah**
Goodbye	Adeus	a-**deh**-oosh
Good morning	Bom-dia	boñ **dee**-uh
Good afternoon	Boa-tarde	boh-uh **tard'**
Good night	Boa-noite	boh-uh **noyt'**
Yesterday	Ontem	oñ-**tayñ**
Today	Hoje	ohj'
Tomorrow	Amanhã	ah-mañ-**yañ**
Here	Aqui	uh-**kee**
There	Ali	uh-**lee**
What?	O quê?	oo keh
Which	Qual?	**kwahl'**
When?	Quando?	**kwañ**-doo
Why?	Porquê?	poor-**keh**
Where?	Onde?	oñd'

Useful Phrases

How are you?	Como está?	**koh**-moo **shtah**
Very well, thank you.	Bem, obrigado/da.	bayñ o-bree-**gah**-doo/duh
Pleased to meet you.	Encantado/a.	eñ-kañ-**tah**-doo/duh
See you soon.	Até logo.	uh-**teh loh**-goo
That's fine.	Está bem.	shtah bayñ
Where is/are . . . ?	Onde está/estão . . . ?	ond' shtah/ shtowñ
How far is it to . . . ?	A que distância fica . . . ?	uh kee dish-**tañ**-see-uh **fee**-kuh
Which way to . . . ?	Como se vai para . . . ?	**koh**-moo seh vy puh-ruh
Do you speak English?	Fala inglês?	**fah**-luh eeñ-glehsh
I don't understand.	Não compreendo.	nowñ kom-pree-**eñ**-doo
Could you speak more slowly please?	Pode falar mais devagar por favor?	pohd' fuh-**lar** mysh d'-va-**gar** poor fuh-**vor**
I'm sorry.	Desculpe.	dish-**koolp'**

Useful Words

big	grande	grañd'
small	pequeno	pe-**keh**-noo
hot	quente	keñt'
cold	frio	**free**-oo
good	bom	boñ
bad	mau	**mah**-oo
quite a lot/enough	bastante	bash-**tañt'**
well	bem	bayñ
open	aberto	a-**behr**-too
closed	fechado	fe-**shah**-doo
left	esquerda	**shkehr**-duh
right	direita	dee-**ray**-tuh
straight on	em frente	ayñ freñt'
near	perto	**pehr**-too
far	longe	loñj'
up	para cima	pur-ruh **see**-muh
down	para baixo	pur-ruh **buy**-shoo
early	cedo	**seh**-doo
late	tarde	tard'
entrance	entrada	eñ-**trah**-duh
exit	saída	sa-**ee**-duh
toilets	casa de banho	**kah**-zuh d' **bañ**-yoo
more	mais	mysh
less	menos	**meh**-noosh

Making a Telephone Call

I'd like to place an international call.	Queria fazer uma chamada internacional.	**kree**-uh fuh-**zehr** oo-muh sha-**mah**-duh in-ter-na-see-oo-**nahl'**
a local call.	uma chamada local.	oo-muh sha-**mah**-duh loo-**kahl'**
Can I leave a message?	Posso deixar uma mensagem?	**poh**-soo day-**shar** oo-muh meñ-**sah**—jayñ

Shopping

How much does this cost?	Quanto custa isto?	**kwañ**-too **koosh**-tuh **eesh**-too
I would like . . .	Queria . . .	**kree**-uh
I'm just looking.	Estou só a ver obrigado/a.	shtoh soh uh vehr o-bree-**gah**-doo/uh
Do you take credit cards?	Aceita cartões de crédito?	uh-**say**-tuh kar-**toinsh** de **kreh**-dee-too
What time do you open?	A que horas abre?	uh **kee** oh-rash **ah**-bre
What time do you close?	A que horas fecha?	uh **kee** oh-rash **fay**-shuh
This one	Este	ehst'
That one	Esse	ehss'
expensive	caro	**kah**-roo
cheap	barato	buh-**rah**-too
size (clothes/shoes)	tamanho	ta-**man**-yoo
white	branco	**brañ**-koo
black	preto	**preh**-too
red	vermelho	ver-**mehl**-yoo
yellow	amarelo	uh-muh-**reh**-loo
green	verde	vehrd'
blue	azul	uh-**zool'**

Types of Shop

antique shop	loja de antiguidades	**loh**-juh de añ-tee-gwee-**dahd'sh**
bakery	padaria	pah-duh-**ree**-uh
bank	banco	**bañ**-koo
bookshop	livraria	lee-vruh-**ree**-uh
butcher	talho	**tah**-lyoo
cake shop	pastelaria	pash-te-luh-**ree**-uh
chemist	farmácia	far-**mah**-see-uh
fishmonger	peixaria	pay-shuh-**ree**-uh
hairdresser	cabeleireiro	kab-lay-**ray**-roo
market	mercado	mehr-**kah**-doo
newsagent	kiosque	kee-**yohsk'**
post office	correios	koo-ray-oosh
shoe shop	sapataria	suh-puh-tuh-**ree**-uh
supermarket	supermercado	soo-**pehr**-mer-**kah**-doo
tobacconist	tabacaria	tuh-buh-kuh-**ree**-uh
travel agency	agência de viagens	uh-**jen**-see-uh de vee-**ah**-jaynsh

Sightseeing

cathedral	sé	seh
church	igreja	ee-**gray**-juh
garden	jardim	jar-**deeñ**
library	biblioteca	bee-blee-oo-**teh**-kuh
museum	museu	moo-**zeh**-oo
tourist information office	posto de turismo	**posh**-too d' too-**reesh**-moo
closed for holidays	fechado para férias	fe-**sha**-doo puh-ruh **feh**-ree-ash
bus station	estação de autocarros	shta-**sowñ** d' oh-too-**kah**-roosh
railway station	estação de comboios	shta-**sowñ** d' koñ-**boy**-oosh

Staying in a Hotel

Do you have a vacant room?	Tem um quarto livre?	tayñ ooñ **kwar**-too **leevr'**
room with a bath	um quarto com casa de banho	ooñ **kwar**-too koñ **kah**-zuh d' **bañ**-yoo
shower	duche	doosh
single room	quarto individual	**kwar**-too een-dee-vee-doo-**ahl'**
double room	quarto de casal	**kwar**-too d' kuh-**zahl'**
twin room	quarto com duas camas	**kwar**-too koñ **doo**-ash **kah**-mash
porter	porteiro	poor-**tay**-roo
key	chave	shahv'
I have a reservation.	Tenho um quarto reservado.	**tayñ**-yoo ooñ **kwar**-too-re-ser-**vah**-doo

EATING OUT

Have you got a table for . . . ?	**Tem uma mesa para . . . ?**	tayñ oo-muh **meh**-zuh puh-ruh
I want to reserve a table.	**Quero reservar uma mesa.**	**keh**-roo re-zehr-**var** oo-muh **meh**-zuh
The bill please.	**A conta por favor/ faz favor.**	uh **kohn**-tuh poor fuh-**vor**/ **fash** fuh-**vor**
I am a vegetarian.	**Sou vegetariano/a.**	Soh ve-je-tuh-ree-**ah**-noo/a
Waiter!	**Por favor!/ Faz favor!**	poor fuh-**vor** **fash** fuh-**vor**
the menu	**a lista**	uh **leesh**-tuh
fixed-price menu	**a ementa turística**	uh ee-**mehñ**-tuh too-**reesh**-tee-kuh
wine list	**a lista de vinhos**	uh **leesh**-tuh de **veeñ**-yoosh
glass	**um copo**	ooñ **koh**-poo
bottle	**uma garrafa**	oo-muh guh-**rah**-fuh
half bottle	**meia-garrafa**	**may**-uh guh-**rah**-fuh
knife	**uma faca**	oo-muh **fah**-kuh
fork	**um garfo**	ooñ **gar**-foo
spoon	**uma colher**	oo-muh kool-**yair**
plate	**um prato**	ooñ **prah**-too
napkin	**um guardanapo**	ooñ goo-ar-duh-**nah**-poo
breakfast	**pequeno-almoço**	pe-**keh**-noo-ahl-**moh**-soo
lunch	**almoço**	ahl-**moh**-soo
dinner	**jantar**	jan-**tar**
cover	**couvert**	koo-**vehr**
starter	**entrada**	eñ-**trah**-duh
main course	**prato principal**	**prah**-too prin-see-**pahl'**
dish of the day	**prato do dia**	**prah**-too doo **dee**-uh
set dish	**combinado**	koñ-bee-**nah**-doo
half portion	**meia-dose**	may-uh **doh**-se
dessert	**sobremesa**	soh-bre-**meh**-zuh
rare	**mal passado**	**mahl'** puh-**sah**-doo
medium	**médio**	**meh**-dee-oo
well done	**bem passado**	**bayñ** puh-**sah**-doo

MENU DECODER

abacate	uh-buh-**kaht'**	avocado
açorda	uh-**sor**-duh	bread-based stew (often seafood)
açúcar	uh-**soo**-kar	sugar
água mineral	**ah**-gwuh mee-ne-**rahl'**	mineral water
(com gás)	koñ gas	sparkling
(sem gás)	**sayñ** gas	still
alho	**al**-yoo	garlic
alperce	ahl'-**pehrce**	apricot
amêijoas	uh-**may**-joo-ash	clams
ananás	uh-nuh-**nahsh**	pineapple
arroz	uh-**rohsh**	rice
assado	uh-**sah**-doo	baked
atum	uh-**tooñ**	tuna
aves	**ah**-vesh	poultry
azeite	uh-**zayt'**	olive oil
azeitonas	uh-zay-**toh**-nash	olives
bacalhau	buh-kuh-**lyow**	dried, salted cod
banana	buh-**nah**-nuh	banana
batatas	buh-**tah**-tash	potatoes
batatas fritas	buh-**tah**-tash **free**-tash	french fries
batido	buh-**tee**-doo	milk-shake
bica	**bee**-kuh	espresso
bife	**beef**	beef
bolacha	boo-**lah**-shuh	biscuit
bolo	**boh**-loo	cake
borrego	boo-**reh**-goo	lamb
caça	**kah**-ssuh	game
café	kuh-**feh**	coffee
camarões	kuh-muh-**roysh**	large prawns
caracóis	kuh-ruh-**koysh**	snails
caranguejo	kuh-rañ-**gay**-joo	crab
carne	**karn'**	meat
cataplana	kuh-tuh-**plah**-nuh	sealed wok used to steam dishes
cebola	se-**boh**-luh	onion
cerveja	sehr-**vay**-juh	beer
chá	**shah**	tea
cherne	**shern'**	stone bass
chocolate	shoh-koh-**laht'**	chocolate
chocos	**shoh**-koosh	cuttlefish
chouriço	shoh-**ree**-soo	red, spicy sausage
churrasco	shoo-**rash**-coo	on the spit
cogumelos	koo-goo-**meh**-loosh	mushrooms
cozido	koo-**zee**-doo	boiled
enguias	eñ-**gee**-ash	eels
fiambre	fee-**añbr'**	ham
fígado	**fee**-guh-doo	liver
frango	**frañ**-goo	chicken
frito	**free**-too	fried
fruta	**froo**-tuh	fruit
gambas	**gam**-bash	prawns
gelado	je-**lah**-doo	ice cream
gelo	**jeh**-loo	ice
goraz	goo-**rash**	bream
grelhado	grel-**yah**-doo	grilled
iscas	**eesh**-kash	marinated liver
lagosta	luh-**gohsh**-tuh	lobster
laranja	luh-**rañ**-juh	orange
leite	**layt'**	milk
limão	lee-**mowñ**	lemon
limonada	lee-moo-**nah**-duh	lemonade
linguado	leeñ-**gwah**-doo	sole
lulas	**loo**-lash	squid
maçã	muh-**sañ**	apple
manteiga	mañ-**tay**-guh	butter
mariscos	muh-**reesh**-koosh	seafood
meia-de-leite	**may**-uh-d' **layt'**	white coffee
ostras	**osh**-trash	oysters
ovos	**oh**-voosh	eggs
pão	**powñ**	bread
pastel	pash-**tehl'**	cake
pato	**pah**-too	duck
peixe	**paysh'**	fish
peixe-espada	**paysh'**-shpah-duh	scabbard fish
pimenta	pee-**meñ**-tuh	pepper
polvo	**pohl'**-voo	octopus
porco	**por**-coo	pork
queijo	**kay**-joo	cheese
sal	**sahl'**	salt
salada	suh-**lah**-duh	salad
salsichas	sahl-**see**-shash	sausages
sandes	**sañ**-desh	sandwich
santola	sañ-**toh**-luh	spider crab
sopa	**soh**-puh	soup
sumo	**soo**-moo	juice
tamboril	tañ-boo-**ril'**	monkfish
tarte	**tart'**	pie/cake
tomate	too-**maht'**	tomato
torrada	too-**rah**-duh	toast
tosta	**tohsh**-tuh	toasted sandwich
vinagre	vee-**nah**-gre	vinegar
vinho branco	**veeñ**-yoo **brañ**-koo	white wine
vinho tinto	**veeñ**-yoo **teeñ**-too	red wine
vitela	vee-**teh**-luh	veal

NUMBERS

0	**zero**	**zeh**-roo
1	**um**	**ooñ**
2	**dois**	**doysh**
3	**três**	**tresh**
4	**quatro**	**kwa**-troo
5	**cinco**	**seeñ**-koo
6	**seis**	**saysh**
7	**sete**	**set'**
8	**oito**	**oy**-too
9	**nove**	**nov'**
10	**dez**	**desh**
11	**onze**	**oñz'**
12	**doze**	**doz'**
13	**treze**	**trez'**
14	**catorze**	ka-**torz'**
15	**quinze**	**keeñz'**
16	**dezasseis**	de-zuh-**saysh**
17	**dezassete**	de-zuh-**set'**
18	**dezoito**	de-**zoy**-too
19	**dezanove**	de-zuh-**nov'**
20	**vinte**	**veent'**
21	**vinte e um**	veen-tee-**ooñ**
30	**trinta**	**treeñ**-tuh
40	**quarenta**	kwa-**reñ**-tuh
50	**cinquenta**	seen-**kweñ**-tuh
60	**sessenta**	se-**señ**-tuh
70	**setenta**	se-**teñ**-tuh
80	**oitenta**	oy-**teñ**-tuh
90	**noventa**	noo-**veñ**-tuh
100	**cem**	**sayñ**
101	**cento e um**	señ-too-ee-**ooñ**
102	**cento e dois**	**señ**-too ee **doysh**
200	**duzentos**	doo-**zeñ**-toosh
300	**trezentos**	tre-**zeñ**-toosh
400	**quatrocentos**	**kwa**-troo-señ-toosh
500	**quinhentos**	kee-**nyeñ**-toosh
700	**setecentos**	set'-**señ**-toosh
900	**novecentos**	nov'-**señ**-toosh
1,000	**mil**	**meel'**

TIME

one minute	**um minuto**	ooñ mee-**noo**-too
one hour	**uma hora**	oo-muh **oh**-ruh
half an hour	**meia-hora**	**may**-uh-**oh**-ruh
Monday	**segunda-feira**	se-**goon**-duh-**fay**-ruh
Tuesday	**terça-feira**	ter-sa-**fay**-ruh
Wednesday	**quarta-feira**	**kwar**-ta-fay-ruh
Thursday	**quinta-feira**	**keen**-ta-fay-ruh
Friday	**sexta-feira**	say-shta-**fay**-ruh
Saturday	**sábado**	**sah**-ba-doo
Sunday	**domingo**	doo-**meen**-goo

FOR PEACE OF MIND ABROAD,
WE'VE GOT IT COVERED

DK INSURANCE PROVIDES YOU
WITH QUALITY WORLDWIDE
INSURANCE COVER

For an instant quote
go to **www.dk.com/travel-insurance**

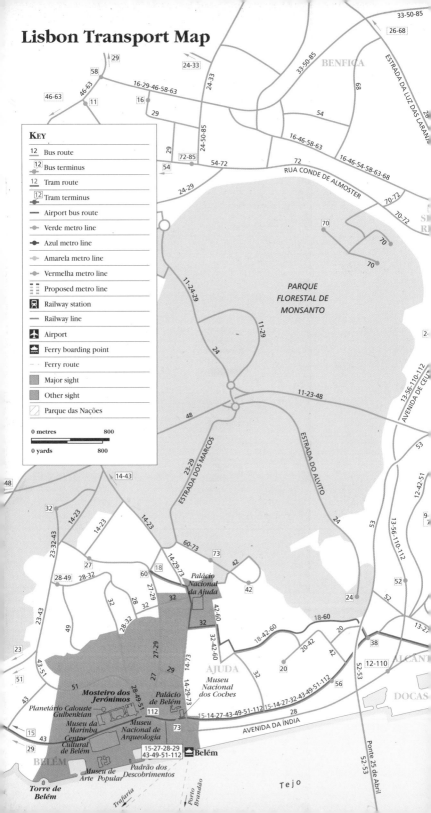